ELY CULBERTSON

TOTAL PEACE

*What Makes Wars and
How to Organize Peace*

Doubleday, Doran & Company, Inc.
GARDEN CITY, NEW YORK
1943

PUBLISHED BY THE BLAKISTON COMPANY, PHILADELPHIA
DISTRIBUTED BY THE BOOK LEAGUE OF AMERICA

Preface

THE TITLE OF THIS BOOK explains itself. In our age of total wars we will need a total peace. Nothing less will do. This means the kind of peace which not only safeguards the essential sovereignty and national interests of the United States and of our Allies, but goes beyond that to establish, by means of a new system of collective defense, the foundations for lasting world peace.

The making of this total peace cannot be unduly delayed, improvised, or left to the hazards of an indefinite future. A new total war will not wait for an instalment-plan peace to evolve gradually from year to year and piece by piece.

Because we have no comprehensive and carefully planned United States foreign policy we are already losing politically strategic positions, thereby making it more difficult to win the kind of peace which is vital to us and to the world. Our government, as Vice President Wallace said recently, is groping in the dark. The real danger is that we may continue to grope in postwar chaos. Those who may seek in this book arguments for partisan politics will be disappointed; the author has no interest in internal politics except as they affect United States foreign policy. If our government has failed to develop a true policy for the postwar period, it is due less to lack of knowledge than to lack of time. Before Pearl Harbor it was necessary to abandon our traditional isolationism and swing Americans toward intervention. During the war there was—and still is—the gigantic task of winning. But the time is upon us when we must, without further hesitation, formulate a new American foreign policy. For even a decisive victory will be in vain unless it is followed by total peace.

This book, *Total Peace,* deals essentially with the problems of world settlement after this war. It is written not from the standpoint of winning the war but from the standpoint of winning the peace, after the inevitable and not-too-distant defeat of Germany and Japan. Adoption of the World Federation Plan may, it is true, hasten our victory, without diminishing its scope, by offering to the German people a better alternative than grim despair. But the general course of the book is set in the direction of the postwar world. It is, I believe, the first comprehensive work on United States foreign policy that begins, so to speak, with the end of the war.

Total Peace is more than a mere elaboration and improvement of the *Summary of the World Federation Plan,* published some time ago. Although a modern plan for collective defense and an international police force is the main purpose of this book, many chapters present new principles of United States foreign policy and are designed to help an intelligent reader find his way in the complex mechanisms of power relations among nations.

It would be unfair to single out anyone who has been helpful to me in improving the World Federation Plan without mentioning hundreds of others, many of them persons of national standing in intellectual, political, and business fields, who have also been most helpful. I am particularly grateful for the fact that so many experts in international politics, some of them with plans of their own, received, judged, and sought to improve the World Federation Plan strictly on its merits, even though its author did come from the bizarre and wholly unrelated field of contract bridge.

As always, I am indebted to Mrs. Josephine Culbertson for her help. This time, however, Mrs. Culbertson was not advising me as a champion bridge player. She insisted upon the role of a "dumb reader," a kind of consumers' delegate, representing the reactions of an average clubwoman who is indeed interested in the problems of the war and of the peace to come, but who is not always versed in the technicalities of these problems. Others assumed a similar role, among them Mrs. Ethel Clyde, to whom I am also indebted. They kept me in leash when I was running away with too many long-winded words.

Mr. Bernie White of the Doubleday, Doran Company translated my word-ideas into the lucid reality of his charts and maps.

Above all, I am indebted to my chief secretary and adviser, Lucinda Jane Hazen, who never let up in her arduous task and without whose help this book would not have been the same. Miss Hazen was assisted, with the same spirit of loyalty, by Miss Elizabeth Grundy and by the staff of the World Federation, a non-profit educational corporation.

Grateful acknowledgment is due to the following publishers for permission to quote: to Little, Brown and Company for the quotations from *United States Foreign Policy: Shield of the Republic,* by Walter Lippmann; to the John Day Company for quotations from *Between Tears and Laughter,* by Lin Yutang; to Harcourt, Brace and Company for quotations from *American Strategy in World Politics,* by Nicholas John Spykman; to the Macmillan Company for quotations from *Conditions of Peace,* by Edward Hallett Carr; and to Henry Holt and Company for quotations from *Democratic Ideals and Realities,* by Sir Halford Mackinder.

ELY CULBERTSON

Contents

BOOK ONE

PRESENT BASIS FOR PEACE: POWER POLITICS

BOOK TWO

HOW TO ORGANIZE PEACE: THE WORLD FEDERATION PLAN

BOOK ONE

PRESENT BASIS FOR PEACE:

Power Politics

I. FORCE AND COUNTERFORCE

CHAPTER ONE

Abstractions and Realities

I BECAME A BRIDGE AUTHORITY very simply and easily. The story is pertinent to this book because it also tells how I came to write *Total Peace*. The revolution I perpetrated in the world of cards came as a strange by-product of my earlier revolutionary activities in social movements of various countries. My system of contract bridge is an echo of the experience I acquired in the study of philosophy and political sciences. My techniques of mass appeal to swell up the name of Culbertson as a bridge idol were developed and tested in the heat of my earlier mass appeals for the brotherhood of man. I even learned to play cards in a czarist jail.

In those days when I was much younger and not so foolish, I was desperately in love with the most beautiful abstractions: Humanity, Justice, People, Liberty, Peace. I hated the tyrants and despised the warmakers. I lived in the shadow of the great gatherers of noble truths, and I sought to follow the precepts of humanity's emancipators. These ideals were my science and my commandments.

In the name of these commandments I violated the commandments of the Czar and was put in jail. The jail was in the city of Sochi, in the Caucasus, the year 1908. It was the saddest year for men of good will everywhere in the vast Russias. The First Revolution was dying in spasms, and all hopes were submerged by waves of black reaction.

In the cell with me were six social revolutionists, condemned to death and awaiting, during appalling weeks, the confirmation of the judge's sentence of execution—a confirmation which was inevitable because the revolutionists, stemming spiritually from the original Rus-

3

sian revolutionary party, the Narodnik or People's party, were too proud either to renounce their ideals or to beg for mercy. They were the salt of the Russian earth.

They were magnanimous to the people who, not understanding, had betrayed them. Often they discussed the causes of the failure of the Revolution, not in bitter recrimination, as with the Occidentals, nor in apathetic resignation, as with the Orientals, but in a relentless spirit of self-searching and systematic criticism. One of them said: "The trouble with us is that we intellectuals are living in the world of shadowy abstractions. This is not a real world. What is the reality behind our concepts of humanity, of justice, of freedom? What is people? What are the real *forces* that move people?"

There were many involved answers, and it was apparent that no one knew the real structure and forces of people, or of the state against which they fought, or of humanity, which was but a cloudy vision emanating from glowing words. They had no doubt of their ideals, since these were built on the highest concepts of social morality, but they had no body of exact knowledge on the behavior and forces of societies. There was no bridge connecting their idealistic peaks with the political realities, and they remained isolated from the people they sought to save. Here were men about to die for the people, with a query on their lips "What is people?"

When I was released from the jail through the double circumstance of being a minor and a native American, I intensified my struggle for the people and sought to learn more about them.

My activities as a revolutionist were, at that time, directed as much against the tyranny of governments maintained by force as against the Marxian dream of a regimented, all-absorbing economic state. I was a disciple of Kropotkin, who opposed the violence of state against man and who proclaimed the supremacy of the law of co-operation. Like the Quakers, we sought to establish a society based on the consent of the governed and the free co-operation of all. I still think that one of the most compelling and truly realistic books of all time is Kropotkin's *Mutual Aid*. In this book, published after Darwin's law of the survival of the fittest had filled all men of good will with despair, the great Russian stated powerfully that mutual aid and not mutual destruction is the dominant law of societies.

We hated war as the breeding place for tyrants, and I gave to this ideal some of the best years of my youth. But as I went on struggling and dreaming against impossible odds, I learned more about the true structure of societies. Bitter experience taught me that the human herd was better adapted for tyranny than for freedom. I began to understand that every society, from a private club to an empire, could function only through its leadership organ; and that this leadership organ, like any human organ, was plagued by corruption and disease. Too often even the noblest of leadership degenerated into a tool of oppression and a source of profit. Inevitably the established leaders sought to retain their privileges of leadership, became exclusive, suppressed the opposition, and fought for power or spoils.

The First World War finally opened my eyes to the shameless exploitation of all peoples by their leaders, conservative, liberal, or radical. I was nauseated by the abject groveling of liberal and socialist "idealists," who overnight gave up their slogans of humanity and peace for the shouts of command by the Junkers of Europe. Although the air was full of propaganda and slogans, calling the world to fight for democracy, I realized that nations had been hurled at each other by one of those inexorable historical cyclones whose real origins were in the Industrial Revolution, and that only might could prevail. It became apparent that there was no escape in this world from the rule of force except within oneself. No nation could long remain prosperous without inviting aggression from others; nor could it long remain indigent without planning aggression against others. Force was the dominant law of societies—brutal military force, vested economic force, subtle poisonous force of ideologies or propaganda, force of inertia or ignorance. Above all the forces ruled the brutal, incontestable military force.

I gave up my revolutionary activities. But it was not a surrender, not even a compromise. It was simply a strategic retreat until I could accumulate more intellectual strength and attack the enemy of peace from a more realistic position. Not for a moment did I doubt that the law of co-operation was the supreme law of individuals and societies. But the same law of co-operation prevailed among the men of violence, who were organized better than the men of peace. My grave error, I reasoned, was in not recognizing the power of force, organized since time immemorial by the few so that they could wage war and enslave the many. These few understood force and knew how to manipulate it. But all men loved freedom, and most men sought peace. If, I reasoned, I could learn all the mysteries and tricks of force, if I could discover a system whereby the overwhelming numbers of men of good will could bring their superior force to bear against the few, then we would have peace and freedom. Organized violence was the enemy of mankind, and I resolved to learn from the enemy.

Thus, as I gave up my "profession" as a revolutionist, I acquired a new and even stranger profession: I became a social engineer, specializing on all problems of force. This was to be, and still is, my real lifework. I carried with my new profession the abiding mistrust of all governments, a conviction that all governments are inherently evil and that even a government of angels would evolve into a government of devils if its leaders remained long enough in power. Twenty-five years later this concept of government served me in good stead when I was drawing the blueprint for the government of the World Federation System.

During the First World War, while others fought each other, I studied the techniques of their fighting and the forces that made them fight. After the war I continued my studies. Force is power in action. It was necessary, therefore, to study the causes of war, the means of making war, military science, the technique of revolutions. I studied all the prophets of force and trickery from the ancients through Machiavelli to Robespierre, Napoleon, Clausewitz, Darwin, Bakunin, Nietzsche, Sorel, Lenin, Trotsky, and Haushofer.

But force is not only power in action; it is also and essentially a social power. It was necessary, therefore, to study the problems of power in societies, and that meant the knowledge of the structure of societies and mass psychology. Here I came up against my first blank wall. Although there were innumerable works on systems of government, there was very little on the inner structure of societies, and even less on mass psychology. What are the magnetic forces that hold individuals together, transmuting them into a social organism as ephemeral as a crowd or as lasting as the Chinese nation? How does a social movement start, and what are the laws of its development? Why are some individuals always on top in a society while others are always on the bottom? These and scores of other questions had to be answered precisely if I was to understand how force works in a business corporation, a village, or an empire.

The same ignorance prevailed, and still largely prevails, in the indispensable knowledge of group and mass psychology. A human body is largely built around the stomach; a social body is built around a special kind of mind—the social mind. Hence the great importance of psychosocial forces and of social psychology. As a revolutionist, I had run up against this mystery of the social mind. I saw that one may have the noblest and the most practical ideals and yet be utterly helpless without the knowledge of the hidden levers that move the masses; that false propaganda skillfully presented is often more powerful than the truth. All around me I saw political charlatans and demagogues drench the people with lies and spits of hatred and yet carry them off their feet, while my teachers floundered although they worshiped the truth and loved the people.

Many practical rules in the art of influencing the social mind, based on crude trial-and-error methods, have been known since earliest times. The structure of armies and churches is unconsciously based on these rules. The communists and feudalists have perfected the methods, and the American advertising industry has brought in a wealth of practical discoveries. A number of psychological laws have been developed, based on statistics and the law of probabilities. But even today our knowledge of the social mind is limited to its superficial layer and is grossly distorted by attempts to apply the lessons of individual psychology to an entirely different kind of mind.

A theory is widely accepted, for instance, that the "average" intelligence of the American nation is that of a twelve-year-old child. The professors who advanced this theory ought to have their own I.Q. examined. For the "average" intelligence of the American nation is the intelligence of the average level of its local and higher leaders— that of a man about forty-five years of age with a college education and a considerable stock of practical wisdom.

As I pursued my studies of societies in Europe after the First World War, it became apparent that all social structures and activities, be they those of a charitable organization, a state, or a revolution, must have underlying laws and methods common to them all. If I could find these underlying laws, I would have the key to the forces operating in all societies. I began to look for this key.

Before I could complete my research I found myself ruined by the Communist revolution in Russia. Our family fortune flowed from the oil fields of Grozny in the Caucasus, which my American father developed. This fortune was expropriated, and in the twenties I returned to my own country penniless, settling in New York. Later I gladly forgave Soviet Russia for expropriating our fortune, in view of their magnificent resistance against Hitler. But at the time I was in a quandary. I did not wish to get any kind of job because it meant curtailing severely my researches on the problems of societies and force. And yet I had to live somehow. It was then that I decided to become a scientific gambler in cards. Spinoza, one of the great teachers to whom I devoted years of study, ground lenses for a living, making enough money in a few hours to devote the rest of his time to philosophical meditation. High-stake bridge flourished in New York. While in the University of Geneva in 1915 I had learned to play bridge; why not grind out bids and plays?

I had always been fascinated by the bizarre world of cards. It was a world of pure power politics where rewards and punishments were meted out immediately. A deck of cards was built like the purest of hierarchies, with every card a master to those below it and a lackey to those above it. And there were "masses"—long suits—which always asserted themselves in the end, triumphing over the kings and aces. In bridge every play was in itself a problem of force and timing. And the inexorable rhythm of the law of probabilities dominated the fall of the cards like the beating of a tom-tom. I was at home in this unique world of cards, and I seldom lost.

Now that cards had become a rather serious matter with me, I drew upon my experience as a student of systems and built a system of bridge for my private use in gambling. But my wife kept disapproving of my playing for high stakes, in spite of Spinoza and in spite of my big winnings. She thought it was a waste of time and that there was another and quicker way to win the necessary leisure for my studies on the problems of force in societies. She insisted that I had a marvelous system of contract bridge and that if instead of playing for high stakes I would teach others how to play for amusement, I could solve the financial problem. Mrs. Culbertson offered to help. I then gave up playing for high stakes and concentrated on the system and promotion of contract bridge. Originally I named our system the Forcing System, but everybody started to call it the Culbertson System, and we followed suit.

When we launched our system toward the end of the twenties, contract bridge was mounting on one of those waves of mass hysteria that suddenly seizes millions in a fad or a political revolution. There was chaos and turmoil in the world of cards. A revolution was brewing. Twelve apostles of bridge, each with his own following, were screaming at the top of their voices their own solutions of the world-shaking problems of contract bridge. Although each authority had something good to offer, none had a specific and comprehensive system. These contract-bridge planners abounded in pointers, suggestions, slogans, and vaporous generalities. We profited by our many years of work in building our bridge system. One cannot build a system for anything overnight nor improvise it from the echoes of the past. The millions of bridge players, in search of a concrete bid or a specific method of play, welcomed our system. Within two years, from 1930 to 1932, a deck of cards was pyramided into a world-wide movement with millions of devotees. I succeeded much too well, and became a victim of my own technique of publicity. Later, because I was "typed," like a Hollywood actor, it would be difficult to convince some people that a bridge authority could also be passionately and intelligently interested in the destiny of the country that showered him with fame and wealth far beyond his humble deserts.

There were two solid advantages I derived from my revolutionary excursion into the world of cards. First, I became the master of my time and could devote myself to more intensive and fruitful research in the problems of force. This did not mean that I abandoned bridge. Bridge is and always will be my hobby, and is still my bread and butter. But the money and leisure that the bridge players gave me permitted me to call upon the best assistance in my research. I was my own master. As a teacher of bridge I was not handicapped, like other professors and teachers, by the routine necessity of teaching classes and correcting papers. I did not depend upon any committee. I knew from past experience that no committee has ever created an organic system or written a poem or composed a symphony. Collective wisdom is indispensable, but it can operate only on the basis of an organic system created by an individual, and it can only modify, criticize, or put into practice. I could choose my own fields of research and make my own tests. All this the bridge players made possible. And, in a way, they must bear their share of the responsibility in the writing of this book and in the creation of the World Federation System.

The second advantage lay in the fact that the promotion of contract bridge offered me a unique opportunity to test practically and to improve the soundness of my theories of social psychology and mass propaganda. I began to put the results of my studies on the structure and dynamics of societies into a book. They dealt not merely with the art of influencing peoples, but with the workings of any one of hundreds of millions of social organisms, from a family cell to the State Department of the United States. In my opinion, at least a cursory knowledge of the elements of societies is an indispensable preliminary to understanding what is going on in this world. One cannot sell soap effectively or launch a revolution without knowing—consciously or unconsciously—how, why, and when the people react to each other.

That book, however, had to be postponed; for the law of military force was again hurling the world into war.

CHAPTER TWO

Nationalism vs. Internationalism

In 1938 I became convinced that the Second World War was inevitable and that history would call upon the United States to play a dominant role in world politics. It seemed even then that the coming decade would establish a pattern of forces for generations to come. The tides of war were rising everywhere, and yet we were drifting planlessly and improvidently toward manifold catastrophes. The reason was (and still is) that we had no foreign policy derived from a scientific estimate of forces that the Industrial Revolution had let loose upon the world, and correlated with our unheard-of industrial power, geographic situation, and historic opportunities.

The years I had spent in the study of the problems of force and international politics would now, I resolved, be turned to account in the self-imposed task of working out a modern system of United States foreign policy. Many of the basic concepts were already there and had stood the test of events. My concepts were based on an enlightened understanding of the rules of power politics that a great state must practice if it is to avoid disastrous combinations of enemy powers or even to survive. Building a system for a foreign policy of the greatest state in the world, in such a manner that it would withstand the stresses and strains of events tomorrow as well as a generation hence, was a presumptuous and awesome task. Only in the spring of 1943 did I complete it, at least in its essentials. After that it was necessary to translate it into this book, *Total Peace*.

Meanwhile the shadows of the coming peace grew larger and more portentous. It was evident that we had no plan either for a consistent policy of power politics or for a workable system of collective defense. We had only principles, good speeches, and better intentions. But a foreign policy cannot be improvised overnight and conducted from day to day. One must look to the coming events with a historical eye and plan months and usually years ahead in order to be prepared for all the possible moves of foreign states, friend and foe.

The fundamental goal of American foreign policy which I envisioned was security for the United States against future short-term and long-term threats. I sought this security first of all in the strength of the United States itself and in a new concept of an American Strategic Zone to guard the Atlantic and the Pacific approaches to the American continent, and secondly in closer co-operation with the states whose selfish interests could coincide with ours.

The foreign policy of the United States, like the foreign policy of any great state, must primarily be based upon its national interests and the play of power politics which is the reality of today. Dominating the relations between states is force—sheer armed force and, so far, little else.

There is no parallel between an individual in a society and a sovereign nation in a society of sovereign nations. Above the individual with his own rights there is a higher law with higher rights, enforceable by police power. There is no higher human law above sovereign states except the empty shell of international law. Inasmuch as there is no international organization to enforce international law, however nobly conceived, its "laws" are largely futile whenever they happen to conflict (and this happens often) with the national interests of any strong sovereign state. A state, in virtue of its absolute sovereignty, is a law unto itself. It is the final arbiter and interpreter of all its treaties with other states. In the supreme anarchy of sovereign states its members can therefore enforce or obey only one law—the law of tooth and claw—and only one foreign policy—power politics.

Power politics is the policy of a state based on the use or threat of force. In this grim game of survival, therefore, the United States also must base its foreign policy on power politics. Only when an adequate substitute for power politics is developed can the United States relax.

American power politics is unique and differs widely from the power politics of other states because its underlying conditions are unique and differ widely from those of all other states, except possibly Russia. These underlying conditions are:

1. With the disarmament of Germany and Japan, the United States becomes the most powerful nation in the world, surpassing the combined strength of the next strongest victorious powers. Her productive capacity of decisive fighting machines will surpass that of the rest of the world; her navies will control most of the oceans, and her air fleets will or could dominate most of the skies of the world.

2. This unparalleled power of the United States will begin to decline in relation to other states a few years after the war. The very fact that the United States is the richest nation in the world, the guardian of the Western Hemisphere, and the principal obstacle to the expansion of other states, exposes her to inevitable future coalitions and aggression. The future security of the United States may be threatened (a) by some of our present allies, (b) by some of our defeated enemies, or (c) by vastly populous nations, now dormant, when they become industrialized.

3. The United States possesses a continental living space, an econ-

omy which is essentially inward-expanding, and a dominant economic position within a zone comprising nearly forty per cent of the livable land area of the world, inhabited by twelve per cent of the world's population. The fundamental problem of American power politics, therefore, is not how to expand into the living spaces of other nations but how to preserve what she already possesses. Thus the main object of American power politics is opposite to that of German or Japanese power politics which is to conquer the living space of other nations.

It follows that the United States must use her present enormous power to fortify herself strategically against future aggressors, and politically to integrate, on the basis of sovereignty and mutual co-operation, the nations within and outside her Strategic Zone. This means that the United States must carry on a policy of militant defense. But this also means that the United States *must base her power politics on renouncing wars for the purposes of economic or political conquest*. Thus an apparently idealistic principle of non-aggression coincides with the obviously selfish principle of power politics.

From these underlying conditions I established three basic principles for American power politics:

The first principle is that *the United States cannot permit any other great state to increase its power materially through conquest or domination*. On this principle are based the methods and rules of American Balance Politics.

The second principle is that *the United States must use its present power to insure itself strategically against possible future aggression by one or more sovereign states*. I included in this strategic concept not only a new American Strategic Zone but the necessity to implement our Good Neighbor policy in Latin America and in the Pacific through Regional Federations on a voluntary basis. On this principle are based the methods and rules of American Space Politics.

The third principle is that *the United States must use its present power to establish, if possible, an adequate system of world collective security*. On this principle are based methods and rules of Collective Defense. If such a system of collective defense could be established, it would constitute an *adequate substitute* for power politics.

Thus the ultimate object of American power politics is the elimination of power politics in relations among states.

Those readers who know of the World Federation Plan may wonder how I can reconcile the principle of power politics with the principle of collective security. During the last generation a new principle appeared, side by side with power politics, in the foreign policy of states—the principle of collective security based on some kind of world organization. This was the noble ideal of Wilson.

A little later I shall show specifically why any system of collective security was impossible in the past. At the same time I shall show specifically that new and unique circumstances have arisen in the last few years which could make an adequate system of collective security not only possible but certain. But—and this is the important point— any future system for collective security must fulfill the double requirements of effectiveness and acceptability. This is the double yardstick for any political system. A system such as the League of Nations was acceptable but wholly ineffective. Some other system, based on the drastic limitation of the sovereignty of states, might be effective in insuring lasting peace, but would be wholly unacceptable. What is needed is a system which will insure the maximum effectiveness and the maximum acceptability.

The great powers would never consent to any system of collective security which means disarming them, or sacrificing their essential sovereignty, or trusting an untried, untested world organization. There would be a considerable time lag between the inauguration of a system of collective security and its final acceptance. The system would have to be tested in actual operation, which would require several years. Meanwhile it would be political folly for the United States or any other great power not to be prepared for possible betrayals even by the administration of the world organization itself. The only sovereign right a great power like the United States would be willing to give up is the right to wage wars of aggression. That right could be yielded provided that in all other respects the United States is fully safeguarded, not only by the articles of a world constitution, but also by her own armed forces and strategic bases. A world co-operative of nations can be established only on the foundation of nationalism.

It follows that the concepts of power politics and national interests of a state would necessarily prevail at least for a period of time, even if some future system of collective security is established. I was therefore on safe ground in developing the new concepts of American power politics, which constitute the *nationalist* basis of American foreign policy. Parallel to that I developed new concepts of collective defense, which constitute the *internationalist* basis of American foreign policy. The nationalist and internationalist requirements for American foreign policy were then integrated in a higher synthesis of the World Federation Plan. In this manner I reconciled the principle of power politics with the principle of collective security.

The nationalist and the internationalist bases are derived from two distinct methods of solving the problem of America's future security. The United States can defend herself against future aggression in one of two ways:

1. The United States can make herself militarily powerful enough to be practically independent of the rest of the world. This she can achieve by creating a new American Strategic Zone and by winning over as permanent allies at least the peoples of Latin America and of the Malaysian region.

2. The United States can protect herself by participating in an international organization, with a strong international police force, together with international agencies for economic and educational rebuilding of the world. This she can achieve by using her tremendous power to help establish, on a voluntary basis, an international organization for common defense.

Which of these two solutions should the American people choose? *The answer is both solutions.* I would give the same answer if I were writing from the standpoint of Britain or Russia, who, also possessing vast living spaces, seek to defend what they already have rather than risk all to acquire more.

To take the nationalist solution and to refuse the added insurance of the internationalist solution would be politically as shortsighted as to pin one's hopes on the internationalist solution without having a safe line of retreat to the nationalist basis.

Strangely enough, my experiences as a scientific gambler have been of great help in planning American foreign policy. I am known as a bold, aggressive player. Actually I never take a serious risk without an "out," some safe line of retreat in case my gamble fails. The trouble with most peace planners is that they put all their eggs in one idealistic basket. They don't know how to expect the unexpected, to count in the incalculable. They are willing to risk the whole future of their country on one single solution without having an "out." On the other hand, the trouble with the nationalist "realists" is that they too have no "out" for the day when the United States cannot stand alone.

The double solution offers not only the maximum of effectiveness but also the maximum of acceptability. There is a compelling psychological reason for it. All ideological considerations aside, there are two basic groups of Americans—the nationalists and the internationalists. This fundamental and traditional cleavage cuts across political lines and will continue to grow, for it corresponds to the two different solutions of the fundamental problem of security for the United States. There are millions of Americans, nationalistically inclined, who have little interest or faith in saving the world. History has convinced them that force is paramount and permanent and that there is no substitute for power politics. They want to know what their own country will get out of this war for its greater security and power. There are millions of other Americans, internationally inclined, who are convinced that old ways mean new wars and that America's security lies in the security of all.

The nationalists are determined that *this time* America's own military security and power shall be perpetuated; the internationalists are determined that *this time* a better and more just world order shall emerge from the war. The nationalists do not want the rest of the world to cheat America; the internationalists do not want America to cheat the world. No plan of world settlement will be acceptable unless it satisfies the essential requirements of both these basic groups of Americans. For, in our democracy, each group is strong enough to prevent the other group from realizing its postwar plans.

We saw this tragic contradiction at work after the First World War, when exactly nothing was settled. We are certain to see it at work in the coming world settlement unless something is done about it now. The division is already bitter and, if allowed to crystallize into set attitudes, might well mean a paralysis of the will of the nation, leading to a postwar settlement that will be no settlement at all.

The true solution is not nationalism or internationalism, but a higher synthesis of the nationalist and internationalist doctrines. Both doctrines are patriotically inspired. Both are indispensable to insure the security of the United States against future aggression. The same cleavage between the two opposing solutions troubles the mind of millions of individual Americans. The wise thing to do, therefore, is to use both of these weapons for our defense. Meaningless compromise or a middle way will not do.

Narrow nationalism is phony nationalism. Brittle alliances of two or three dominating powers for "the good of others," economic alchemy to remove the immemorial causes of war in a decade, or appeals for the Parliament of Man are varieties of phony internationalism. But if we combine sound nationalism with sound internationalism, we can establish a *unified* American foreign policy providing the maximum of effectiveness and the maximum of acceptability.

Democracy is an unstable equilibrium of pressure groups. To the American nation, unity is even more important after the war than during the war. A war can be carried on and won by a minority of the nation. Peace can be won only by a majority of the nation. The only way to maintain that unity long enough to win the peace is by establishing a positive ideal wherein both nationalists and internationalists will have an equally vital stake. The nationalists may scoff at the pound-foolishness of the internationalists' proposed system of collective defense, but they will be paid off in the national coin of the American Strategic Zone and safeguards of the national sovereignty. The internationalists may scorn the penny-wiseness of the nationalists, but they will be paid off in the international coin of a world order that makes sense.

CHAPTER THREE

The Dilemma of the International Police Force

SEVERAL TIMES in the preceding pages I have mentioned a new system of collective defense. How did this new system come about?

The answer to this question is also a story of the most revolutionary event in the history of the world, an event which has occurred before our very eyes but the full significance of which is understood only by a few. This significance lies in the fact that whereas only a few short years ago lasting world peace between states was *impossible,* it has now become *possible*.

I was one of those who correctly believed that any effective system of collective defense to insure lasting peace was futile. The reason was not that "war is human nature"; I have no patience with people who seek to solve specific problems with vaporous generalities about human nature. Much of "human nature" is the result of conditions created by human beings themselves. For thousands of years human sacrifice was "human nature" to the bloodthirsty priests. Nor have I any patience with diehards who reason that because a certain thing has never happened in the past it cannot happen in the future. That type of mentality was meat to me in bridge, for while they always played for the average run of cards, I played for both the average and the highly improbable. There are thousands of things that are happening around us which have never happened before, and more will happen yet.

WHY LASTING PEACE WAS IMPOSSIBLE

There was a specific reason why I was convinced that all plans for lasting peace were hopeless. The specific reason lay, until very recently, in the nature of weapons that man used. Lasting peace was impossible because lasting disarmament of states and groups within states was impossible. After the revolutionary appearance of iron weapons and the horse, thousands of years ago, any blacksmith could forge the weapons necessary for war. In the Middle Ages anyone with wealth enough to buy a horse and armor became a moving fortress. Later almost any industrial shop could produce the rifles, machine guns, and artillery which, though cumbersome, were adequate. There was no way of disarming effectively even the small states, let alone the large states. And without effective disarmament of the world there was no way of preventing one state from attacking another. In early medieval times, when the Catholic Church was supreme in Europe, kings were made and unmade by Rome. Repeatedly the church sought peace between the peoples. But there was no means of *disarming* the men of violence. There was no way to stop all the blacksmiths and armorers from forging weapons. Much was achieved in humanizing war, but nothing could be done toward abolishing war.

Thus there was never a moment in history—including the 1920s—when a system of collective defense could be established that would adequately insure the states against aggression. Even the First World War was essentially a war of mass armies armed with easily procurable weapons.[1]

WHY LASTING PEACE IS NOW POSSIBLE

Since the 1930s it has become apparent that new and extraordinary circumstances have taken shape which make the establishment of a system for lasting peace entirely possible. After the blitzkrieg in Poland an idea was born in my mind which stirred me more deeply than any I have known. I became convinced that a new era had dawned upon humanity, an era which might terminate in the destruction of our civilization or in the establishment of lasting world peace. *Lasting peace has become theoretically possible because science has revolutionized the structure and the technique of modern weapons, developing a new age of heavy fighting machines.* The Industrial Revolution has finally caught up with military weapons. It revolutionized them too, creating gigantic, intricate fighting machines

[1]World peace is possible, of course, if we have a world state, like ancient Rome. That was "peace" under the self-perpetuating tyranny of the Roman military clique. I am dealing with the collective defense of sovereign states.

which require for their production and use vast industrial plants, based on tremendous living space.

As a result all but a few of the nations of the world have become automatically disarmed, since they have no capacity to produce in adequate quantities the war-winning fighting machines. For the first time in history the monopoly of world power has become concentrated in the monopoly of heavy weapons—armored ships of air, sea, and land.

I then drew the conclusion that peace has become a theoretical possibility because *for the first time in history it has become possible to disarm the world by segregating the decisive, deadly engines of destruction in the hands of a few*. These "few" may be either the governments of two or three leading powers, or victorious future conquerors, or *the trustees of a world co-operative of nations*. It is the last possibility—collective defense—that carries the hope of lasting peace. Just how this possibility was to be realized, and I knew it was extremely difficult, was another question.

The Principle of the Segregation of Weapons

There was nothing really new in my discovery of the principle of the segregation of heavy weapons. All its elements—the gasoline engine, the deadly planes and tanks, the intricate instruments of precision—were there for everyone to see. But I felt like a scientist who had made an electrifying discovery that a certain vital theory which heretofore had been untenable on theoretical grounds had become, because of changed conditions, theoretically possible. What stirred me so deeply was the overwhelming fact that lasting peace—that Great Peace about which philosophers and common men have dreamed since the dawn of civilization—had become at least a *theoretical* possibility. The Beast of War could at last be isolated, his deadly weapons *segregated* in the safekeeping of men of peace. Thus not only the war lords, but war itself, could be put into a strait jacket.

Modern science has made a thorough job of revolutionizing weapons of war and communications. There is a revolution in the hitting power of steel and in the burning power of fire. Guns and bombs reach invisible targets with deadly accuracy. There is a revolution in the time and distance factors: the strategic hour does the job of twenty hours; distances of thousands of miles are telescoped into hundreds or scores of miles; oceans become seas, and seas become lakes. There is a revolution in military strategy. For the first time in history war is truly three-dimensional. The height of man-made walls has risen from ten or twenty feet to twenty or forty thousand feet, and they have changed the walls of stone to walls of fire. A fortress or a ship can be blown up not only from below the ground or the sea, but from the skies above. Man has acquired a celestial cavalry. And the god of war, who in Napoleon's time was "on the side of the largest battalions," is no longer there. He now flies.

The decisive weapons of a few years ago have become like a bow and arrow before the fighting machines of today. That is why there is a millenarian gulf between the years 1918 and 1939. The industrial potential has become equal to the military potential. The Second World War is the first Battle of Weapons. Always, in the past, war was essentially the fight of men against men. Now war has become essentially the fight of machines against machines. Not only have all but a few states become effectively disarmed, but the masses within the states have also become disarmed.

Four principal conclusions are inescapable from this revolution in military weapons and communications:

1. Democracy everywhere will find itself in increasing peril.

2. All but a few states of the world will become satellized around protector states.

3. The monopoly of heavy weapons, after this war, will have passed to Britain, Russia, and the United States. And, of the three, the United States will possess a controlling monopoly.

4. This monopoly of heavy weapons by the three victorious powers will be temporary. Vastly populated, hitherto dormant nations are becoming rapidly industrialized. When they are even partly industrialized (and that will be soon) the combination of their fighting machines with their inexhaustible man power will be well-nigh irresistible. If they fall under the sway of some future Hitlers (which is highly probable), our civilization will be in grave jeopardy.

For the first time in history, two things have become possible:

either the conquest of the world by one dominant state, or a co-operative of nations of the world based on the segregation of decisive weapons.

Is Democracy Doomed?

The first and almost immediate threat is to democracies everywhere. Some liberals with ideological fixations are so saturated with "the economic interpretation of history" that they are blind to the most obvious threats to democracy. My differences with them arise from the fundamental difference between their and my diagnosis of the ills that beset the world. They ascribe the profound perturbations of the world today to social injustices, and they valiantly strive to remedy them. I am ready to travel that far with them. But social injustices have always existed, and yet we have not always had the incredible world-wide horrors of today. There is something happening in the world which is so pregnant with danger to democracy that the liberal or socialistic economic formulas do not suffice.

Our modern democracy was born in the smoke of gunpowder, when bullets pierced the armor of the knight and cannon balls destroyed his castle. *Bullets, not ballots, are the true sentinels of democracy.* Today the peoples and their true leaders are virtually disarmed by tanks, planes, and modern propaganda. In the past, democracy flourished where the nature of weapons and military structure favored the defense of freedom by the peoples themselves under their freedom-loving leaders. Such conditions no longer prevail. Everywhere violent minorities can seize the levers of the state and deprive the people of all hope of redemption. The day of barricades is over, and so is the day of barricade revolutionists. The only forces still working to preserve our democratic freedom are the psychosocial forces of habit and tradition. *The reality of physical force is leaving the peoples.*

Many think that this is a world revolution of the peoples on the march toward their final liberation. I say this is a world counter-revolution against the peoples everywhere, who are more and more disarmed. The probabilities are strong that the neo-feudalists will be the victors in the continuing postwar struggle, even though the democracies and Soviet Russia have won the war.

If by a miracle some democracies escape tyranny at home, they must inevitably face future dictatorships if they wish to survive in the ever-widening swings of greater wars to come. Another war like this one and democracy will be a hollow word, even in the United States. Thus all freedoms depend upon Freedom from War. And Freedom from War can be secured only by segregating the decisive heavy weapons and making it impossible for any government or clique to use these weapons for aggression.

The Quota Force Principle

No sooner did I establish the principle that effective world disarmament, and therefore collective defense, had become theoretically possible than I encountered an obstacle which apparently made the *practical* application of that principle impossible. This obstacle is the great dilemma of an international police force, and hence of lasting peace. For without a powerful international police force, in control of all the heavy weapons, to support a system of collective defense, there can be no lasting peace. By an international police force I mean, of course, what has always been meant—that is, an armed force under the control of a world organization with well-defined though limited powers, *separate* from the sovereign states. Any other use of the term "international police force" is either ignorance or a willful attempt by politicians to fool their people.

Such an attempt might be made because Dr. George Gallup's polls have shown that seventy-four per cent of the people in the United States and in Britain approve of establishing an international police force. Late in September 1943 a special test was made of reaction to the Fulbright and the Ball-Burton-Hill-Hatch resolutions in Congress. Of this survey, made among "informed groups," Dr. Gallup writes:

"The vote came out almost precisely the same as that recorded in a recent survey of the whole nation.

"The vote of the 'informed' is:

For	75%
Against	17%
Undecided	8%

"When the Institute recently polled the whole country the vote was seventy-four per cent in favor, fourteen per cent opposed, and twelve per cent undecided."

From the standpoint of public acceptance, the problem of lasting peace is thus well on the way to solution.

The great dilemma of an international police force arises from the contradiction between the necessity to disarm all the states as far as heavy weapons are concerned and the impossibility that the leading states would consent to such disarmament. This contradiction may be stated as follows:

First Premise: An effective international police force is possible only if the government of a world organization has the monopoly of the production of heavy weapons (armored ships of air, sea, and land) and their exclusive use for its international police force.

Second Premise: It is impossible for the great powers to consent voluntarily to such disarmament and thereby entrust their destiny to any powerful international body.

Conclusion: Effective segregation of decisive weapons under an international police force is impossible; hence any effective system of collective defense is futile.

A proud and mighty nation, such as the United States, Britain, or Russia, would never consent to disarm herself effectively and thus place her own destiny in the hands of an international body. If a powerful and prosperous nation were foolish enough to do this, it would, in effect, be conquered without firing a shot; wholly disarmed, it would be at the mercy of an international organization composed largely of foreigners and, to some extent, of enemies.

It may be argued that it is better to trust an international organization for peace than supinely to await new and devastating wars. But this argument defeats itself. Any international organization for peace, in possession of an overwhelming military power, might well become an international organization for tyranny and hopeless enslavement of the world. It is better for a nation to win a devastating war than to disarm herself and thus become a possible prey to a possible clique of international politicians and war lords.

No matter how many checks or balances are applied to a world government, or how strict are the limitations of its powers, its mem-

bers are only human. The nature of all social organisms, from private club to world government, is such that those in control inevitably tend toward the formation of cliques, so as to perpetuate their own power and privileges. The government of a world organization, once in possession of an overwhelming armed force, would sooner or later corrupt itself, becoming the breeding place of greedy politicians and power politics combines. Even if the government of such a world organization were made up of the purest of idealists, the dangers would be as great, because in that case the world organization might lead to the worst kind of tyranny—the tyranny of fanatic reformers who, conscious of their immense power and impelled by this or that ideology, would not hesitate to tear up any constitution or break up any nation. These reformers might compel the United States to dissipate its wealth for the benefit of the world, or they might declare Soviet Russia to be the world's public enemy number one.

But the greatest danger for the leading powers, if they disarm themselves, would lie in the international police force itself. The international police force, controlling the disarmed individual nations, might easily evolve into a corps of Janizaries or a Praetorian Guard, and its High Command could easily conquer the world and seize its riches.

Hundreds of books are written on the problem of lasting peace in which an international police force is taken for granted, leaving the "details" to be worked out later. It is astonishing with what glib nonchalance these experts prattle about an "international police force" without realizing its sinister implications, if it is to be a *real* force, or its hopeless futility if it is to be a token force.

It is on the rocks of this contradiction that any effective system of collective defense must founder. No matter how perfect a plan may be in other respects, if it fails to provide for the collective defense of the world *without disarming* individual nations, lasting world peace is but a dangerous delusion.

This inner contradiction was inherent in all the past systems of collective security, from the first plan of Pierre Dubois in the fourteenth century to the League of Nations. Since effective world disarmament was not possible anyway, because decisive weapons could not be segregated, it did not matter. I had hoped that I could

find a way out of the impasse now that world disarmament had become theoretically possible. But again I was facing a blank wall. After
trying hundreds of solutions I reluctantly gave up. Logic compelled
me to admit that there was no solution to this inner contradiction
and that therefore any practical solution of the problem of world
peace was impossible.

Yet the solution was always there, so extraordinarily simple and
so transparently obvious that it never occurred to me or to anyone
else. I actually stumbled on it largely by sheer luck and only partly by
knowing what I was looking for. One day I was thinking about the
National Guards of our states and the Federal army. I remembered
how much fear there was, when our Constitution was being established, lest the Federal government, with its armed forces, should
encroach upon the freedom of the states, and how finally each state
kept its own militia under the orders of the governor in peacetime,
while in time of war it was incorporated in the Federal army. This
was the clue!

The solution finally came to me. Of course the problems of an international police force were entirely different and vastly more complex. But what mattered was the fact that in the days when our states
took their sovereignty very seriously their National Guard, or State
Militia, was a *two-way army*. In time of peace it served as a state defense against the possible betrayal or tyranny of the Federal government with its army, and in time of war it became a part of the collective defense against the foreign aggressor.

The international police force could also be a two-way army. It
would consist of National Contingents armed with heavy weapons,
recruited from the citizens of the country and stationed in its territory. In time of peace each National Contingent would be subject to
the orders of its national government. But in time of war it would
automatically form part of the international police force. The number of these National Contingents would be limited to a few great
powers, and the strength of each would be determined on the basis
of a quota derived from the present relative armed strength of each
great power.

But there was a possibility that, in spite of a solemn covenant, some
of these National Contingents might be prevented by their national

governments from joining against the aggressor. A separate force would be needed to act independently of the National Contingents—similar to our Federal armed force, but of course not proportionately so powerful. Therefore, in addition to the National Contingents, there would be a special Mobile Corps (International Contingent), made up of regiments of *small nations,* which would be at the direct disposal of the international organization in war and in peace. This Mobile Corps would be stationed on extraterritorial bases and would function as the *shock troops* of the international police, with the National Contingents as the reserves. In both cases the sole purpose of the international police force and the sole enforceable power of the international government would be to prevent a state from waging war against another state.

How would the heavy weapons be segregated? The government of the international organization would set up a World Armament Trust, divided into subsidiaries located in the territories of the National and International Contingents, with production apportioned on the same quota bases as that of the Contingents.

It is clear that this solution consists of *a new system of composition and distribution of national armed forces based on the segregation of heavy weapons.* It is so arranged that the existing relative strength of the great powers is not diminished, while, in addition, a powerful new *collective strength* made up of small nations is established against future aggressors. This point is of vital importance to a basically non-aggressor nation like the United States, which will thus secure, through an integrated system of collective defense, the perpetual alliance of the small nations of the world with a population of over three hundred million. The highly trained volunteers from the small nations, recruited for the International Contingent, will always fight against any aggressor, since the only hope of the future survival of the small nations lies in a system of collective defense.

The capacity of each great power to defend itself is not only preserved, but, is in fact, increased. The quota of the United States National Contingent, for instance, will be at all times twenty per cent of the total armored force of the world and twenty per cent of the production of warplanes, warships, and guns. Together with the Mobile Corps, which will constitute twenty-two per cent of the

world's heavily armed forces, the American defensive power will be enormously increased. At the same time the possibility of tyranny by the international organization is eliminated, since each great power not only retains its national armed force but will have the automatic support of many other contingents.

In this manner an international police force, consisting of several National Contingents and one International Contingent, can be established. The terrifying heavy weapons can be segregated once and for all, for the sole purpose of collective defense. A new, permanent, standing armed force of shock troops can be developed from the freedom-loving small nations, who, although weak *individually,* become *collectively* a powerful ally against all future aggressors. Yet neither the essential sovereignty nor the capacity for resistance by individual great powers will be diminished.

The great dilemma of an international police force seemed to be solved,[2] at least in its essential outline. But before I could be scientifically certain, it was necessary to test thoroughly the Quota Force Principle. No one but a fool would rush into print with the glad tidings of his discovery, only to find out later that somewhere he had made a grievous error. When I had completed the blueprint of the Quota Force Principle and had tested its theory in every conceivable manner, I was certain that the solution would work and that its adoption would involve no risk whatsoever for the United States or any other power. But a scrupulous scientist—or a scrupulous scientific gambler—doubts even the rigorously logical deductions of his own mind, allowing margin for error.

"Perhaps," I said to myself, "there is a false link somewhere in the chain of my thoughts."

My first step was to select a number of truly brilliant minds who did not have any vested intellectual interests of their own and who were strangers to me. I submitted the formula to them, asking them to break it down. To my great satisfaction (and surprise), they found little to criticize.

My next step was to send out the formula (and the World Federation Plan) to five thousand experts in universities and elsewhere.

[2]This solution, called the Quota Force Principle, is fully explained elsewhere in this book.

Their response was similar. Since then, although many features of the World Federation Plan have been criticized, the Quota Force Principle has withstood the tests in all its essentials.

I am now convinced beyond any doubt that the solution of the dilemma of an international police force and of collective defense exists. Thus, as a result of new and unique circumstances, caused by the Industrial Revolution, lasting peace is not only theoretically possible but feasible, and not in some remote future, but in our time.

Only the unexpected or the humanly unforeseeable stands in the way. But I have provided even for that, in the nationalist basis of American foreign policy, by establishing an American Strategic Zone, to which we could "retreat," and by maintaining the strategic zones of other great powers.

There were many problems other than that of an international police force to be solved and tested. There was particularly the problem of the sovereignty of states. This problem was solved by depriving the states of one sovereign right only—the right to wage war of aggression and to manufacture heavy weapons. Thus the government of the World Federation is in reality not a government at all but a Peace Trust to which each nation entrusts a part of its sovereignty (the right to wage war of aggression), receiving in exchange a greater value (the right to be defended against aggression).

In my concept of collective defense I did not seek to abolish sovereignty. I sought to reinforce it. I did not seek to abolish nationalism. Nationalism is the most powerful force today. Abolishing nationalism is like trying to abolish love. We can abolish love only by abolishing women. And we shall abolish nationalism only when we abolish nations. I sought to distill from the poisons of nationalism the antidote for war.

To me these problems and many others which had baffled the experts for many years had seemed insoluble. The main reason was that the central problem of the international police force was not solved. Once this problem was solved all other solutions fitted in easily and naturally.

Thus an effective plan of campaign for the coming Battle of Peace—the World Federation Plan—was ready.

The Mood of Acceptance

It is not enough to have an effective plan of campaign. There must also be, among some great powers at least, the mood of acceptance. A plan of collective defense would not have suited Germany or Japan. In the future it may not suit some great power which harbors aggressive designs. The mood of acceptance exists today. Through an extraordinarily favorable conjuncture of events each of the five great powers which will have a say during the next few years— Britain, France, Russia, China, and the United States—will or should favor a satisfactory system of collective defense. None of these powers is land-hungry. Each is immensely wealthy, actually or potentially, and the security of each is sorely threatened in the future, unless a system of collective defense is established. France, with her limited population, is condemned to oscillate between vassalage to a re-vived Germany and dominion annexation by Britain. China, with her unlimited man power, is condemned by the inexorable mechan-ism of the world balance of power to future partition, as soon as the fruits of her industrialization begin to ripen dangerously. Britain, with her vast empire standing as an inverted pyramid on the over-populated island of England, will be the first victim in any future world war. Russia's dominant fear today, as in 1919 (and the key to her foreign policy), is her fear of a world coalition against the Soviet Union. The United States, because it is the most powerful, is potentially the most threatened of all. Never before has the world situation been so propitious to collective defense. Today the yearnings for lasting peace by the peoples of the world have coincided with the power-politics interests of the leading states. In American hearts the determination that *this shall never happen again* is writ in letters of fire. The American nation will tolerate neither the indefinite delays of a long armistice nor the false internationalism of alliances.

Another factor may prove decisive in the establishment of collective defense. It is the unparalleled present power of the United States, which many American politicians underestimate. The same Industrial Revolution that made Germany the greatest military power in Europe, and the deadliest threat to all the nations of the world, has made the United States the greatest military power in the world and the only hope of all nations. The United States has enough power to establish a system of collective defense with little help from outside. If, for instance, Britain and Russia should abstain, for reasons of power politics or for lack of vision, from joining such a system, then their assistance will not be indispensable. Their sovereignty and rightful territories will be respected. But the United States is sufficiently strong, physically and spiritually, to be invincible in collective defense with China as a partner or with France and smaller nations. Similarly, the United States could draw enough support from the outside to form, with Britain alone or with Russia, a system of collective defense just to all. In any event, it will not be necessary for the United States to ride on the coattails of the Anglo-Russian Alliance in order to organize a world that makes sense.

CHAPTER FOUR

Blind Alleys in Our Foreign Policy

HISTORY HAS DEALT to the American nation the biggest hand of all time. It is a grand slam. But it is not a lay-down grand slam. It can be beaten. It can be muffed. To win, this hand must be played with consummate skill. And it must be played against tricky, skillful adversaries, well stocked with trumps.

Never before was a nation in such a unique position to do so much good or to commit irreparable blunders. And never before was the gigantic power of a nation so ephemeral and so inexorably limited by time. Other yet undeveloped nations will soon learn most of our industrial techniques and surpass us with their vast man power. If we play our game badly, we may be, in a quarter of a century, where Britain was in 1940.

Today our greatest danger is not from outside; it is from within. And especially it is within our national leadership—officials, politicians (Republican and Democrat), experts, writers, intellectuals, businessmen, and the legion of others. All love their country. Most are highly intelligent. But few know the intricate game of power politics.

We did not mature gradually, as England did, into the exalted and highly dangerous position of leading power of the world. We inherited the scepter while still in our adolescence, and there was no time to learn the rules of the power-politics game. We seem also to have lost the bold pioneering spirit and the sure political touch of our Founding Fathers. Our foreign policy, whether it was on the side of power politics or on the side of international co-operation, has been too often timid, imitative, anemic, and inconsistent. We echoed and still echo the policies of other foreign powers, even though our conditions are vastly different and our circumstances unique.

Our State Department published a White Paper pointing with pride to the fact that for years they were aware of Japan's preparation to attack us. We attended innumerable futile conferences, signed all kinds of childish pacts like Kellogg's, in which the leading powers, including Germany and Japan, "renounced" war as an instrument of national policy—just like that. This much ado about nothing made the American public believe that something profoundly significant was going on behind closed doors and that far-reaching plans were laid for years to come. Actually our diplomats were diving deep into the ocean only to bring up empty shells. They are still bringing them up.

Much of what has happened and is still happening is not the fault of the State Department or of our government. A number of brilliant men have accomplished a great deal of what is useful and necessary for our foreign policy. To a certain extent the fault is inherent in our internal political structure, where the vital questions of foreign policy are determined on the shifting sands of local politics. But the principal fault lies in the lack of a continuous organic system of American foreign policy, flexible enough to meet changing conditions and inflexible enough to oppose the selfish power-politics moves of other states.

It is already apparent that the leading nation of the United Nations is more unprepared for the peace to come than it was for war. There are, indeed, in the United States, government agencies and private societies in which hundreds of committees are working on the problems of the postwar world. But they have no organic and specific plans, in the sense of a general's plan of campaign. Theirs are vague, noble resolves, "declarations of intent," plans to make plans in some more or less remote future; or they deal with specialized parts of the complex edifice of war and peace. It is truly tragic for our nation that, while the campaigns of war are calculated in detail and far in advance, the most important campaign of all—the Battle of Peace—is to be conducted without any comprehensive master plan. And because time is pressing relentlessly, no better "plan" has been devised so far, in official and semiofficial circles, than to move back to the power-politics alliances of the early nineteenth century.

It is no secret that we have no strategic plan for the world settlement, either in the government or in the opposition party. Instead the government has worked out, under military and economic experts, a technique for a prolonged and indefinite occupation of the defeated and even liberated countries. We have worked out to the minutest detail our plans for dealing with the population of Dresden, for instance, when our troops march in. But we have not worked out, even in the broadest outline, any plans for our postwar relations with each and with all the nations of the world.

The "Improved" League of Nations

All kinds of fallacies dealing with international politics block the approaches to a sound American foreign policy. Elsewhere I discuss in detail most of these fallacies. Every one of them, if it should prevail, would drive the nation into a blind alley. Here I will briefly consider a few of these fallacies.

The League of Nations was and still is a dangerous delusion that affected some of our best-known national leaders and had adverse repercussions on our foreign policy. Nor is there any hope in an "improved" League. Architects of the League of Nations sought to reconcile two incompatible principles: the principle of *unlimited* sovereignty of nations, and the principle of a sovereign law over nations. As a result the League was, and always will be, a Babelian assembly of ambassadorial puppets.

The toil and sacrifice contributed to the cause of the League of Nations by men and women of good will has not been in vain. Wilson and his co-workers for the League have awakened a world consciousness that will never die. For the first time humanity has beheld a world center around which the civilized forces of peace and freedom might crystallize against the primeval forces of war. But the solution of the world's problems does not lie in futile attempts to resurrect the League of Nations, whose bullet-riddled covenant has been buried with military honors. It lies in trying to build a new House of Nations on the imperishable foundations of Wilson's great ideal.

PEACE BY PIECE

Another fallacy is primarily a state of mind, which does not make it any less dangerous. It is what one might call the theory of gradualism. According to it, we should do nothing definite after this war in connection with the problems of the world settlement. For many years we should settle nothing of importance. Instead we should have a long armistice, so that passions can "cool off" and economic reconstruction can "take hold." Little by little, and piece by piece, the vast problems of the postwar world will gradually work themselves out, somewhat like porcupine quills from a dog. This is world peace on the installment plan.

This fallacy will fritter away the most precious few years of our history. Our power and influence in the world will rapidly decrease as other nations recover their strength. Our chances of making a settlement right for us and for the world will progressively decrease. Once the heavy blanket of war is lifted, the foreign states, armed and fed by our Lend-Lease, will have less and less need of our help. Confused and weakening struggles for power will be resumed by the political parties and ideologies within our democracy, and among nations there will be no effective force other than power politics, leading inevitably to war.

CAUSES AND MEANS

If our economists knew more about military science and our generals more about economics, we would be better off. Then there would not be such hopeless confusion between the economic *causes* of war and the military *means* of making war. To say that the causes of war are largely economic is a truism. Economic causes, like the air, are everywhere. To assume that the cure for wars is *first and foremost* an economic cure is a fallacy. No one can deny the vital importance of the economic approach to the problems of peace. But the fallacy of certain economists is in putting an economic cart before a political horse. If we are to wait until social injustice is removed or even reduced, then the greatest of social injustices—war—will destroy our way of life.

For there is no more dangerous fallacy than to assume that only poor and suffering nations start wars. As a rule, the contrary is true. Modern war is a big business, requiring vast amounts of equipment and therefore a fairly high degree of industrialization and prosperity. Neither Hitler's nor the Kaiser's Germany, nor Mussolini's Italy, nor the militarists' Japan was impelled to war by insufferable economic stringency. Whatever the *indirect* causes of war (and there are scores of such causes, especially economic), the *direct* cause of this war, and the usual cause of all wars of aggression, resides in a purely psychological mechanism: a clique, in control of a nation, accumulates enough decisive weapons and enough malleable cannon fodder; having done so, it proceeds to solve the economic "problems" that perpetually beset the nation by the simple expedient of looting other nations. But a clique does not drag its country into war because it is impelled by an inexorable economic determinism; it does so because it *calculates* that it is stronger than its neighbor and that it can get away with the booty. If the clique *calculated* that its chances of winning were slim, then no number of "economic causes" would induce its members to risk their own heads.

Wars cannot be reduced, let alone abolished, by appeasing with waves of abundancy the ever-greedy cliques of leaders and their party followers. So long as the leaders of a state can obtain enough decisive weapons to attack another state and get away with the loot— *just so long will there be wars of aggression*. Economic conditions do create a *climate* favorable to wars of aggression, but only the possession of decisive weapons by those in control of a nation and lack of an international police force can make such a war possible.

The first thing to do, therefore, in seeking to solve the problem of lasting peace, is not to attack the *causes* of war (which are myriad), but the *means* of making war (which are few). This is the first time in history that it has become possible successfully to segregate the means of making war. Then, and only then, can we organize the economic and educational rebuilding of the world, which is the *second* line of our attack upon war.

It will take generations to eliminate the causes of war; it will take but a few months to put an unbreakable stranglehold on the means of making war. Before liberating the peoples of the world from economic enslavement we must chain the war lords. Before Freedom from Want there must be Freedom from War.

The Postwar Troika

The most dangerous of all the fallacies is the proposal of Mr. Walter Lippmann and many others that the United States enter into a postwar alliance with Britain and Russia. There are variations on this theme, running from an Anglo-American alliance to the Big Four—China being the fourth to whom lip service is paid.

No more dangerous fallacy exists than the naïve assumption that three world powers—Britain, Russia, and the United States—each in full control of its powerful armed forces, each fearful or jealous of the other, and each under incessant internal pressure from shifting groups, could long remain in blissful accord. It is only human that Mr. Roosevelt would expect to be the trotter in this postwar troika, with Mr. Churchill and Mr. Stalin as side-kicks. It is equally human that Mr. Churchill would expect to be the trotter. It is not less human that Mr. Stalin has the same idea. All are good trotters. None is a good side-kick. Mathematically, two out of three will be disappointed. Mathematically, also, the odds are overwhelming that this postwar troika will not last for more than a stretch.

No one is more ardently desirous than I for a permanent arrangement with the British Commonwealth of Nations, which is today and has been in the past one of the greatest civilizing and stabilizing forces in history. A way must be found by which we insure an intimate, perpetual co-operation between all the English-speaking commonwealths as an imperishable foundation for a world that is free, humane, and just to all. This way exists. But it does not lie through the antiquated machinery of a power-politics alliance between Britain and the United States, either with or without the participation of Russia or China. Such an alliance defeats its own purpose and destroys all hopes of a lasting co-operation, on the basis of equality and the preservation of sovereignty, between the English-speaking nations. It also destroys all hope of a new world order in which no combine of nations, however powerful, can dominate the rest of the world, and where there is no danger of the breakdown of all-too-temporary alliances leading to new wars.

THE SYSTEM OF NO SYSTEM

If some of our political writers lack a sense of historical perspective, many of our statesmen confuse the power politics of their home states with the power politics of the world. They apply to the vast architecture of war and peace the techniques they learned as local politicians. Many of our Republicans think that all problems of the world settlement will be adequately dealt with once Mr. Roosevelt is dislodged. Many of our New Dealers keep fiddling their ideological tunes while the world is ablaze. And, judging by his pronouncements, even our President is not wholly immune from looking upon the historical problems of the coming peace as a simple business proposition or clever political horse trading. Mr. Roosevelt has been a great war president, and before the war he had the vision to see the coming dangers and to prepare the country for them. It is to be hoped that he will have equal foresight in meeting the vast problems of the coming peace.

But so far we have been drifting planlessly and improvising our foreign policy from day to day. Except in purely technical matters, we seem to be constantly surprised by events which we could easily have anticipated, since the very object of our fight was to create them. One may be sure that both the British and the Russians have carefully calculated plans for any contingency, prepared sufficiently in advance. For instance, Russia and Britain have long ago taken their stand on the vital question of their strategic zones.

Not to have any system is also a system. I met many bridge players who were proud of this "system," but invariably they were the biggest losers. In international politics, also, a system not to have any system means only one thing—you are forced to play the system of the other fellow.

The foreign policy of a great state is a symphony of force and counterforce, of political point and counterpoint. Mr. Roosevelt is a great improviser. In internal affairs this has worked sometimes brilliantly, sometimes not so well. But one cannot improvise for long in international affairs. The stakes are destiny. The pit into which Mr. Roosevelt might fall (and the country with him) is psychological. He might look upon the problems of the world settlement as a matter to be settled amicably among brother politicians, a family affair. Frankie and Winnie can meet, this time, somewhere in the Pacific Ocean and settle the whole business in a few all-night sessions. Then they'll have a chat with Joe Stalin. And we'll all be set for a brave new world.

If only things were that simple!

Moral Defeatism

Our national leadership is even more unprepared in the field of collective defense than in the field of straight power politics. The great majority of American people are instinctively convinced that somehow a system of world co-operation can be worked out that will make lasting peace possible. This is blind faith. The great majority of our national leaders are convinced that no system of lasting peace can be worked out. This is blind cynicism. In official and private circles there are few among our leaders who honestly believe that lasting peace is possible, and there are some who doubt that it is desirable. But this gangrene of moral defeatism has touched not only the politicians; it has spread throughout our national leadership, among intellectuals as well as among businessmen. Lack of reasoned faith in lasting peace paralyzes their creative efforts. Because many of our national leaders and intellectuals lost the first battle for world peace, fought with the defective weapon of the League of Nations, they have jumped to the tragic conclusion that lasting world peace is impossible, except in some remote future. Surely this is defeatism of the worst kind, because it is founded on superficial assumptions. The irony is that many of the same leaders who fought for the ideal of world peace a quarter of a century ago, when it was virtually impossible, are now—when lasting world peace can be made a scientific certainty—fighting against it, or are content with ersatz plans and proposals for futile alliances.

Thus, because so many of our national leaders are too naïve about the implacable forces of power politics and too cynical about the *reality* of lasting peace *now,* we are facing once again a paralysis of will of the leadership and a world un-settlement.

In Book II of this work I take up the concrete discussion of the problems of the world settlement and offer their solutions. But even if all the solutions were perfect (and this is far from being the case), it would be but a part of the road toward the establishment of a world settlement satisfying to our country and just to the world. In our democracy paralysis of the will can be averted, but only on the condition that the citizens make a study of the problems of the peace to come and the writing of the peace their own personal concern. They should trust no single authority, accept no important concept without a free and specific discussion of its merits. Otherwise the peace will again be written by the politicians and the visionaries.

It is in this spirit that I offer the results of my lifelong study of the problems of force which began when I was a revolutionary youth, continued through my bridge years, and now have ended with *Total Peace.* If force is to prevail among states in the postwar world, then above all things I want my own country to be the strongest. And if, as I firmly believe, an adequate counterforce for the anarchy of sovereign states can be developed in a new system of collective defense, then it is again my country which must assume the leadership.

There are overwhelming forces for peace which we can organize if we have a practical plan, a bridge into the future. The World Federation Plan is the first comprehensive and yet specific blueprint for such a bridge. I cannot begin to say how many things are wrong with the blueprint. But it works, and the bridge is anchored not in dreams but in the realities of today and tomorrow. Once over this bridge, the peoples of the world, during two or three generations at least, can achieve Freedom from War; and once the nations are free from this social cancer they can start, each in its own way, and all together, building a new world of economic and political justice. Better planners and builders will come who will improve immeasurably this new bridge into the postwar world, provided a start is made and made now. This is the start.

II. OUR ERA OF GREAT WARS AND TURMOIL

CHAPTER FIVE

Modern Machinery for War

THERE ARE three great cycles of civilization. During the first, lasting scores of thousands of years, men as hunters followed food plants and animals wherever they could find them. During the second or agricultural cycle, which began at least ten thousand years ago and is still in progress today, men domesticated the plants and animals and became rooted to the land. Great plains of the world filled up with tillers of the land, while less and less room was left for the nomads in the plains and for the hunters in the forests and mountains. The third cycle began less than two centuries ago with the industrial civilization and is now in its first volcanic stages of development.

More progress in science has been made in the last hundred years than in the five thousand years preceding. We live in a civilization undreamt-of except by a few Da Vincis. It seemed a short generation back that this new civilization would solve, in a few more decades of science and co-operation, the uglier problems of humanity. We could multiply our food a thousandfold and, by means of molecular architecture, create many of our raw materials, so liberating ourselves from the tyranny of the land. We were in a fair way to conquer all scourging diseases, and we had nearly doubled the span of the average life. We had abolished the physical enslavement of man by man, and torture had receded into the incredible past. The beast in man was humanized everywhere, and we knew ourselves to stand on the threshold of even greater discoveries, whereby every man would at last attain his full dignity and happiness would be denied to no child. With confidence we predicted a rising spiral of human progress and anticipated that the human race might, after all—despite the germs of decay and the recurrent tyranny of leaders—become a family of Abels.

And then, unbelievably, millions of Abels became Cains.

In a few short years humanity traveled back beyond Genghis Khan and even beyond the Assyrians. They too knew how to exile conquered peoples, but it never occurred to them to decapitate entire races by mass murder of their intelligentsia.

What happened? What are the causes of these cyclonic wars and revolutions which, setting afire the West and the East, have already swept away kingdoms and republics and crippled empires? What is the malignant virus which so suddenly paralyzed the most ancient and the most modern social organisms and which threatens, after this war, even greater wars and revolutions in which even the mightiest of nations—the United States—might perish?

There are, of course, scores of causes. But they have their roots in the Industrial Revolution itself. The general cause is the breakdown of the pattern of the agricultural civilization. The walls of the agricultural age, ten thousand years high, are crumbling all around. This half-archaic, half-modern civilization of today left the agricultural civilization in the eighteenth century, but will not complete its tumultuous journey until perhaps the twenty-second century. The pattern of the agricultural civilization, which scores of times repeated itself in Asia, in Africa, in Europe, and only yesterday in America, is being torn apart. Old ways of life and old techniques have broken up; new ways of life with new techniques are still in the process of formation.

From the mother source of the Industrial Revolution came revolutions in hundreds of fields of human endeavor. But the specific field where the Industrial Revolution had the most profound effect on the power relation among the states and on the people within the states was the military field. *The machine age revolutionized the structure and the technique of modern weapons,* creating a new military age of heavy fighting machines. We shall see that the very machine age which brought so much promise and so much hope to the world carried within it the seeds of its own dissolution.

In order to understand the effects of this military revolution, we must consider briefly the effect of weapons and techniques of warfare on states and peoples in the past. Of course no single factor determines history. However important was the military factor, there were other factors—political, economic, and psychosocial—which made the military influence dominant.

Now and then in history a nation, often insignificant or obscure, develops, by accident or by slow evolution, new military weapons or methods that place it at a tremendous advantage over other nations. Then attack and conquest follow automatically. If the other nations are slow to catch up and adapt themselves to the new military technology, they are beaten and enslaved. Often it is impossible to adopt the new military system in time. More and more nations are conquered, and sometimes the world. The Macedonian phalanx under Alexander destroyed scores of kingdoms and brought the "new order" of Greece to the empire of the Medes and the Persians. The more flexible structure of the Roman legion smashed the rigid Greek phalanx, and Rome inherited the world. The Germanic and Slav cavalry finished off rotting Rome. Another revolutionary technique of the man on the horse brought the greatest conqueror and strategist of them all—Genghis Khan and his "Mongolian hordes," which were small, compact bodies of mounted troops, always fighting against apparently overwhelming numbers. The tactics of Genghis Khan and his high command anticipated the blitzkrieg by seven centuries. The armored man on the horse and the impregnable castle dominated the feudal age. The armor of the feudal age, already threatened by the English longbow, was finally pierced by the bullet, and the walls of the castle crumbled before the cannon. The tradesman, the craftsman, and the scientist came into their own. The liberation of the middle class, the industrial production of artillery and better roads made possible the appearance of Napoleon, with his mass armies and grand strategy. The First World War was the last of the Napoleonic type of warfare. It was dinosaurishly overdeveloped, with its thousands of cannon and millions of cannon flesh hurled by one group of stupid generals against masses headed by another group of stupid generals. Already it was a bloody triumph of the machine gun against which there seemed to be no adequate weapon. Then came the first clumsy tanks, which groaned in their steel bellies at ten miles an hour, and airplanes, as stable as kites, from which the pilots took aim with revolvers and rifles. These new, crude machines were harbingers of the military revolution.

This was the end of the old warfare and of the old world. This was also the end of three wonderful centuries of relative freedom, when the masses and their true leaders could take up arms when pressed too hard by their rulers and defy them successfully. The new feudal age—the age of irresistible armored machines for the few—was in the making.

THE BAIT AND THE TRAP

In general it can be said that people, not leaders but ordinary people who carry the brunt of the fighting, do not want wars. There is only one way to make them fight a war of aggression: that is by totalitarian control or a promise that war will remedy conditions even more intolerable.

The cancerous overpopulation of Europe formed the sinister background for the rise of neo-feudalism and the Second World War. There were other somber colors in the background, but the pressure of overpopulated and ill-adjusted millions remained as a constant cause. The greatest trap of all time was built in western Europe by the machine age during the nineteenth century. In it more than one hundred million Europeans were trapped. They were unwelcome in their own homes. Their countries could find no markets for the export of their surplus goods or land for the export of surplus populations even for a temporary relief from pressure. In Germany alone there were between twenty and thirty million such people, and Germany was not the most densely populated nation of Europe.

The foundation for this gigantic trap was completed by the early part of the nineteenth century. England was prospering; its population grew by leaps and bounds. New millions were born, not because England could feed them but because a wonderful new trick had been discovered: England could sell its industrial products all over the world at a good profit, and with that profit buy raw materials, food for its workingmen, opulence for its capitalists, and power for the state. With that power more markets were developed by military or economic conquest, more products could be exported, and more Englishmen were born.

But soon other countries learned the wonderful trick. Machines are exportable and so are the blueprints. Machines multiplied everywhere, but never so fast as babies.

Germany, France, Italy quickly followed the British lead. At first there was enough for everyone. Populations in all western Europe more than doubled in less than a century. The standard of living increased rapidly. But still more countries learned the trick, and the tremendously expanded markets began to contract. The United States came in, with its formidable competition of mass production. Then came Japan, and scores of small countries. The doors to markets and emigration began to be closed and bolted everywhere. The trap was sprung. England had its empire, the United States had its continent, and France had its economy beautifully balanced between industry and agriculture. But Germany, Italy, Japan, and some smaller European countries were trapped.

The bloodletting of the First World War was but a momentary relief. Some of the superfluous millions found place in new industries, created by new discoveries. But the bulk lay heavily on the stomach of each country like an undigested meal. The superfluous masses fermented. They pressed hard against their own fellow-workers, forcing the standard of living lower and lower. They also pressed upward against the higher strata of society, forcing them to divide. Under a leader who might convince them that there was a way out, they were ready to give up the luxury of freedom and coagulate into an anonymous mass of proletarian machine slaves, in the factories or on the battlefield.

Side by side with the struggle of the lowest classes for bread was a silent, ferocious struggle by the middle and upper classes to maintain their precarious standard of living. Once a man tastes the better things of life, he becomes a revolutionist or a traitor before he becomes a slave. The time of blood and man-made thunder was approaching.

Therefore it was pathetically futile for the politicians of the world to assemble around conference tables in order to solve the problems of the day in a businesslike manner. You couldn't really invite the nations to chop off the heads of millions of their superfluous people, or suggest to England that she give up the gains of centuries and reduce her population from forty-five million to twenty million or less. The problem was one which might well occupy a world co-operative of nations over a period of a century. It could not be solved quickly, under threat of war, by diplomatic negotiations or tariff concessions.

Meanwhile, in Germany, the pressure from unwanted men began to dislocate the whole nation and it rapidly neared explosion. One did not know then whether the blow of the explosion would come outward toward war or upward toward revolution. For while the Weimar Democrats talked and talked and talked, the climate of the country grew more and more ominous. Communists multiplied, and later came the Nazis. With the Nazis, Germany exploded in both directions, first upward into a totalitarian revolution and then outward into a totalitarian war.

The New Speed of Disaster

The First World War let loose upon the world war-trained leaders with no one to lead and little enough to eat. They looked for followers who could be organized into any kind of movement, and they found them among young men who, with fewer and fewer jobs and more and more frustrations, went to swell the restless masses. The Second World War will release upon the world another and greater army of well-trained leaders of the officer type, with new habits of command and a new sense of power. Many of them too will look for a cause and a supreme leader. And in so doing they will add to the fermentation of the masses and in the struggle for power do their part in accelerating revolutionary movements in the neo-feudalist direction.

In the nineteenth century three types of societies emerged from the Industrial Revolution: the feudalist, the capitalist-democratic, and, later, the socialist-democratic. Around these three divisions, rather than into the simple Right-Left, Fascist-Communist division of popular argument, social organisms rallied and sought some unity of purpose in the era of change.

The American and French revolutions, both against the feudalist order, were the first rehearsals of the era of great revolutions staged by the industrial civilization. The feudalist order was as old as warrior castes; after considerable battering during the French revolution it gradually recovered, in Europe at least, most of its power and privileges.

The Right or capitalist democracy and the Left or socialist democracy were relatively new. They sprang from the same concepts of the sovereignty of the people and equal rights for individuals. They were made possible by new social organisms, the bourgeoisie and the artisans developed by the earlier Industrial Revolution.

The feudalists, as always, based their society upon control of the state from the top by a special privileged class. The Left democracies sought to shift this control to the bottom under the leadership of intellectuals. The Right democracies sought, in the name of freedom for the individual, to maintain a balance between all social organisms within the nation, and to prevent any social organism or class from tyrannizing the others.

For more than a century Left democracy had no home of its own until Lenin and his group of brilliant intellectuals established the proletarian dictatorship of Soviet Russia. This gave to the neo-feudalists their biggest trump in the ideological struggles within the nations before and during the Second World War. Napoleon's rallying cry was "The Cossacks are in Europe!" The clash of Left and Right democracies after the First World War accelerated the rise of neo-feudalism. The anti-communist crusade was even more effective in screening the designs of Hitler and other neo-feudalist power politicians in Europe and Asia.

That different social and political concepts now involve us in an era of wars is due to a tremendous change in what I will call, for want of a better term, the velocity of social movements. In the same way that the strategic military hour does the job of twenty hours before, the *social* hour in social movements does the job of about twenty hours before. This revolution in the social hour comes as a result of the revolution in transportation and in communication of the spoken and printed word. Christianity required at least three centuries to spread over the world; the communist and fascist revolutions were born and grew to maturity in less than ten years. In this short space of time, equal to a schoolboy's growth, both revolutions solidified two enormous nations with iron organizations, armies and bureaucrats and soldiers, and a complete mystic cult of the state. Without telephone, radio, loud-speakers, automobiles, accelerated printing, easy financing, and scores of other technical improvements in social contacts, Hitler would probably have met the fate of an obscure hero in a local beer-hall putsch; Mussolini would have been mussed up by the *carabinieri,* or elected a deputy; and Stalin might have become vice-president of the Federated Republic of Georgia.

Today the new techniques may be used for many purposes. Roosevelt or Hitler delivers a fireside or a cannonside chat to untold millions all over the world. A cute new hat launched in New York today is worn in San Francisco tomorrow; a complicated bridge system girdles the world in two short years and draws in millions of followers. The mass climate can be changed in months instead of decades; national leaders spring up in a matter of months to drive the masses, and movements spread at new speeds of disaster.

Not only did the Industrial Revolution take from the masses the physical means of defending themselves; it broke down their will to resist. It created vast proletarianized blocs of people, huddled in the cities, who could be easily dominated by radio and press propaganda and by specialized police. It brought the magic of radio and moving pictures. It multiplied the power of the written word. But all this it placed at the disposal of the dictators. As a result the will of the masses is divided by far-reaching distortions and the mass mind is corrupted by a knowledge worse than ignorance because it is false. In the totalitarian countries millions marched with hypnotic exaltation to an inglorious death.

The Industrial Revolution gave its best help to movements such as neo-feudalism, spreading from the top down. It became easy for small, virulent minorities, in control of propaganda, police, and modern weapons, to capture the nerve centers of mighty states and hold their peoples in subjection. When the dying order of the aristocrats revived around Hitler as a messiah, it was revitalized by the industrial civilization and its frustrated millions until the new feudalism became powerful.

But it was not "the wave of the future." It was a wave from the past. It came, armed with new weapons, as a tidal wave of counter-revolution against democracy. It is a fatal illusion to assume that these powerful forces of neo-feudalism will vanish after the defeat of Nazi Germany and Japan. On the contrary, with the entrance upon the world industrial arena of the now half-dormant Far and Middle East, they will be revived more violently than ever.

The same velocity of change apparently favors democratic movements. But the victory of a democratic movement, by its very nature, does not insure the liquidation of feudalism; while the victory of a feudalistic movement means the hopeless enslavement of the people by a dictatorship of a minority supported by irresistible fighting machines. Thus there will be, after the war, tremendous clashes over the control of the masses by various ideological groups, in which the totalitarians, and especially the neo-feudalists, will have a tremendous advantage.

DISARMAMENT OF THE STATES

Thus the main and specific cause of our era of great wars and turmoil is the scientific revolution in military weapons and communications. It transcends the political, the economic, and the psychological causes: the struggle for power, and *the new means made available by the industrial civilization for the use of power* by predatory minorities in control of states, dominates and integrates all the other causes. In the last analysis, the struggle for power among the leaders of the same nation or of opposing states is dominated by the power of military force. And now this immemorial military force has become irresistibly powerful through the concentration of intricate fighting machines in the hands of a small elite within a nation and of a small minority of nations in the family of nations. The peoples and all but a few of the states are effectively disarmed.

The scientific instruments of precision that conquered vast new worlds in the physicochemical sciences also built the deadly fighting machines for the enslavement of peoples by their own leaders and of states by the few industrial giants. The same gasoline engine and electronic tube that ring the world with bands of intimacy have turned those bands into shackles for the peoples and for the states disarmed. Obstacles of man or of nature have lost their exclusive meaning. Japan, a second-rate industrial power, with her second-rate planes and tanks, conquered the Dutch East Indies, the Philippines and the Malay States in less than three months—a feat that neither China nor India was able to accomplish in two thousand years.

In the First World War it took Austria and Germany fifteen months to conquer Serbia. In the Second World War two weeks sufficed to overthrow Yugoslavia. When one tank division calls for resources of a small kingdom to equip, small nations with their population armies are virtually disarmed by armored tank divisions and plane squadrons. Germany herself was doomed by the greater mathematical weight of armor plate and firing power of the Allies. When the monolith China and hundreds of millions of Hindus, Mohammedans, and other nations become industrialized (and this is a matter of the next twenty or thirty years) their greater mathematical weight of armor plate and firing power, *plus* their vast man power under predatory minorities, will doom the Anglo-American empires as surely as Germany and Japan were doomed in this war.

The disarmament of all small states and most of the large ones paved the way for the rise of modern horde states. For the first time since the formation of the horde states of the Romans and the Mongolians, modern and more terrifying horde states emerged in Germany and Japan. It is a paradoxical but true fact that the Industrial Revolution created almost perfect conditions for such horde states in which satellite states (subjugated or voluntary) revolve around the powerful nucleus of an industrial military state, and the proletarianized multitudes are shackled together more strongly than Rome or Babylon ever dreamed. Each of these horde states rests upon a strict hierarchy of nations and of men within these nations. Enslavement of all nations by a few nations can now be accomplished by remote control—simply by sending a squadron of bombers, by shifting the heavy industry, or by manipulating money. A modern horde state by its very nature will irresistibly tend to become a world state or else be destroyed by a rival horde state.

The nature of modern fighting machines and the vast amount of them needed are such that the industrial giant states require the resources of continents to wage a winning war. For the first time in history the battle for loot has become the battle for weapons. All the gigantic battles of this war—the Battle of France, of England, of the Atlantic, of Russia, of the Pacific, of the Middle East, of India, and of Europe—are but incidents in the continuous battle for weapons. The Second World War was not fought for this or that province, a country, or even a bloc of countries. It is the first war of continents and oceans. In such a war, empires such as France, China, or Italy are but pawns, and empires such as England, Russia, or Japan are but castles, bishops, or knights. From time immemorial, men fought against men, and weapons were but accessories; in this and in the future wars, machines fight against machines and men are but their auxiliaries. Vast mechanized blocs of workers and soldiers fight under their leaders to produce and use still more of the engines of destruction which devour their substance. The strategy of war and the strategy of economics and politics will be built around the central mathematical fact that the greater weight of organized metal and scientific chemicals will prevail. Unless something equally revolutionary is done to segregate the fighting machines, even this war may be but an incident in the continuous struggle for the monopoly of heavy weapons. To the winner must eventually go the dominion of the world.

These implications of the revolution in military weapons should concern those economists who think we can cure wars by economic means, or those men of good will who think that we must first change the hearts of men. There is great merit in both proposals as far as they go. But much more than that will be needed to avert the future catastrophe of war. Stuart Chase, an outstanding economist and liberal, said in connection with the thesis I advance here:

"It is all very well to talk about the steady march toward enlightenment which will someday reach its goal of permanent peace. The steady march is a matter of decades, while the elapsed time from a bomb bay to its target is a matter of split seconds. . . . Mr. Culbertson takes us as we are, God help us, with little or no reliance on that higher nature which, like prosperity, seems always to be just around the corner."

These implications should also concern those "hardheaded realists" who are not wholly convinced that war is harmful. There is a decisive difference between the wars of the past and the wars of today and tomorrow. This difference is one of magnitude and malignance. The Second World War is but one of a gigantic, mechanical series, mounting with inexorable force toward the next, even deadlier war, and ushering in a new dark age wherein a few parasitic organisms will sap all the strength and all the beauty of the world.

CHAPTER SIX

The American Superstate

THE OUTSTANDING political event of this century is the emergence of the United States of America as a superstate. This turn of destiny exceeds in importance the birth of the Soviet state or the rebirth of feudalism. The shifting of the center of gravity from the great powers of the Old World to the superstate of the New World will prove to be, in the course of future history, the more decisive factor.

For whatever happens to America today will happen to the world, and whatever happens to the world will happen to America. Today the world is a disunion indivisible. Whatever America does or fails to do in relation to the world will start a chain of events binding future generations to the present, twisting them into patterns of human happiness or misery which, this time, will probably remain unchanged for generations.

A superstate is a modern phenomenon, arriving in the wake of the Industrial Revolution. Its essential characteristic is a highly integrated, scientific industrial production. There are three basic requirements for the existence of a superstate:

A very large, homogeneous population;

A large, continuous living space;

A highly developed machine production.

All three requisites are necessary; lack of any one of them must seriously handicap the modern state in its struggle for existence.

Germany, Japan, and England have large homogeneous populations and high machine production, but they lack continuous living space. Under modern conditions a country that is forced to obtain most of its essential raw materials from across the seas can never be a superstate. It is at the mercy of any powerful foreign nation or combination of nations able to cut its umbilical cord. Germany and Japan are but *rump* superstates. England is in a class by herself. She has a vast overseas living space, but it is thousands of miles away across the oceans. England is further handicapped by the fact that her population is rather small for a superstate, and yet she must import food for millions of her people and at the same time compete in trade with her own Dominions, to pay for the food and raw materials.

Russia and China are *incomplete* superstates. They possess very large homogeneous populations and living space of continental dimensions, containing most of the essential raw materials. At present they lack the highly integrated machine production. Russia, however, will soon overtake the United States.

Thus the United States today is the only superstate.

The United States has a large homogeneous population. Of her 138 million people, the core is made up of the English, who have contributed the language, the culture, and above all the Anglo-Saxon institutions of freedom and self-government. The middle layer is made up of Irish, Scots, Germans, Scandinavians, and other sturdy, vigorous peoples. The outer layer is made up of Slavs, Latins, and others who have added to the temperament and the imagination of the newly molded nation without affecting its basic homogeneity.

The United States has a large, continuous living space. Geography played no mean tricks on America. Enviable resources lie below the earth; on top there are immense forests, long navigable rivers, and rich earth. With the initiative, science, and inventiveness of a free people these virgin lands became the foundation for an unprecedented industrial civilization. The continent of Europe, exhausted after thousands of years of digging for ore, and lacking food for its overpopulated nations, turned naturally to the new land. Furthermore, the geographical position of the United States could hardly have been improved had it been designed by American military strategists. During its precious formative years the country was sheltered by the oceans and by distance from the greatest single evil that can befall a nation: aggression. Unimpeded by pressure of hostile nations on its periphery, the young community was able to give practically all its productive and creative powers to the task of building up a great nation. While in the Old World the expenditures for war or preparations for war were consuming the bulk of each country's productive resources, war expenditures of the United States in the past were relatively insignificant. For many more years the vital nerve centers of the American nation cannot be conquered or destroyed by an enemy.

For many years England was in this enviable position. With one foot in the English Channel and the other in the Atlantic Ocean, she could strike out from her little island wherever she chose, and no enemy could strike back at her vital nerve centers. Now the United States, with one foot in the Atlantic and one foot in the Pacific, with a continent instead of islands as a fortress, and thousands of miles from any aggressor, is in a position to manipulate the levers of history with overwhelming effect.

The United States owes this extraordinary position largely to the third basic factor in a superstate—the highly developed machine production which enables a nation to produce fighting machines. It is supremacy of hitting and fighting power in fighting machines which wins the battles, and the side which produces substantially more of the fighting machines will necessarily be victorious. In trying to re-create the Roman Empire in the age of Detroit, Mussolini failed to learn this fundamental lesson of modern warfare: for the first time in history, *industrial capacity has become synonymous with military potential*. And the United States, which was one of several great world powers, has become the first superstate.

The Threats to the American Superstate

This theory of superstates is important. In it is contained the geo-political background of modern power politics.

In the West, Germany, with its giant industrial head, had a pygmy body. It could attain its continuous living space only by conquest of neighboring lands. And the only neighbor offering adequate living space for the would-be German superstate was Russia, a territorial giant with a small industrial head. In the East a parallel situation was shaped between Japan and China. The march of industrial civilization determined the moment in history when this double drama was to be played. The German militarists had to strike at Russia before she became fully industrialized. The Japanese also knew that it was now or never in regard to the control of China, necessary as a preliminary step to the conquest of possessions held by the European powers. The German and Japanese states coveted more living space in order to be superstates; the German and Japanese militarists coveted more power. Both ends could be served by successful wars of conquest against Russia and China respectively, before these territorial giants became superstates themselves.

History also determined the final act in this ironic drama by bringing in at the last moment the overwhelming power of the American superstate against Germany and Japan. The United States could not, in self-preservation, permit either Germany or Japan to conquer too large a living space.

Russia, after the United States, comes closest to being a true superstate. In spite of devastation, she will probably emerge from this war only two decades behind the United States in industrial development. When she achieves her industrial development she will be the second superstate to emerge—and potentially a more powerful one than the United States, because of her larger population and larger living space. China lags far behind Russia. However, under the compression of war, her industrialization is proceeding at a rapid pace. The time necessary for any country to become industrialized will be much shorter in the future than it was in the past. It took England a century and a half to get into the industrial swing. Germany and the United States required three quarters of a century. Russia traveled the same industrial road in less than a quarter of a century, in spite of a revolution, famines, and epidemics. The new industrial states benefit by the experimentation of the older ones; the blueprints are there ready-made, and modern techniques make it possible to export entire plants with teacher-engineers and all. It will not be very long, therefore, before China, with her vast and highly intelligent man power, will surpass Japan many times over and approach the United States as a formidable industrial and therefore military power—a third superstate. Behind China there looms the subcontinent of India.

and in the Middle East the Islamic peoples—heretofore dormant populations—await industrialization.

During the next two decades the American superstate will stand supreme and unchallengeable as the leader of the machine age. No parasitic clique of nobles dominates the nation, sapping its strength. The pressure groups are fairly well balanced. Never in history has a nation been so powerful, so prosperous, so democratic.

Never before has the nation's future existence been more gravely jeopardized by the very forces of the Industrial Revolution which created its greatness. The same industrial hourglass that ran in our favor to the doom of the German and Japanese militarists will, soon after this war, inexorably run against us. One of two things will happen: (1) the now incomplete superstates, with their vast living space and population, will become industrialized; (2) the rump superstates will form the nuclei for new totalitarian horde states, gaining more space by conquest. In either event the American superstate is doomed as a first-rate power. For these new superstates will be able to produce many times more fighting machines than we could produce, even under dictatorship and a low standard of living. Our oceans will no longer be capable of protecting us against the onslaughts of overwhelming numbers of men and machines launched against us. The conquest of the rich lands of the American continents will become as feasible in 1975 as it was in 1675—and therefore as probable. Against the industrialized hordes of Europe and Asia our 150–160 million people will have to wage a desperate and ultimately losing war.

The Time Is Now

Today the American superstate towers above all the other nations. Geographically it stands in the center of the world, at the great crossroads of the Atlantic and Pacific oceans. Economically it stands in the center of the industrial civilization. Militarily it stands in the still center of cyclonic wars and revolutions raging in Europe, Africa, and Asia. It is the depository of decisive weapons and of all the hopes of humanity.

But it is only for a few ephemeral moments of history, a few short years, that the American superstate stands supreme and unchallenge-able.

The time limit of America's power is no more than twenty-five years. *But the actual time limit in which the United States can use her present power to insure her future is probably no more than five years.* Everything will depend upon the kind of world settlement that emerges after this war. And the kind of world settlement which emerges depends primarily upon the American nation.

How can the United States save herself, after winning this war, from the mortal threats to her very existence which are to come? What kind of foreign policy should she follow? What kind of peace must we have after the defeat of Germany and Japan?

In a matter involving the destiny of our nation, we must examine the answers without passion, without hatred for any people. And without trust in any people. We must act as though the future war lords were here today. For, unless we take steps now to prevent it, they will be here in our children's day.

CHAPTER SEVEN

Future of the United Nations

THE HOPES of the democratic world are now centered upon the United Nations and their Atlantic Charter. More hopeful than any other member of the United Nations is the government of the United States. There never was a coalition of nations whose leading member banked so heavily on the lasting union of its allies. While other members of the coalition have advanced cautiously, the American government has gone all out for the United Nations—not only for winning the war, but as a foundation on which to build the vast architecture of the postwar world. The various political and economic plans for world-wide reconstruction now advocated by American officials are based largely on the concept of a self-perpetuating and harmonious United Nations, managed by Britain, Russia, and the United States in the name of and for the good of all. All utterances of the American government assume as an axiomatic truth that, after the war as during the war, the United Nations offer a solid and lasting foundation on which to build a new and happier world. The United Nations are to be a new, "improved" League of Nations—more united, more enduring, more powerful, because *this time* it will be under the benevolent leadership of the United States. Compared to these fervent planners, Wilson was a hard-boiled realist.

Since so much depends, for the United States, upon this concept of the United Nations, it is necessary to scrutinize it coldly, without fear or prejudice. How strong and lasting will this union be for the purpose of establishing a kind of peace different from that made after the First World War? What will be the anticipated behavior of

Russia, Britain, China, and other members of the United Nations? To answer these questions we must consider the mechanism of the United Nations and the hidden motors that turn this mechanism.

The United Nations is an alliance, or a coalition, of thirty-odd sovereign states. An alliance, or a coalition, is a union of sovereign states for the purpose of defense against common danger or for some other specific purpose of mutual advantage. An alliance, or a coalition, by its very nature is temporary, since there is no higher separate body to interpret the terms of the alliance in case of disagreement and to enforce observance of the terms.

The United Nations, therefore, is a large, loosely held combination of sovereign states with a "nucleus" of three leading powers. This "nucleus," in turn, is not a nucleus at all; for it also consists of sovereign states, each in control of its own armed force and each the final interpreter of the terms of the alliance.

The common purpose which gave rise to this coalition and which holds these strangely assorted states together was the common danger from the Axis aggressors. However, each nation possesses its own national common purpose around which is built a complex of national interests, selfish policy, hatreds, and fears. These thirty-odd common purposes have been temporarily submerged by the terrifying wave of German-Japanese conquests. The leadership mechanism of the United Nations consists of thirty-odd separate, isolated "cylinders," each motivated by its own national interests. Under the relentless pressure of the common enemy these thirty-odd "cylinders" have hit together more often than not, even though with a staggering waste of energy. The coalition, however, possesses no integrated, central leadership organ, no higher authority, no court of last appeal.

Within this loose mechanism of the United Nations there is a smaller mechanism. It consists of three leading sovereign states—the United States, Britain, and Russia. Since the military voice of other member states is too small to be heard, the war is largely managed by these three powers. But here again we have not one higher leadership organ, but three separate and often contradictory leadership organs, trying hard to synchronize their sovereign beats in the rising heat of mutual rivalries and recriminations. Being sovereign states, each may oppose the other or abstain from action agreed to by others. This has already happened several times in spite of the enormous common danger.

By all rights China, who suffered the most and fought the longest, should have a powerful voice, even in such an embryonic council. But, although much praise is showered on heroic China, she is only hovering on the threshold of the council's chambers. With Hollywood stars it is only the reality of the box office that counts; with leading states it is only the reality of force that gets the top billing. China has not enough fighting machines to be heard.

Even the influence of the United States over her sister members of the United Nations is rapidly diminishing. All governments, from the Prime Minister of Luxembourg to the Prime Minister of Great Britain, are extremely sensitive about their national interests and will grow more so as the need for American Lend-Lease grows less and less. Much is being made of the joint British-American High Command and various joint economic boards and agencies, in which Russia "assists." It is hoped that all these war organizations, instead of being demobilized, will be remobilized for a long armistice. But here again the unanimous agreement of three sovereign powers is indispensable on a thousand and one questions that will be raised, and there is no machinery to settle even a single disagreement.

Such is the mechanism and the leadership organ of the United Nations. From the standpoint of integrated organization, the United Nations have not attained even the status of a simple village, with its selectmen, judge, and constable. Nor could they ever attain any lasting organization, since each member is a sovereign state and therefore a law unto itself.

Yet, for the purpose of waging the war, the United Nations have done remarkably well. A combination of extraordinary reasons made this possible. The reasons are:

1. The ruthless, terrifying menace from the common enemy.

2. The power of the United States that has overflowed into the war theaters of the world.

3. The world-wide extent of the war, which made it actually five different and loosely connected wars fought on widely separated battlefronts under independent high commands: the Western Euro-

pean War, the Russian War, the Mediterranean War, the Chinese War, and the Pacific War.

4. The brilliant war leadership of Roosevelt, Churchill, Stalin, and Chiang Kai-shek. Blunders were made, of course, and the part contributed by each national leader is not of equal value; nevertheless, the foursome of the United Nations showed overwhelming superiority to the trio of the Axis powers.

5. The irreparable blunders of strategy and psychology committed by the Nazi, Fascist, and Japanese cliques.

6. Last, but equally important, the occupation by the Axis of vast parts of the British Empire, Russia, and China, and the enslavement of their peoples, thereby strengthening the common purpose to a point at which it was almost unbreakable.

The United States did not need to fear that any of her important allies would sign a separate peace. There were other reasons for this besides solemn agreements. In the earlier stages of the war her allies had lost too much to think of a satisfactory separate peace. At the later stages of the war, with a total victory in sight, her allies have regained too much to place themselves in double jeopardy between the not-yet-defeated Axis powers and the growing might of the United States and her remaining allies.

In the case of Britain, a separate peace would have been unthinkable. She was deeply committed, not only to the United States, but to her own Dominions, and a separate peace would have meant the eventual disintegration of her empire.

In the case of Russia, only a conviction that the British and the Americans were preparing a postwar coalition against her with Germany's help could have induced her to sign a separate peace before Germany's defeat. Even had Germany, on the brink of her defeat, offered to Russia the restoration of Russian territories, Poland, the Balkans, and the Middle East, and a large part of Germany's industrial plants to boot, it would have been idiotic for Russia to accept. Let us assume that Soviet Russia, ignoring the five million Russian ghosts, accepted Germany's offer. In that event she would have to continue fighting on Germany's side. For if she did not assist the greatly weakened Germany, Germany alone would be defeated by the Anglo-

Americans, who are in control of the seas, the air, and vast mass armies. And once Germany was defeated, Russia would be facing a world coalition headed by the Anglo-Americans, probably assisted by Germany. If Russia should assist Germany, as an ally, then one of three things would happen: (1) Russia and Germany would win the war, (2) there would be a stalemate, or (3) Russia and Germany would be defeated. If Russia and Germany should win the war, then Russia would still have to face, sooner or later, a powerful Germany in control of western Europe, and hostile Anglo-Americans. Not only that; the Anglo-Americans at any time could offer to Germany far more at the expense of Russia than Russia could offer at the expense of the Anglo-Americans, who would still be in control of their possessions, largely dominating the seas and the air. Thus a move by Russia to conclude a separate agreement with Germany could always be met by the countermove of the Anglo-Americans offering to Germany at least a part of Russia's *lebensraum*.

A similar situation would develop in case of a stalemate between the Russo-Germans and the Anglo-Americans. Finally, if (which is likely) the weakened Russians and the Germans both were defeated, then the world settlement would be made chiefly at the expense of Russia, and her Communist government would be destroyed.

This does not mean, however, that a conflict will not arise between Russia and the Anglo-Americans once Germany recognizes her defeat, withdraws to her own territories, and establishes a democratic (not communist) government. On the contrary, such a conflict is probable. The considerations of Russian power politics require, after Germany's defeat, the preservation of a strong, non-fascist Germany as an additional bulwark against the utter domination of western Europe and the rest of the world by the Anglo-Americans. On the other hand, the Anglo-Americans are heavily committed to the "unconditional surrender" of Germany and her total disarmament. Russia, therefore, may well refuse, after consultation with Britain and the United States, to carry too far either the dismemberment or the crippling of Germany. The seeds of conflict exist. But this will no longer be a problem of a separate peace, but a problem of the postwar settlement.

There is even less danger of a separate peace between China and

Japan. China would have little to gain from a separate peace with Japan, and everything to lose.

If I have discussed this question of a separate peace by Russia or China somewhat in detail, it is not because I mistrust in any way the words of either Soviet Russia or China—the two countries who have not yet been known to break their formal agreements. The reason I have taken up this question of a separate peace is because some Americans in public life have been trembling in their boots throughout the war lest Russia or China sign a separate peace. This pusillanimous and unreasoned fixation had, indirectly, a paralyzing effect upon America's dealings with her allies. Sometimes it is as dangerous to appease one's friends as to appease one's enemies. During the war we have failed to reach distinct understandings with our British, Russian, and Chinese allies on many of the vital questions of the postwar settlement. While the Russians and the British acted differently and more wisely in their own national interests in territorial and other matters, we kept silent for fear of "rocking the boat." As a result, our postwar united front will be seriously threatened.

What will the situation of the United Nations be after this war? How far can the American nation bank on its present allies in order to get the kind of peace it desires?

It ought to be obvious to anyone that there is a fundamental difference between the strength of a coalition such as the United Nations *during* a war, when the fear of the common enemy binds them together, and the same coalition *after* the war, when the cementing fear of the common enemy is eliminated, leaving only vague aspirations for a general peace. The magnetic force of the common purpose will no longer be there. Each of the thirty-odd sovereign cylinders will again start pumping feverishly for its own national blood stream. Yet American statesmen, in their plans and speeches, dangerously confuse these two different *kinds* of United Nations, treating them as one and the same body.

How strong will the union of the United Nations be *after* the war? Will Britain, Russia, and the United States continue to maintain a common front for the Battle of Peace, based on justice to all? Never in history has there been a coalition of powerful sovereign states which has for long survived the defeat of their common enemy. There has always been a postwar scramble for spoils and more power, maneuvers for stronger strategic positions. Will this be an exception?

The foreign policy of a state has always been determined by the rules of power politics as applied to its existing geographic, economic, and psychosocial pattern. What will be the postwar policy of victorious Britain, Russia, China, and other members of the United Nations? Upon the specific answers to these questions will depend the answer to the question: What shall America do?

CHAPTER EIGHT

Power Politics—The Law of Nations

THE PAST, THE PRESENT, and the future of any state are twisted and shaped by the international struggle for power. Power politics is the polite name for that struggle.

Power politics can be defined as *the foreign policy of a state when based on the use or the threat of force*. Power politics is, then, a subtle international variant of the immemorial law of tooth and claw.

The interests of a state may be conquest, in which case we have the politics of aggression; or they may be maintenance of the *status quo*, in which case we have the politics of defense. The power politics of the self-styled "have-not" nations, such as Germany, Japan, or Italy, is based on expansion by force; the power politics of the "have" nations, such as Britain, Russia, and the United States, is based on defense against the aggressive expansion of rival powers. The former nations seek to get by force what they believe they need; the latter seek, by force if need be, to keep what they have.

Their relatively passive policy does not mean that the peaceful nations must meekly await the blow from a future aggressor before they resort to force. Good power politics anticipates the behavior of rival states and acts accordingly. Its rules may well impose on the most peaceful state the necessity of a preventive war in order to check the strength of a potential enemy. Fundamentally, the present war waged by the United States against the Axis powers is a gigantic preventive war. The rules of power politics demand that a great nation, such as the United States, should not permit other great nations, such as Germany or Japan, substantially to extend their power over Europe or Asia. Should we allow them time in which to organize their vast conquests, we would face, in ten or twenty years, an irresistible combination of hostile powers which might conquer us, or at least cripple us and destroy our way of life. France suffered the greatest disaster of her history because her national leaders missed a score of opportunities to apply intelligently the principles of preventive war against the obviously arming Germany. Russia, on the other hand, survived because realistic power politics, and not communist ideology, guided her foreign policy. Regardless of whether a nation is essentially peaceful or essentially aggressive, its foreign policy is based on the ultimate resort to force.

There are many who condemn power politics for ethical reasons. Actually, in a world in which the dominating factor in relations between states is force, power politics is an indispensable condition for the survival of a state.

There is *no adequate substitute for power politics* in the family of nations today. Even if a great majority of states were to agree to "renounce" war (and therefore power politics) as an instrument of national policy, it would be but a futile gesture. As long as there is one single great power that may make a sovereign choice of violence, all other states must prepare to follow. There is a fatal chain of war, stretching from one end of the earth to the other and binding the politics of every great state with links of violence. In relations between sovereign states the measuring rod of any state—its influence, its very survival value—is not its culture, its spirituality, or its wealth. It is the amount of military force it possesses and can use. This is not a question of good or evil; it is a question of what is. Until an adequate substitute for force is found, therefore, power politics will remain the basic policy of any state that seeks to survive—including the United States.

This does not mean that in a nation's foreign policy there is no room for enlightened idealism. Nor does it mean that the German and Japanese type of power politics, based on enslavement and terror, should be condoned. But democratic slogans and noble resolves are pitiably inadequate. Only a true collective force, organized around a higher but equally relentless concept of power, can defeat the anarchical terrorism of individual sovereignties.

Power politics rests upon the historical axiom that *there will always be states who seek to expand beyond their own frontiers at the expense of other states.*

In the past there were two principal obstacles to expansion—the resistance of other states, and natural limitations such as seas, deserts, mountains, jungles. The revolution in communications is rapidly reducing the natural obstacles to zero; it will soon eliminate the frontiers of continents and subcontinents. The natural frontiers of China and India are being obliterated; the great desert ocean of Gobi no longer separates the Slav and the Mongol. The seas of the Pacific and the Atlantic are open roads, and their islands mere stepping-stones. The great new era of migration of peoples is even now being inaugurated behind the armored ships of land and sea, under the gigantic canopy of warplanes. In the past the freedom of a great country was more effectively defended by the obstacles of nature than by the skill of its generals. In the future every state will find itself stripped of its immemorial armor of seas, mountains, and deserts. Only the will of the people and their skills will stand between their freedom and possible destruction.

This makes even more important the understanding of the aggressive and the defensive types of power politics.

The same state may, at different periods of its history, shift from an aggressive policy to a peaceful one, or vice versa. Rome was the most warlike of ancient states until the first century; later, in spite of new worlds still to be conquered, Rome renounced aggression, and its power politics consisted of vigilant frontier defense. Russia's power politics was violently expansionist for more than a thousand years; now, and in spite of her earlier fit of messianic ideology, her power politics is definitely defensive. China and India, for thousands of years pacifist, may become, because of their already enormous and rapidly increasing populations, the greatest "have-not" nations in history. Then their "inherent" pacifism will melt away, and, in possession of modern fighting machines, they might move with aggressive energy.

These shifts from an aggressive to a defensive type of power politics, or vice versa, find most of their impulses in the basic economy of the state.

POWER POLITICS AND THE ECONOMY OF A STATE

The profound differences between the aggressive and the defensive patterns of power politics derive mainly from the two fundamental types of a state economy, inward- and outward-expanding. The economy of a state like the United States or Russia, with a vast self-contained living space and adequate sea outlets, is basically inward-expanding. Its power politics, therefore, is essentially defensive. The economy of an industrialized state like Japan or Germany, with only rump living space and dependence upon other states for important raw materials, is essentially aggressive.

The concept of the relation between the economy of a state and its foreign policy goes much deeper than the fascist rationalization of "have" and "have-not" nations. The concept also goes further than the theory of the economic interpretation of history, which fails to take into account the leadership factor and the enormous importance of psychosocial factors in shaping the behavior pattern of a nation. With these modifications, we can say that there is a basic long-term relationship between the kind of economy of a state and its foreign policy. For example, the basic conditions that led to the growth of the American superstate and of the Russian near-superstate are similar in many respects; their long-term foreign policies are, therefore, likely to be similar. Different basic conditions and different inner necessities, in the case of Germany and Japan, have produced a different type of policy. The roots of American or Russian power politics (based on defense against aggressors) and the roots of German-Japanese power politics (based on expansion by force) are sunk deep in the economic situation peculiar to each state, and are held fast by the psychosocial and geographic factors.

Other and important causes exist, of course, to explain a policy of aggression. Violent minorities may seize control of a state and use its resources for selfish purposes. But they could not seize the levers so easily, or so quickly turn a great nation into the road of war, without a favorable psychosocial and geo-economic climate.

Also, a state such as Germany, whose economy is outward-expanding, may seek new solutions when repeated attempts at plundering other nations prove disastrous. In fifteen or twenty years Russia and China will be so far advanced industrially that there will no longer be any hope for Germany and Japan to dominate them. Germany and Japan will, in effect, become big satellite states, and they might seek to adapt themselves to the new conditions by an entirely different foreign policy.

Thus there may be exceptions to the theory that the power politics of a state (aggressive or defensive) corresponds to its general economy (inward- or outward-expanding). But exceptions and fluctuations between the types are but indirect confirmation of the basic concept.

Power Politics and Idealism

Power politics, by its very nature, is limited to the goals and interests of the state. In a democracy private citizens and societies may have the right to place the higher interests of humanity above the interests even of their own country. But in the higher politics of the state all interests, however lofty, and even consideration of humanity itself, must be subordinated to the security of the state and its people. Only when that security is firmly established, with maximum precautions against future contingencies (including betrayal by allies), may the leaders of a great state turn their eyes toward the distant horizons of the world as a whole.

America's vast industrial, inward-expanding economy, plus an oceanic geography around the American continental island, created the special conditions for American power politics, in sharp distinction to those of German power politics. German power politics is based upon the necessity of continental *lebensraum* for her so-called master race, from which inevitably follows the attempt to conquer the world. American power politics is based on the sovereign principle that nations shall not be enslaved by other nations, from which inevitably must follow defense against any potential conquerors of the world. This fundamental opposition between American and German power politics does not lie in the natural world idealism of millions of Americans, nor does it rise from the purely ideological conflicts of the two great nations. Beneath the superficial soil of political ideologies one quickly reaches the hard rocks of power politics.

In the past there have been a few rare moments of history when the purely selfish interests of a great state coincided with the purely humanitarian interests of the world. During these moments a great state, clad in the armor of the chivalrous knight, constituted itself the defender of the people's liberties and the protector of smaller states against tyrants and war lords. The results were beneficial to humanity as a whole. The task of the defender state was facilitated by a powerful element of true idealists everywhere, who are always on the side of the weak and the oppressed. Thus from time to time, by a combination of selfish and idealistic motives, humanity advances to a higher plateau.

Such a moment of history is in the making today. Three powers, Britain, Russia, and the United States, are becoming the joint masters of the world. In their hands is the reality of force, and they will dictate the coming world settlement. Each of these sovereign states is, or should be, moved by considerations of its own national interests and safety. Yet these very national interests dictate, temporarily at least, the higher interests of freedom and justice for all the nations of the world. All that is needed is to integrate these similar national interests into a system of a true co-operative of nations, before mutual rivalries, fears, and ambitions, inherent in the relations between powerful sovereign states, regain the upper hand. It is a unique and auspicious conjunction of the events of history that the national policies of all three of these leading powers are the policies of land-satiated states, so that the principal goal of each power is not preparation for conquest but protection against future aggression.

Now, for the first time in history, hard-boiled power politics and humanitarianism can go hand in hand. If, in the next few chapters, I seem to overlook this happy point, it is only because I feel that clarity will best be served by discussing realism and idealism quite separately. Hence let it be understood that many of my comments in the power-politics field apply *only* to that field, and that I do not mean that we, or any other nation, should live under a jungle code. As a matter of fact, I stress the stark realism of power politics because Americans, and others, will eventually have to choose between this brutal, historic "solution" of world settlement and the alternative of a collective-defense system that combines justice and humanitarianism with realism and practicality.

THE TWO DIVISIONS OF POWER POLITICS

A sovereign state is a social organism, endowed with vital organs of growth and existing in the midst of actually or potentially hostile states who at one time or another are likely to seek its destruction. The world of today is a world of dynamic changes, and a great state which ceases to grow, expanding inwardly or outwardly, is doomed to become a satellite state or to be destroyed.

The fundamental principle from which power politics is derived is this: *Great nations have been destroyed or enslaved either (a) because they stopped growing or (b) because other nations grew faster and became more powerful.*

A nation which follows the rules of power politics, therefore, will always endeavor (a) to increase its power by expanding either outwardly (into more land) or inwardly (by industrialization), and (b) to keep other strong nations from materially increasing their power through conquest or domination.

Power politics, consequently, has two basic divisions: space politics and balance politics. Space politics, or geopolitics, is concerned with the expansion of the state itself. Balance politics, or balance of power, is concerned with preventing other nations from growing too powerful by conquest or threat of conquest.

Balance-of-power politics has been prominently associated with England. Geopolitics has been identified with Germany, as a pseudo science which her militarists developed to rationalize their yearnings for conquest. Actually both of these divisions of power politics, which I have called balance politics and space politics, have existed since states began the struggle for power among themselves. Although both are based upon the use or threat of force (power politics), each has its own mechanism and its own methods.

The Mechanism of Balance of Power

Balance of power, or balance politics, may be defined as a fluid division of power among sovereign states, the effect of which is to prevent a dangerous preponderance of military strength by any state or combination of states.

The *object* of balance politics is *to prevent the accumulation of preponderant power by another state or states*. It does not matter whether the state in question is friend or foe, nor does it matter whether it is likely or unlikely to make use of its increased power. From the standpoint of power politics, all sovereign states are potential enemies and all sovereign states will or may make use of their power against the interests of another sovereign state. The skill of balance politics consists precisely in preventing a situation in which another state, having grown too powerful, *might* threaten the existence of the first state. Had we played the game of balance politics more skillfully with Japan during this generation, we would have avoided the sinister menace and saved thousands of American lives.

How does the mechanism of balance of power operate? A classic case history is the problem of a two-front war, which Germany sought to solve during the last half century. This purely strategic problem of a simultaneous war against Russia in the East and the European powers in the West is tied to the purely political mechanism of the European balance of power.

Here is the balance pattern of Europe before the First World War, which was essentially repeated in the Second World War: In the center of Europe lay a Germany militant, powerful, and land-hungry. In the East lay populous Russia with her vast, beckoning living space. But in the West stood France and Britain, often unwilling but always inevitable guardians of Russia.

Scattered between these four giants were the pygmy states whose principal function was to retard invasion by precious weeks or days. On the flanks hovered secondary great powers, Italy and Austria-

Hungary. On the dim horizon, thousands of miles across the sea, lay the United States and Japan.

But the real world drama was played in the theater of Europe, where the four great powers were tied to each other by invisible strings in such a manner that if one moved, the others must move also. France and Britain could not permit already powerful Germany to conquer any substantial part of Russia. If they did, Germany, enriched by her conquests, would reduce the relative position of France and subsequently Britain to that of secondary powers, and eventually conquer them as well. On the other hand, neither Russia nor Britain could permit Germany to conquer France. If they did, Russia would be helpless before a Germany dominating continental Europe, and Britain's turn would be next.

Bismarck understood this inescapable mechanism of balance of power far better than Hitler fifty years later. Although in 1871 France was prostrate before the Prussians, Bismarck contented himself with an indemnity and the disputed province of Alsace-Lorraine and modestly withdrew. The German High Command also understood the mechanism, and the famous Schlieffen Plan, with which the Germans inaugurated the First World War, was based on a quick defeat of France and Britain in the West while the slower-moving Russians were held off in the East. This brilliant plan, prepared by the high command years before its execution, worked beyond expectations. But the Germans lost the First World War largely because they failed to realize that beyond the European balance-of-power mechanism existed an even greater and equally inexorable world balance of power. In that world mechanism the balancing wheel was the United States, with the rising might of its industrial power.

So long as there were no drastic changes in the European balance-of-power mechanism, the war was of no urgent concern to the United States. But with Russia prostrate and France and Britain on the brink of defeat, the historic European mechanism was threatened with collapse. There loomed the possibility of a Germany dominating Europe and large parts of Africa and Asia. Then it would have served no useful purpose for the United States to "take" Latin America and to "inherit" choice morsels of the British Empire. Within two decades or so the Hohenzollerns' United Kingdom of Europe would have outbuilt the United States in guns and ships, driving Americans from the seas of the world and trapping them within their own borders to be taken care of at leisure. Power politics demanded that the European balance of power, and that of the world, be re-established by the United States.

After the defeat of Germany the European balance mechanism was given back by the United States into the keeping of the British and French politicians, who did with it what a stupid child does with a watch and hammer. Twenty-one years later the power pattern was repeated in Europe with essentially the same balances and the same checks. There was an even heavier shift in favor of Germany, this time with strings attached to Japan. Again the world mechanism was threatened with a breakdown. Again, anxious as were Americans to stay out of "the European mess," the world-wide play of the power mechanism compelled the United States to throw her weight against the dictators of Europe and Asia.

Thus balance politics, operating as a magnetic force, fixes each state in its orbit; it establishes regional mechanisms of balance of power in which mutually attracting and repelling states are held together, and it ties up these regional mechanisms into a single world mechanism.

The case history of the two-front war illustrates the dynamic principle which governs the mechanism of balance politics. It has always existed and always will exist, so long as there are two sovereign powers left in the world able to fight. It is the iron law of great sovereign states that the price of their existence is prevention of the hegemony of any one of their members. The underlying conditions and the number of great states within the mechanism of balance of power will vary from time to time, but not the automatic play of the principle itself. This principle dominated the struggles of the Romans and the Carthaginians for two centuries, until Carthage was plowed under; it was at the heart of the rivalry between Athens and Sparta, and, in the larger world sphere, between the Greeks and the Persians. It brought us to the Second World War, and in any future world war it will again compel the United States to intervene, whatever the cost.

The balance-of-power mechanism operates not to prevent war but to make preventive wars successful. It is designed as long-term insurance against losing a war. It cannot control or regulate the sovereign states; it can only register their mutual fears. And at times it can bring the threat of a pack against the overambitious wolf. But by its very nature the balance-of-power mechanism means instability, and when the inevitable war comes the mechanism continues to operate, only this time in the field of battle. When peace arrives the balance mechanism starts all over again, only at a slower tempo and with a power pattern heavily weighted in favor of the victors. Sooner or later, however, demoralized by their triumph or torn by internal dissensions, the victors dissipate their advantages and are attacked in turn. In spite of its crude construction, the balance of power is the best political mechanism that history has so far devised for canalizing war among the sovereign states.

In the Shadow of the Giants

The mechanism of balance of power would not be complete without a complicated system of small states, who add their tiny weights and counterweights to the balance scale of the greater states. All lesser states, down to the tiniest, seek to maintain themselves by precarious balances and holds on their bigger brothers. They live in the shadow of the giants. The smaller states survive and thrive mainly as a by-product of rivalries among the great states. Thus Uruguay has survived because it is in the dead center of the struggle between Argentina and Brazil for the domination of South America; and Argentina has prospered in the shadow of clashing interests between Britain and the United States.

In the past the national armies of the lesser states added a substantial weight on the scales of the greater states. Many of them were militarily hard to get, and all of them had either a nuisance value or value as buffer states. But something has happened to throw all the lesser states off balance. Their territories can be overrun in a matter of days and even hours. Such a catastrophe has never happened before in the history of the smaller states. The Latin-American countries, for instance, received a double blow: the planes and tanks have nullified their national armies with their rifles. and the European balance of power, upon which they relied to shield them from the Yankee Colossus, will become useless to them after this war.

WHEELS WITHIN WHEELS

The complex world mechanism of balance of power consists of several regional mechanisms. In the world mechanism these regional mechanisms operate like wheels within wheels. Each of these regional mechanisms possesses its own system of balance of power. When a regional mechanism breaks down we have a local war, which may or may not spread to the world at large.

There are today, for instance, four such regional mechanisms, each balanced by its own system of sovereign states: the western European, the eastern European, the Far Eastern, and the American. In the last case there is only one balancing wheel—the gigantic one of the United States.

The balance within these regional mechanisms and between them has always been in a state of change. Some of the great powers disappear, new ones rise, while the center of gravity gradually shifts over the globe. History suggests to me that the world balance of power is subject to a broad cyclical law, its operation as clearly discernible as larger economic cycles. In certain periods, such as the early feudal ages or the eighth century B.C., the world balance mechanism consisted of a great number of states, of about equal power. Then the different states began to be gradually absorbed, or satellized, by two or three leading powers. Finally the struggle narrowed down to but two powers. The end came, after centuries of strife, either with a world state (as in the case of ancient Persia, Greece, or Rome) or a total breakdown of the balance mechanism, leading to complete fragmentation of states and the start of a new cycle.

We are now at the stage of the historical cycle when the smaller states are being absorbed by larger ones, leading rapidly toward a "galaxy" system of three or four giant states. The regional mechanisms of old have now become industrial *power centers*. The elimination of physical obstacles and the revolution in military weapons enormously accelerate this process of "agglutination." It will come to a climax with the partial or complete industrialization of the vast man power of Asia. Who will agglutinate whom remains to be seen. But it is certain that the mass of small states is being rapidly eliminated and that states which heretofore played the role of great powers are being reduced to the status of secondary and even satellite powers, while new giant states are rising.

The Twilight of Europe

For more than three centuries the world was largely dominated by the events in Europe and by the interplay of forces in the purely European mechanism of the balance of power. Europe, herself but a peninsula of the world island, ruled the five continents. There was only one balance mechanism for the world, the European. During these centuries the European mechanism shifted slowly. Spain, bled white by imperial adventures, left the family of great powers early in the eighteenth century. Turkey, once the menace of Christendom, was gradually beaten down by her hereditary enemy, Russia; she miraculously escaped extinction because the other European powers preferred her to Russia as keeper of the Dardanelles. And when she cut the imperial cloth to fit her size, becoming one of the smaller powers, she grew healthy and prospered. The peoples of the Far East were still dormant, and in the West, across the Atlantic, the United States was too busy digesting a continent. But Britain, France, the Germanic states, and Russia still played the leading roles, balancing each other and the world.

The nineteenth century was the Golden Age of Europe. Great states held each other in check, while smaller states thrived on the beautifully balanced scales of Europe. And when wars broke out, upsetting the balance mechanism, it automatically righted itself, keeping the world on a fairly even keel. After a Napoleonic flurry—the first ominous sign of the catastrophic wars to come—there were long lapses of peace, during which science leaped forward and the Industrial Revolution charged its batteries. For thirty-eight years, between 1815 and the Crimean War in 1854, there was no war in Europe. This was the century of stately diplomatic conferences and balls, of leisurely intrigues, of the Holy Alliance of the Russian, French, and

Austrian emperors, of the concert of Europe, with British ministers as concertmeisters.

Conditions were ideal for the play of balance of power. There was time for everything. Armies marched on foot or sailed on slow-moving ships. Distances were enormous, physical obstacles almost insurmountable, and it took years to reduce any one of hundreds of powerful fortresses. It was still the war of men against men, armed with nothing better than rifles and cumbersome cannon.

Leading powers were fairly equally balanced in arms. The greater industrial concentration of Europe was balanced by Russia's greater space, an almost decisive strategic weapon of defense. Britain's dominant sea strength was balanced by the military strength of the continental powers. The small nations, with their armies and fortresses, played an important planetary part around the great states. All this kept the plague of war in an endemic state. There was time for the balance mechanism to keep on righting itself.

Then, in 1914, came the first devastating explosion of the time bombs accumulated by the Industrial Revolution. Forces far greater than paper alliances and ambassadorial conclaves began to operate. The concert of Europe, played for so long in contented adagio, speeded up its tempo and crashed into discords.

There was a shift from war by fighting men to war by machines, and a parallel shift in power potential from domination by nations specializing in fighting men (such as France) to domination by nations specializing in heavy industrial production (such as the United States). For the first time in history, industrial production became exactly equal to the military potential.

Certainly the delicately balanced mechanism of the semi-agricultural, semi-industrial European era could no longer check the epidemic spread of total war. It was one thing for that mechanism to operate across enormous distances, at the leisurely pace of the foot soldier; it is another thing for it to operate in a world of intricate new machines moving at ever-increasing speed. When oceans shrink and continents are flanked by air, empires collapse in a few weeks. The British estimates of a power balance favorable to Britain must be altered in view of the fact that cities can be devastated in thirty minutes, and American plans for cushioning this continent must be revised when defense of the Dutch East Indies becomes more important strategically than defense of western Canada.

In the last thirty years the world power mechanism has been changed more drastically than in the three hundred years before. It is certain that during the next thirty years there will be even more violent oscillations in the world power mechanism. These shifts of power and the appearance of new power centers in America and Asia spell the doom of European domination, the supremacy of the United States during and immediately after the war, and the end of American supremacy once the enormous man power of Asia is even partially mobilized by industry.

CHAPTER NINE

Tomorrow and after Tomorrow

THE MIGHT of the western European powers, undermined by the rapid growth of powers outside Europe and shaken by the First World War, will be broken by the Second World War. Our own time sees the end of an era that lasted for half a millennium. Western Europe, no longer the balance mechanism of the world and of modern history, will become one of several world power centers.

The props have been knocked from under France by Germany, and from under Germany by the Allies. In western Europe will remain only Britain, in the flush of her tremendous victory, but facing a superhuman task of feeding and maintaining her overpopulated island, holding together her empire, and preparing to defend herself against rising industrialized superstates.

While western Europe will thus lie prostrate except for Britain, at its eastern end a new and mighty power center—the Eurasian—will rise in victorious Russia and will operate like a powerful magnet on neighboring countries in both Europe and Asia. In the Far East, although the Japanese power will be destroyed, a new and mightier power center—the Chinese—is being forged. And on the American continent a power center with an industrial potential of fighting machines superior to the rest of the world is already in operation, and will continue to balance the world for at least a decade.

Thus a new, much more complex world mechanism of balance of power, with four power centers instead of one, is in process of formation. Western Europe has become but one of the four, and not the strongest. Even when its three hundred and fifty million highly civilized and industrialized people recover from the Second World War, Europe will never again play the dominant role it played before, unless controlled by one or two single powers. It will remain as tragically overpopulated as before, depending upon the outside powers for its essential materials and food. There will be the same traditional animosities, power politics, and turmoil. Defeated France, Germany, Italy, and their satellites, perhaps with victorious Britain, will seek to renew the struggle for European control of the world mechanism of balance of power; but it is too late to stop the rise of superstates elsewhere.

The Germans in Russia and the Japanese in China tried in vain to push back the clock. Practically singlehanded, Russia withstood the might of Germany in continental Europe, and China withstood for six years the industrial might of Japan. Within a few years after the Second World War both Russia and China will be impregnable on their home grounds. A few years later the decline of the western European powers will turn into a fall precipitated not by their failure to grow, but by the irresistible growth of nations in possession of vast, unified man power and space. The heretofore first-class powers, Germany, France, possibly Britain, will become second-class powers, as will Japan in the East, and cede first place to new industrial super-states—the United States, Russia, and China. Industrially integrated European nations of forty, fifty, and sixty million population will rate only second class when compared to industrially integrated continental blocs of one hundred and fifty, two hundred, and five hundred million.

These profound changes in the power pattern of the world are taking place under our eyes. In the future development of the world balance mechanism we can anticipate two different power patterns at two different time periods. The first, established immediately after the war, will be dominated by the United States. The second will develop in the next two or three decades and will be characterized first by the rise of Russian might and subsequently by the entrance upon the world stage of a new leading actor, industrialized China.

Chart I shows the world power pattern of 1900, when Europe dominated the world. Chart II gives the world power pattern of 1945, when the United States will be the dominant power. Chart III gives us a picture of the world power pattern of 1975, when the center of gravity shifts to Asia. These three charts will give us a graphic picture of the decline of Europe, the rise of the United States, and its anticipated decline relative to the industrial rise of Russia and China. That picture will give us also a yardstick by which to measure the foreign policy of the United States in 1945, when she is at the height of her power.

THE WORLD POWER PATTERN OF 1945

From the standpoint of force (the reality that counts in power politics), the United States will emerge from this war by far the most powerful state. Alone, it will be considerably more powerful than Britain, Russia, and China combined. Since the United States will have no dearth of natural allies who may fear either Britain or Russia, and will still be far from the peak of her potential industrial production, the postwar power of this country will be overwhelming. No combination of powers outside the United States will be strong enough to shatter or even weaken her dominant position during the next several years.

As the principal dispenser of food, capital, and materials needed for postwar reconstruction, the American economic arm will powerfully support its military arm. And the wide sympathy and confidence enjoyed by the United States, who is too young as a world power to have accumulated many hatreds and fears, will be a powerful moral support to both the military and economic arms. Most of the nations of the world know that the only profit which the United States sought in the First World War and in the Second World War was security for others and therefore for herself.

CHART I: THE WORLD POWER PATTERN OF 1900

In this period Europe dominated the world. Estimates are based on relative military and naval strength.

That there is always a danger of underestimating the strength of other states, Germany and Japan found out with the United States. But an equally serious blunder could be committed by overestimating the strength of other states and underestimating one's own strength, as is the case today with many American statesmen and writers who can find no better solution of America's security than to ride on the coattails of the Anglo-Russian alliance or to dream about a world co-dominion with Britain. The chart of the power pattern of 1945 does not tell the whole story of the tremendous power of the United States to forge her own destiny, with Britain and Russia if possible, without them if need be.

Britain in 1945: For the first time in three centuries, Britain has lost command of the oceans. The British army and air fleets will still be strong enough to command the waters around the British Isles, parts of Europe, the Mediterranean, and the Indian Ocean. But the American five-ocean navy and world-wide air fleets will effectively control the vital ocean routes upon which Britain depends for her final survival. Except for the few die-hard Tories, this need not unduly alarm the British people. They and the American people remember that American trade and prosperity flourished during long periods when Britannia ruled the waves.

Russia in 1945: Russia will be the mightiest land power in Europe and Asia. Her land armies will easily number twenty million soldiers. Within two decades two hundred and fifty million Russians will equal and probably surpass American industrial power. The question here, however, is how strong Russia will be during the decisive few years immediately following Axis defeat. Certainly not as strong as claimed by the fanatic Communist supporters who have their hearts on their sleeves, or the equally fanatic Communist haters who might have something else up their sleeves. Russia will have even less effective power than Britain to upset the dominant influence of the United States. The Russian industrial machine was just strong enough to stop Germany before Moscow, but too weak to prevent Germany and her satellites from ravaging some of her best lands. This was a triumph of heroic Russian resistance, but in the postwar power pattern her vast ravaged territories will be a big minus. It is true that the theory of "war exhaustion" is largely fallacious; never-

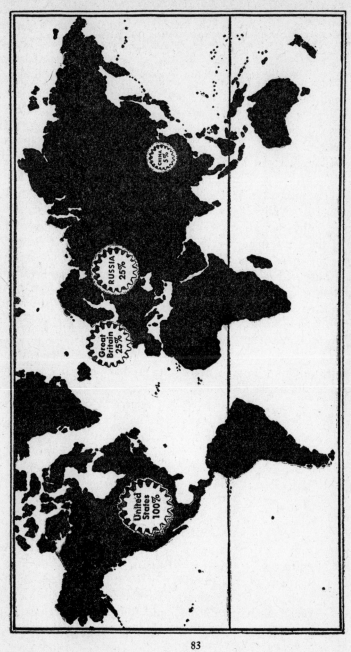

CHART II: THE WORLD POWER PATTERN OF 1945

Estimates of combined industrial and military strength here make the United States the dominant power.

theless, the Germans inflicted deep wounds on Russia, and even with ruthless Russian organization several years will be required to heal them.

Two other important factors, one military and the other psychological, tend to limit Russia's influence outside her own territories and those of her immediate neighbors. In the case of Russia, more than with any other country, a sharp strategic distinction must be made between defense of home territory and offense outside it. Everybody knows about Russia's historic defender, General Winter. But Russia's greatest and most powerful defender is and always has been General Space. A nation collapses when its vital nerve centers are occupied or paralyzed by the enemy. For centuries England's vital nerve centers were unreachable over her channel moat. England developed the greatest empire in history largely because she could hit anyone she chose and not be hit back. Not so with the continental powers of Europe; France and Germany repeatedly collapsed because their vital nerve centers were but a few days' march from the enemy. With Russia, space is the greatest strategic asset; there is a natural dispersal of nerve centers and ganglions throughout the gigantic body of the country. Ten Russias may be conquered, and still new Russias must be conquered. Too late Hitler realized this elementary strategic truth. Only the vital nerve and production centers of the United States are better distributed and less accessible.

But there is this difference between the American and the Russian spaces: The American continent is closely knit by a marvelous network of rail and road communications, thus greatly reducing the space; while the Russian space is enlarged by lack of adequate communications. As a result, the American space is highly "mobile," while the Russian space is static. Translated into strategy, this means that the same space which operates in favor of Russia when in defense of her vital centers will operate against her in attack on the European countries. Any Russian invasion of western Europe must start with weak lines of supply extended many hundreds of miles. The Russian space will cling to the boots of every Russian soldier, weighing him down like the mud of his steppes. While Russian armies shift slowly and ponderously, European armies will be backed up by a network of communications permitting rapid shifts and concentration against Russia's weakest point. This greater mobility would enable a European army, though inferior in number, to defeat a Russian army piece by piece.

All this does not mean, of course, that Russia after the war will be reduced to a passive role. However one may discount the exaggerated statements as to Russian military power, there will be enough real power left for Russia to cause, if she chooses, quite a disturbance in Europe. But it is very doubtful whether Russia will choose to do so while Stalin is guiding her. Of the many reasons for this, the principal one is psychological. Russia's foreign policy is seriously handicapped by the existence of an enormous world-wide pool of hatred, distilled from years of anti-Communist propaganda and resulting in part from Russia's own earlier attack on both fascism and democracy through the Communist International. There are many to whom Russia is guilty of an unforgivable crime in being officially a Socialist republic and a focus of Socialist infection. To them this ideological crime is more important than all the power politics in the world. There are others who, for reasons of power politics, are still dreaming about a limited partition of Russia. In any event, during the next several years Russia must step carefully and warily, lest she find herself facing (after reactionary elections in the United States and Britain) a world united front that might crush her. Stalin's Russia will defend her national interests ruthlessly, energetically, and very skillfully, on the basis of strict power politics. But until her inner power pattern greatly improves she will have neither the capacity nor the recklessness to challenge seriously America's ephemeral role of world arbiter.

How ephemeral this role is we shall see by comparing the world power pattern of 1945 with an anticipated power pattern only thirty years later, when our young children have grown up. The chart of the world power pattern for 1975, unlike the charts for 1900 and 1945, is based on the approximate estimate of the rate of industrialization of various countries and is correlated with the industrialized man power available to each of these countries. It is not possible to estimate in detail the actual military standing of each leading country for 1975, as was the case of the charts for 1900 and 1945; but since the industrial potential of a country, together with its man power and material resources, has become the index of its military strength, the result is the same.

THE WORLD POWER PATTERN OF 1975

The power pattern of 1975 here discussed will be predicated upon the assumption that in the meantime China will not be partitioned and that furthermore no adequate system of collective security will be established. In that event, as after the First World War, the victorious United Nations, having concluded the ever-disastrous peace of power politics, will continue to shift within the balance-of-power system, in preparation for the inevitable Third World War.

1975 in the Chinese Calendar: Our habit of looking at China through the mind of the past is so ingrained that it is difficult to adjust ourselves to the picture of the industrialized China of the future. Yet China of 1975 will be as different from the weak, bulky, and still patriarchal China of today as is Russia of 1943 from the Russia of 1923.

China in 1975, we may reasonably suppose, will be unified by a strong central government and a well-developed network of communications. China will have a pool of several million technicians and specialists in every field of scientific and industrial activity. By 1975 the industrialization of China will be far from complete. But the weight of Chinese man power is so enormous and its cost is so low that even if China is no better industrialized than was the United States forty years ago, it will be able to play a dominant military role in the world power mechanism. Japan proper, with a seventh of China's population and less than seven per cent of America's industrial production, became one of the world's great powers—and that in spite of the enormous handicap of lack of raw materials. China in 1975 will throw as much decisive weight on the side she supports as does the United States today.

On the other hand, it will be difficult to overwhelm China except by the firm alliance of all western Europe and Russia, or western Europe and the United States, or perhaps the United States and Russia. A Chinese-Japanese alliance, supported by other Asiatics, would require for its defeat a solid front of most of the rest of the world. In any event, the China of 1975, as the United States of 1945,

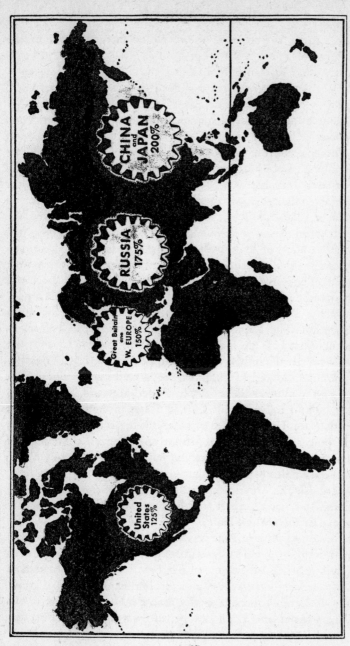

CHART III: THE WORLD POWER PATTERN OF 1975

Approximate ratios of industrialization and population increase show the emergence of Asia as a world power.

will be able to tip the scales of the world balance of power as she chooses.

All this assumes, of course, that China's postwar industrial development will not be thwarted by a prolonged civil war or hampered by power politics played by her neighbors. It further assumes that we cannot count upon a peaceful, democratic China always to prevail. But in power politics the security of a great state such as ours can never be based upon the hope that another sovereign state is likely to be friendly. It can be based only on estimate of the physical capacity of another state to do harm.

The United States in 1975: In the year 1975 the population of the United States will be about 155,000,000. The country will weather successfully its usual cycles of depression, and great new industries will boom. The standard of living will be high. But there will be a hard struggle for the rapidly shrinking world market, in competition with the vast autarchy systems of Britain and two newcomers, Russia and China. Economic aggressiveness by the United States will sharply increase in Latin America, which also will enter the stage of rapid industrialization. The Latin Americans will continue, as before, to fear and therefore hate the powerful North Americans. By 1975 the hostile bloc of partly industrialized Latin Americans will number at least one hundred and fifty million people and may easily prove a fatal drag on the military power of the United States.

Industrially and militarily the United States of 1975 will be more powerful than the United States of 1945. But her relative standing in the world power pattern will drop from unchallenged supremacy to bare equality with several other leading powers. There will be a new industrial and military power center in China, strong enough to threaten seriously the American position in the Pacific. Another industrial and military power center, the Russian, will at least equal and perhaps surpass the United States.

In western and southern Europe will be a third power center. The industrialization of the agricultural parts of Europe will be complete, and a fully industrialized Europe of five hundred million population, using raw materials from Africa and the Middle East, will become, if united, considerably more powerful than the United States. It will probably be a better integrated Europe, and it will certainly be a desperate, overpopulated Europe threatening America across the Atlantic as Asia will threaten across the Pacific. In addition there will be smaller but important centers of power in the rapidly industrializing India and the Middle East.

Thus the world balance-of-power mechanism of 1975 will probably consist of four principal industrial-military power centers and three secondary ones. The United States will be but one of the four centers, and not the strongest. In 1975 it will not even be necessary for the power centers of Europe, Russia, and the Far East to combine in order to defeat the United States. Any single one of them will be a formidable danger, and any two of them combined, with the third neutralized, would make the military defense of the United States very difficult, even with Britain on our side.

The contrast between the United States of 1945 and its probable position in 1975 is ominous. In 1945 the United States will produce by itself as many fighting machines as the rest of the world put together. But in 1975 it is doubtful whether the United States will be able to produce more than twenty per cent of the total fighting machines produced in the world. This will not be because the United States will stop growing, but because other states with vast, hitherto dormant populations will have learned the magic trick of industrialization and will then outproduce the United States. The same thing will happen to us in 1975 on a gigantic scale that happened to Britain at the beginning of the twentieth century: England did not stop growing, but the United States, Germany, Japan, and Russia grew much faster, and, having caught up with industrial England, played their highest trump, which is man power.

The position of the United States in 1975 will be more difficult than was the position of England. Britain was faced with German and Japanese blocs of seventy million people each, which were severely cramped by a small living space. And behind Britain stood the United States. In 1975 the United States will be dealing with blocs of five hundred million partly industrialized Chinese and two hundred and fifty million fully industrialized Russians, not to mention the power centers of western Europe and of Latin America. And there will be nothing but a weakened Britain to stand behind in case of need. This means that toward the end of the twentieth century the position of the United States, from the standpoint of security, will revert some-what to its position at the beginning of the nineteenth century, when only the mutual rivalries of foreign powers permitted its survival.

In fact, the position of the United States after ephemeral years of supremacy will be more hazardous than at any time in the past. For oceans and distances will no longer be decisive barriers. Instead of a weak Canada and Mexico on the northern and southern frontiers, the near neighbors, in effect, will be powerful industrialized masses of Russians pressing from the north, the Asiatics from the Pacific, and the Europeans from the Atlantic—nearly two billion against little over two hundred million Anglo-Americans. In the tragically over-populated world the North and South American continents stand out as a new promised land of milk and honey, a land that today is beyond the reach of despairing millions but tomorrow will be within their grasp.

There will be no reason why the other leading nations, except perhaps Britain, should strive desperately to preserve the Western Hemisphere under the domination of the United States. There will be, instead, good reasons why the leaders of proliferating masses in Asia and Europe should seek to break through American defenses in order to occupy the semivirginal lands of South America and the enormous productive zones of the semipopulated North American continent. The United States of 1975 will have to depend upon the good will of a number of foreign powers. It is more than likely that such good will will not be available. The powers of Europe and Asia may well find it to their advantage to combine among themselves to partition the American continent, reducing the United States to the role of a secondary power, or even destroying her.

It may be that, as in the nineteenth century, the rivalries of foreign powers will prevent any one of them from dismembering the American continent. But it is more probable that, as in the partition of Poland, the powers of Europe and Asia can safely divide the Western Hemisphere among themselves without affecting their *relative* strength. The United States of 1975 may well become a gigantic Poland standing between the West and the East; and an integrated Europe, a fully industrialized Russia, and the partly industrialized Mongolians may well play the role that Austria, Prussia, and Russia played in the several partitions of Poland.

This is no more fantastic than the attempts to partition Russia and the British Empire during the First and Second World Wars. The partition of Russia was the dominant issue during and after the First World War, and only the internal dissensions of foreign powers and the brilliant leadership within Russia saved the Soviet Union from reduction to a Volga state. The partition of the British Empire was one of the dominant issues of the Second World War, since the Axis realized that control of the European continent or China was not possible unless the British Empire was first eliminated.

The dominant issue of the Third World War may well be the partition of the Western Hemisphere and the elimination of the United States as a balance wheel in the world power mechanism. Thus, as vast newly industrialized states come into play, the balance-of-power mechanism breaks down in successive world wars. With each war an attempt is made to remove the most powerful state, which blocks the expansion of rising rival states. In 1975 the United States will be the nation most favored for removal.

IV. UNITED STATES FOREIGN POLICY

CHAPTER TEN

American Power Politics

WE HAVE SEEN that power politics has always been and still is the true law of nations. United States foreign policy, therefore, must be based on power politics.

The basic principles of American power politics are derived from the general principles governing the power politics of any great state. But it is futile and dangerous to seek the solutions of new problems of the American future in the antiquated machinery of the European past. American power politics must be based upon the conditions peculiar to the United States. It must not imitate the techniques of European power politics—techniques which are based on different history and different geography from the American. A more modern, more scientific, and more effective system of United States foreign policy, or American power politics—at present the same thing—can be established, and is discussed in this and succeeding chapters. That system must be based upon the unexampled power of the United States in 1945, and not upon the good will of our allies, present or future. A great power cannot lean too heavily on the promises and agreements, however solemn, of other powers. Behind the written articles of all covenants, agreements, and alliances there is the unwritten article whereby a great and prosperous nation that does not know how to stand alone and fight alone, if need be, shall have her territories and her wealth partitioned by others.

The goal of American power politics is security. The new system of power politics must offer a definite solution to the fundamental problem implicit in the comparative study of the world power patterns of 1945 and 1975. The problem is: *What use of American supremacy in 1945 will best prevent the dire threats to American security in 1975?*

In other words, how can we protect our children from immense future dangers by making use of the immense present resources at the disposal of their fathers?

Previously I have briefly stated the three basic principles of American power politics. American balance politics, space politics, and collective defense are derived from these three principles, respectively. For the convenience of the reader I shall repeat these three principles here and establish the three main divisions of American power politics (foreign policy).

First principle: *The United States cannot permit any other leading state to increase its power materially through the domination of other sovereign states by force or threat of force.* From this principle is derived the methods and rules of American balance politics (balance of power).

Second principle: *The United States must use its present power to insure itself strategically against possible future aggression by one or more sovereign states.* From this principle is derived the methods and rules of American space politics (geopolitics).

Third principle: *The United States, as the strongest and therefore the most threatened state, must use its present power to establish an integrated system of effective collective defense against wars of aggression.*

The first two principles deal with the individual security of the United States as a leading state. They constitute the *national* basis of American foreign policy. The third principle deals with a system of collective defense to insure the security of the United States as part of an international organization. The third principle constitutes the *international* basis of American foreign policy.

There are two corollaries derived from the third principle of American power politics.

The first corollary is that *a system of collective defense, in order to be acceptable to the United States, must provide for all possible contingencies, such as future betrayals and coalitions of other powers, and must not deprive the United States either of its sovereign rights (ex-*

cept the right to wage war of aggression) or of its own military power to defend itself. If such a system of collective defense is theoretically feasible, then the United States must seek to establish it at once. For the only lasting guarantee of the security of the United States lies in the lasting peace of the world.

The second corollary is that *until a system of collective defense is fully established and thoroughly tested in actual operation, the United States must not abandon the first and second principles (balance and space politics).* In practice, this corollary means that the United States must not, in the hope of collective security, sacrifice *prematurely* its present enormous military and political superiority as the leading world power, and that the requirements of the American Strategic Zone, as well as other requirements necessary to insure the *individual* security of the United States, must be incorporated in the world settlement and in any future system of collective defense.[1]

Thus the United States foreign policy makes use of three distinct instruments of American power politics in order to insure maximum security: balance politics, space politics, and a system of collective defense.

Those authorities who have announced the demise of the balance-of-power principle are a bit premature. However the individual states may rise or fall, combine into alliances or isolate themselves, the balance of power will always operate as a regulating mechanism between states until an adequate substitute for power politics is found.

A great nation can survive only on the basis of its own strength. But—and this is the main point—the strength of a great nation is relative; it is measured not so much by its own resources as by those of other states. The example of Japan and Germany proves that a modern state can multiply itself many times in a few short years by conquest, jeopardizing the existence of all the other states.

The increase in power of another sovereign state through conquest proportionately decreases the relative power of the United States. It follows that the United States must use armed force, if need be, while

---

[1] The World Federation Plan embodies both the national and the international requirements of American foreign policy. Of course it also embodies similar requirements of Britain, Russia, and China, including their strategic zones (territorial frontiers). At the same time the national interests of all states are fully safeguarded.

she is superior in strength, to prevent the imperialistic increase in power of another strong state.

The whole principle of American balance politics hinges on the definition of *material increase*. For instance, if in the coming settlement Russia should increase her territories by the addition of Latvia, Estonia, Lithuania, Bessarabia, and the Polish Ukraine, this would still not constitute a material increase of her power. We might oppose any of these additions by diplomatic or economic resistance, but we certainly would not go to war against Russia on this issue.

If, on the other hand, Russia, in addition to these increases, should establish control over a communist Germany, through military occupation or domination, this would materially increase her power. If we permitted such an increase of Russian power we might be faced, in ten or twenty years, with a formidable Russo-German combination that would rule Europe and Asia. It would be cheaper insurance to use our superiority of strength to block Russia (or any other power) from dominating Germany.

Again, we should not permit Britain to control, under one guise or another, the nations of western Europe. This, in addition to her empire, would give Britain an enormous increase of power that might eventually threaten our safety. We have a special relationship with the British, who are our kin, and we would probably not go to war with them even if they sought the domination of western Europe. But, short of war, we should use all the means at our disposal to prevent such control. Balance politics demands that we must be prepared for any contingency, including a totalitarian Britain.

Had we applied this elementary principle of balance politics to Japan, say twenty years ago, we might still have had a war; but that war would have been immeasurably less costly in lives and wealth. And if the extreme isolationists had prevailed upon the United States to refrain from "irritating" Japan, we might still have had peace; but at a cost in lives and wealth immeasurably greater for our children, who would eventually be forced to defend themselves against a Japanese superstate.

It would be criminal folly for an American statesman to assume that this or that foreign nation, fed upon conquests, would be sufficiently appeased so as not to seek to conquer the United States. No conqueror has ever been appeased. No great nation has been or ever will be left alone by other great nations. And the more powerful the nation, the greater the chance of coalitions by rival states against her. The United States, as the most powerful state in the world, will also be the most threatened state. We must therefore prepare ourselves, by a judicious use of balance politics, not only for the wars of tomorrow but for the wars of day after tomorrow.

Timing, and the principle of preparedness, is as important in balance politics as it is in the strategy of war or bridge. A nation is a continuing organism. The growth of nations and the shifts in their power patterns must be anticipated many years in advance and prepared for accordingly. Balance of power is perspective of power—a long perspective.

But diplomats cannot consider long perspectives. In America they have often been helpless before waves of public opinion whipped up by politicians whose sense of timing and perspective never went beyond the next election. There are two fallacies that in the past dominated large sections of American public opinion and will dominate them in the future. Both have a bearing on American balance politics. One is imperialism, which is an attempt to cripple or destroy the world mechanism of balance of power. The other is narrow isolationism, which is an attempt to escape from the inexorable world mechanism of balance of power.

CHAPTER ELEVEN

Ourselves Alone

IN THE UNITED STATES, as a natural result of the war, we now have an increase of patriotism and nationalism. Diseased nationalism may express itself in various ways—as racism, as imperialism, as narrow isolationism, as pseudo internationalism. Not from an ethical standpoint but from strict considerations of national security, let us look at two of them—imperialism and isolationism—as instruments of American power politics.

Imperialism may be defined as the policy of acquisition of territory or economic advantage by the use or threat of armed force. If, for instance, we compel Mexico by threat of force to conclude an economic treaty advantageous to us, this is imperialism; if, on the other hand, we lease a base from Cuba or Britain for vital strategic defense, this is not imperialism within the definition.

It is easy to prove that imperialism is without advantage to American national interests, that it would serve no practical purpose for the United States to conquer Mexico or Argentina. Not the American nation as a whole, but only a few big companies and their stockholders could possibly profit from exploitation of native labor. To exterminate the millions of natives in order to settle American farmers on their land would not sit well on American stomachs; morality aside, Nazi experience proves the difficulty of such resettlement. A much more profitable idea is to build up the productive and consuming capacity of our Mexican and Argentine neighbors and thus utilize their man power for the free and mutually beneficial exchange of goods.

Apart from the fact that conquest of populated foreign lands would bring only grief and expense to the American nation, more immediate considerations of national security demand definite renunciation of American imperialism. The economy of the United States is inward-expanding, with a vast and still partly unexploited continental space. At the same time, as the wealthiest and most powerful nation, the United States is the nation most exposed to future aggression. We need friends and allies everywhere; we can obtain them only by removing their fear of aggression by us. A policy of imperialism would not only deprive us of natural allies but would generate hatreds and encourage hostile combinations. The more imperialistic our policy, the more mountainous would become the hostile resistance, requiring in turn a greater and more brutal effort of force on our part. At some point the vicious circle would snap, hurling us to destruction along with the Germans, the Japanese, and other would-be world conquerors.

In short, a policy of American imperialism would signify that we are not content to keep what we've got and prefer to risk all in order to gain more. As what we've got already is more than any nation has, American imperialism would be decidedly bad power politics.

In the heat of political passions engendered by this war, the word "isolationism" has been stamped with so many different and contradictory meanings that it is impossible adequately to define it. But the prewar meaning is clear: isolation is a historic American policy of aloneness, of withdrawal into our own continental shell. This traditional policy was based on our refusal to participate in European power politics or add weight to the European balance of power. In order to emphasize this refusal, the circle of the Monroe Doctrine was drawn around the American continent.

This was no foolhardy defiance; it was a logical result of conditions. The founders of the new republic were masterful power politicians. They saw the two great maritime powers, Britain and Spain, defeated in the North and in the South of the American continent. They were conscious of the strategic advantage of distance from the power centers of Europe and of the growing strength of the United States on land and in adjacent waters. They well calculated that so long as the great powers of Europe largely neutralized each other by mutual suspicion and war, the United States could successfully isolate the American continent from the play of the European mechanism of balance of power and from feudalistic ideologies.

This policy of isolation, dictated by the rapid, inward-expanding economy of the United States, succeeded brilliantly and became traditional. It kept the United States out of European civil wars, and European power politics out of the American continent.

Then, in 1898, still in its teens as a world power, the United States liquidated the remains of the Spanish Empire in the Caribbean and the Pacific. Although this expansion was accompanied by imperialistic overtones, it was dictated more by the strategic considerations of a rising world power. The waters of the Pacific were still untroubled, but Russia threatened Manchuria and the sun of Japan was rising. The United States was conscious of its position as a great Atlantic and Pacific power. It became necessary to be interested in the oceanic approaches to the American continent.

Thus a new pattern of American power politics became dimly discernible, but it was still essentially a continental and not an oceanic policy. The American people were much too busy developing their continent, spurred to explosive activity by the vision of untold wealth created by the Industrial Revolution. Until 1917 American foreign policy continued to be isolationist; then threats of German domination of Europe, together with heavy financial involvement on the side of the Allies, swung the United States into a European coalition.

At the time of the armistice the United States—a dreamy, awkward giant in a world of European power politicians—indulged in wild and clumsy internationalism. For a few brief months the American nation and the peoples of the world lived, as though in a trance, in the hope of lasting peace. Then came the Treaty of Versailles to smash this hope on the rocks of national interest. Disillusioned, the United States withdrew from traditional European power politics into traditional American isolation.

When the Second World War broke out in 1939 the overwhelming majority of Americans were isolationists still. But history had already set for the United States a contrary course. Regardless of the grim determination of Americans not to become involved in either the European or the Asiatic war, the compass needle pointed toward intervention and internationalism. Bitter struggle between the war and peace parties ensued. Strange bedfellows in the isolationist camp included a small but vociferous minority of communists, a small but voracious minority of fascists, millions of sincere pacifists, and millions more of equally sincere nationalists. In both camps there was confusion, sedulously cultivated by foreign propaganda.

With the fall of France in June 1940 and the perceptible tottering of the British Empire, a tremendous military fact became clear: If Nazi Germany and militarist Japan could consolidate their conquests, the United States could be placed in grave jeopardy in fifteen or twenty years. The world of industrial civilization had shrunk, becoming one little world. In it, non-intervention or inaction meant that the United States must sooner or later find itself at the mercy of would-be conquerors. There was no love for blundering British diplomats or for communist allies, but Pearl Harbor only hastened inevitable war.

This time it was a definite break from traditional isolation, without hope of return to the world of ocean bulwarks and agreeable protective distances. The argument that the United States was impregnable within her own continent was no longer valid. It was apparent that if the United States should go into a Rip Van Winkle sleep for a quarter of a century, she would wake up half conquered. *This* isolationism was dead.

Nor was there any hope of escape left in hemispheric isolationism. For the Western Hemisphere can be effectively defended only, if at all, from strategic bases on the Asiatic mainland and in the islands of the Atlantic. *That* isolationism was also dead.

Millions of Americans, formerly isolationist, changed their minds. But at the core of American isolationism were two powerful forces: one a great spiritual force, the pacifists; the other a great patriotic force, the nationalists. Neither of these two powerful groups has changed its basic attitude. It is obvious that the realities of war make true pacifists more anti-war than ever, even while they wish and seek victory for their country. Similarly the nationalists, though defeated in their mistaken opposition to this war, are unconvinced that nationalism itself was defeated or is wrong.

What nationalists as well as internationalists now realize is that henceforth American foreign policy, be it power politics or welfare politics, must be international. Narrow nationalism in any form is dead. The Industrial Revolution has pierced our continental cocoon, and the peculiarily American luxury of being the white-haired orphan of the world is no longer possible.

The difference between nationalism and internationalism has become one of emphasis. Both nationalists and internationalists are anxious to co-operate with the rest of the world, but from different ends and by different means. There are many kinds of internationalism and many different degrees of world co-operation, but the internationalist philosophy is that the world has shrunk and become *one world*. The internationalists seek to save the world and thereby save America.

The nationalists seek to save America first and then the world, if anything is left over. Their philosophy is that this is one world, all right, but the smaller it becomes, the more the need to draw back into isolationism. It is a hostile world of concentrated hatreds, a world where selfish national interests prevail and where the rules of the game are the rules of power politics. The nationalists claim that international co-operation does not mean that they must throw to the winds traditional American principles and embrace any kind of internationalism, concluding postwar alliances galore and participating in all sorts of international schemes.

Few would dispute this author's internationalism. He fought the prewar isolationists, and his postwar plan is called World Federation. For this plan it can be said that no reasonable nationalist can object to a system of collective security with an adequate world organization, provided such a system respects the full sovereignty of the nation (except for the right to wage a war of aggression), retains a powerful American armed force, calls for a greatly improved American Strategic Zone in the Atlantic and Pacific oceans, and fully protects the security of the United States against all possible betrayals. Under these conditions the added collective security would be welcomed by the most extreme nationalist.

But most nationalists are certain to object to phony systems of collective security, such as a revived League of Nations or, worse, a postwar alliance with Britain and Russia. There are, indeed, new and weighty reasons why, if we wish to realize our hopes of lasting peace, we should avoid any variety of pseudo internationalism after this war.

V. AMERICAN BALANCE POLITICS

CHAPTER TWELVE

Pseudo Internationalism

NICHOLAS SPYKMAN, in his *America's Strategy in World Politics,* correctly observes that the postwar United States will have to operate in a world of power politics. But he blunders in assuming that the historical and economic conditions underlying the balance-of-power mechanism will be, after the war, "very similar to those that prevailed before the outbreak of the conflict."

There is no more dangerous illusion than to assume that because the balance-of-power mechanism has operated in a fairly safe, happy-go-lucky way in the past, it will continue to operate in a similar manner in the future. Yet many of America's students of international politics have fallen, with Spykman, into this trap. Spykman and others are oblivious of the changes brought about by the Industrial Revolution, changes which are still in progress at a much accelerated tempo.

Starting with this basic fallacy, Spykman proceeds to outline the American policy of balance of power after the Second World War in terms of the British policy after the First World War. He foresees three power zones—in Europe, in Asia, and in the Western Hemisphere. He advises that the European power zone be organized in the form of a regional "League of Nations," with the United States as an extraregional member. In Asia he advises an Asiatic "League of Nations," again with the United States as an extraregional member. It is his desire that the nations comprising each of these zones shall be "units of approximate equality in military strength and power potential." In order to achieve this internal stabilization, Spykman wants to preserve Germany as a military power to balance Russia, and similarly expects a "strong Japan" to balance China.

In the Western Hemisphere he would have a third "League of Nations"; but in order to neutralize, at least in part, the enormous predominance of the United States over her Latin-American neighbors, he would like to "accept" an extraregional member (probably Britain) "in the political organization of the Western Hemisphere." Finally, to render the operation of this balance machine more smooth, Spykman advocates satellizing the smaller states, who "in the days of three-dimensional warfare are a political hazard to the whole international community."

Thus each of the three power zones—the Western Hemisphere, Europe, and Asia—will be delicately balanced internally, and at the same time the United States, like a skillful juggler, will keep the three balls in the air by "extraregional membership" in two of the three leagues!

Nicholas Spykman was a distinguished authority on international politics, and his teachings are widely followed. But it is unnecessary to analyze his scheme in detail to see that, confused by ill-digested theories of Germanic geopolitics, he advocates a policy disastrous even if the United States were a defeated power, let alone a victorious one.

At the basis of the Spykman errors lies a lack of perspective and sense of timing. In the first place, we certainly don't want to introduce through the front door a European power into our Pan-American councils by accepting an "extraregional" member from Europe. Least of all would we want a "strong Japan" as a counterweight to China. It would more likely become another millstone around our neck.

But these objections assume the proportions of details when compared to his principal fallacy. His whole system of delicately balanced power zones would collapse in a decade or two, when both Russia and China become more industrialized. In his calculations he failed to take into account the ever-increasing velocity and volume in the dynamic shifts of power patterns. History can be the worst of teachers if the pupil seeks blindly to repeat the patterns of the past, without considering the play of entirely new factors in the present and future.

Spykman and many others are oblivious to the tragic failure of the British balance-of-power policy, a failure that began in the last century. The English blunders, like Spykman's, were largely those of timing and perspective. Twice British diplomats allowed foreseeable events to crowd them into a desperate corner, while they toyed with the early-nineteenth-century technique of the balance of power centering around palace intrigues, parliamentary cloakrooms, and board meetings. In this generation they armed Japan, sought to disarm France and rearm Germany. In the case of Japan we helped a little with scrap metal, but it was Britain's game of balance politics, not ours. And when the real balance of power twice showed its teeth, to the astonishment of the British experts, we were twice dragged into war. It is not certain, of course, that these two wars could have been avoided even with the best of British policy. It is certain, however, that their tragic extent could have been greatly minimized if fewer blunders had been committed bv the British and French diplomats.

THE PROPOSAL FOR A TRIPLE ALLIANCE

The issue of a postwar alliance with Britain and Russia (written, implicit, or disguised under some convenient league) is on the agenda of America's postwar policy. It is apparent that some such alliance is contemplated, and it is already implicit in a number of measures for postwar reorganization proposed by the American and British governments. To oppose it does not mean that we should not co-operate with our war allies, or that we should deny them full justice in the coming world settlement. It does mean that we must be realistic and that we must not become involved, in the name of false internationalism, in any postwar adventures which might jeopardize rather than increase our individual security and which certainly offer no hope of collective security.

An alliance may be defined as a temporary union between two or more sovereign states for the purpose of defense or attack against another sovereign state or states. Thus an alliance is an instrument of power politics. A sharp distinction must be made between an alliance and a more permanent type of union such as the Swiss Confederation, founded in the year 1291 as a "perpetual alliance" of sovereign states, or cantons. What made this union different and permanent was the establishment of a higher government with strictly limited powers, *separate* from the governments of the sovereign cantons and maintained by a *separate* armed force. The original Swiss "alliance" lasted for more than six centuries.

What makes a power-politics alliance between sovereign states uncertain, treacherous, and temporary is the fact that each sovereign state is a law unto itself. An alliance of sovereign states is a union of jealous gods. Each state is its own supreme interpreter of the conditions of the alliance. The sovereign state interprets these conditions by consulting primarily its own selfish national interests, which as a rule are in opposition to those of other great states, allies but rivals. Thus an alliance is like a contract between several individuals involving their entire future but which can be neither interpreted nor enforced by law. The members are like poker players in the old wild-West days, when to continue playing they had to be quicker on the draw of the guns than cards.

The government of a sovereign state is subject to ceaseless fluctuations from pressure groups within and tempting offers from without, resulting in constant variations in the interpretation of an alliance, or in its abandonment or even its betrayal. More, a fatal inner contradiction limits the life of an alliance: although the sovereign states are juridically equal members, they are not equal in strength or in the benefits they derive from the alliance. As a result a constant stress of power politics within the alliance eventually destroys it.

Only a great danger from a common enemy, or prospects of rich and easy loot, can hold sovereign states under the temporary bond of an alliance. But a victorious war alliance destroys itself almost immediately after the victory is consummated. Once the danger from a common enemy is removed, the only danger left is from one's own allies. The problem then facing each victorious power is how to increase its own strength while preventing rival powers from increasing theirs. New combinations and tacit alliances within the formal alliance are formed, resulting in new alignments. Thus an alliance is invariably destroyed by the same power politics that created it.

Yet it is this kind of alliance which powerful groups in official and private circles advocate for the United States after this war, as a way to maintain the lasting peace of the world. Propaganda for a postwar United Nations, for a revived League of Nations, for a European or an Asiatic league, for a collectivist international and for a long armistice comes from groups who seek, in one form or another, a power-politics alliance of the United States with Britain, Russia, or both, to "organize" the world on the shaky foundation of the bayonets of their troops. There is no question of the sincerity and patriotism of the men and women forming these groups. Such alliances, however, are neither good power politics nor good collective security, and the projects based upon such alliances are not true but phony internationalism.

The basic proposal is that we journey back more than a century to revive the Holy Alliance, this time with Britain, Russia and the United States as benevolent protectors of the world. Inasmuch as Britain and Russia have already concluded a twenty-year alliance, the real issue is whether or not the United States should join them.

Mr. Walter Lippmann, a brilliant writer and a distinguished authority on international politics, and one of the outstanding spokesmen for powerful groups in both political parties, believes that the United States should join such a Holy Alliance after the war. Mr. Lippmann's arguments for this proposal are found in his book *U.S. Foreign Policy,* subtitled "Shield of the Republic."

Seeking to reinterpret the traditional American policy of "no entangling alliances," Mr. Lippmann argues that the Monroe Doctrine was made possible only by a tacit alliance with Britain and the help of the British fleet, which was our true "protector" during most of the nineteenth century. He finds American foreign policy before 1941 "insolvent" because it failed to achieve a balance between national power and national commitments in the Western Hemisphere and in the Philippines. The necessary increase in power would be achieved not by greater individual strength but by alliances in "adequate combination," that is with the two strongest powers—Britain and Russia —who will protect our "commitments" while we protect theirs.

Dealing first with Mr. Lippmann's history, it was not the British fleet which sustained the Monroe Doctrine, but the disunited states of Europe against the United States of America. The power politicians of Britain, France, and Spain kept looking with covetous eyes on the fabulous Americas, but they never had enough surplus strength left from their mutual rivalries for the big job of reconquering their lost empires. The one notable exception occurred when the United States became temporarily disunited during the Civil War; whereupon the British fleet neglected to protect us from Napoleon III's expeditionary force for the invasion of Mexico. Both Britain and France hoped for a new partition of the Americas; but in Canada the United States had an effective mortgage against the recurrent imperialistic ambitions to dominate the Americas, displayed throughout the nineteenth century by successive British governments. With Canada we found lasting peace, but those three thousand miles of *unprotected* common frontier did more to maintain the Monroe Doctrine than the tender mercies of British Tories commanding the fleet.

The test of Mr. Lippmann's concept of the subtle and intricate game of power politics comes in his proposals for the future. Here he urges that after the Second World War the victorious United States will have the same commitments to defend the Western Hemisphere and the "Philippines salient," and will still require the help of strong allies for their defense. Since South America contains "no principal military power" to assist, its defense "depends upon whether, in our relations with the great powers, our friends outweigh our foes."

But with whom shall an alliance be concluded? Only with the greatest victorious powers, "for only the great powers can wage great wars." Therefore, Mr. Lippmann concludes, "Our two natural and permanent allies have been and are Britain and Russia. . . . Here then, founded on vital interests which have been tested and proved in the course of generations, is the nuclear alliance upon which depends the maintenance of the world order in which America lives." But Great Britain certainly was not our ally through the nineteenth century, and least of all between the end of the First World War and the late thirties. Russia, though consistently friendly to us in the past, except during the days of the European Holy Alliance, did not consider us as her natural and permanent ally. Our actions toward Russia since 1917 until June 1942 were certainly not those of a natural and permanent ally.

Mr. Lippmann apparently does not consider China as our natural ally. In his book, and as though an afterthought, he adds to the nuclear alliance "if possible, China . . . as she becomes a great state."

In such a "nuclear alliance" of the big fellows, so big that even China would have to wait her turn to grow up, what will happen to

Poland, the Danubian states, and the Balkans? Mr. Lippmann recommends "their neutralization in the realm of power politics." In plain English, they are to become part of a Russian "zone of influence." He admits this is not an easy solution, but, "unlike Switzerland and the Scandinavian states, they do not have the ideas and the usages which are necessary to the practice of genuine neutrality." In other words, the eastern European nations are neither big nor respectable. Mr. Lippmann adds that this is "the only form of security we are able to offer them." The main thing is to preserve at all costs the nuclear alliance of the Big Three. So anxious is Mr. Lippmann to do this that he forgets that Russia herself never made such demands for the "neutralization" of her neighbor states and that in fact Stalin even offered a permanent alliance with Poland.

THE TRIPLE ALLIANCE AND POWER POLITICS

Mr. Lippmann claims that he bases his arguments for the Triple Alliance largely on power politics. "The statesman," he says, "who means to maintain peace should not, to be sure, frivolously 'play power politics.' But he must with cold calculation organize and regulate the politics of power."

Examining Mr. Lippmann's power-politics arguments with cold calculation, we find a number of fallacies. His underlying fallacy is in assuming that we have a great deal to gain from an alliance with Britain and Russia.

Mr. Lippmann greatly underrates the power of the United States while overrating that of Britain and Russia. He is so impressed with the power of victorious Britain and Russia that he is ready to commit the United States to guarantee permanently the territories of two vast empires whose foreign policies we do not control in exchange for a promise from them to protect our "commitments" in the Western Hemisphere and in the Philippines. Let us see whether we will need the protection of Britain and Russia and whether they could (assuming they would) deliver such protection should we need it.

Immediately after this war, and for some time to come, the United States will have effective control of the seas and the air. She will always be able to count on a far greater number of natural allies than

Russia and Britain. In Europe, Asia, and Africa there is no country that need fear the United States for reasons of power politics or past history; practically all nations fear either England or Russia or both. China, for instance, fears both the British and the Communists but would willingly throw in her lot with the United States. During the next fifteen or twenty years there is no power or combination of powers (including Britain and Russia) that could seriously threaten our position. Therefore during this postwar period we will not need the alliance with Britain and Russia to defend our commitments in the Western Hemisphere and in the Philippines.

It is true that in two decades or so the industrial picture will begin to change, and the United States will then be placed in jeopardy. The time will come when we will need all the allies we can get. Could an alliance with Britain and Russia concluded today be of value then? Certainly not with Britain. Reasons of balance politics have twice compelled us to help England in her hour of crisis without any alliance. Reasons of very survival will compel Britain to help us when our hour of crisis comes. Long before the enemy reaches the shores of the continental United States he must conquer or occupy many of the vital nerve centers of the British Commonwealth which surround the United States. In a future world war Britain could not remain neutral or ally herself with enemies of the United States. Such a policy on the part of the British diplomats would not only be courting disaster but raping it. For, should the United States be defeated or eliminated, Britain's turn would be next. We need not tie ourselves hand and foot to the British Foreign Office now, when no one threatens us, in order that two decades later we may be assured of Britain's support, forthcoming anyway because of mutual necessity.

Perhaps Russia could compensate for the deficiencies of Britain's contribution to the alliance, from the standpoint of power politics. As with Britain, during the next fifteen or twenty years, there is very little that Russia could offer to us in the form of security against America's enemies in exchange for our military alliance. After that the mere articles of a twenty-year-old power-politics alliance will not suffice. Russia may or may not help us, depending on our own behavior meanwhile and especially on the *logic of the situation* in which Russia then finds herself. An alliance is merely a formalization of the logic of the situation existing between the states at a given time. In the case of the Triple Alliance, each of the three sovereign states, in full control of its own armed forces, will interpret the alliance in terms of its own national interests. One need not doubt the integrity of the governments who pledge their word, but even their word will be subject to honest differences of interpretation and emphasis, as the meaning of national interests is subjected to shifting weights and changes from pressure groups within. It certainly would be as fool-hardy for us to expect Russia twenty years hence to help protect the Western Hemisphere as for Russia to expect us to defend the vast lands of Russia. In two decades the United States will need something much stronger and much more durable than a mere power-politics alliance.

The short- and long-term gains to Britain and Russia from an alliance with the United States are obvious. It is equally obvious that the United States would have nothing to gain from the alliance during the next fifteen or twenty years, after which period she would begin to draw indefinite and highly problematic dividends. During the all-important period of the world settlement there is nothing we could gain *with* an alliance that we could not gain *without* it. What we would lose is enormous. We would lose the respect of all the nations who are excluded from this alliance of three dominant powers. Above all, we would lose our freedom of action during the decisive years of the world settlement. This freedom means an opportunity to establish on new strategic foundations our own security and at the same time to organize, with Britain and Russia if possible, without them if necessary, that system of true collective security which we have implicitly promised to the peoples of the world in the Atlantic Charter.

But regardless of any system of collective security, by entering into an alliance with Britain and Russia the United States would be violating two basic rules of power politics: (1) she would be entering into an alliance with the only two powers in the world who should and probably do look upon the United States as a formidable rival during the postwar period, and (2) she would be renouncing the advantage of her present enormous superiority in power and accepting a one-third voice in the world settlement.

Mr. Lippmann criticizes Wilson's conception of collective security because Wilson mistakenly held that "there should be a union of fifty juridically equal but otherwise unequal states . . ." The nuclear alliance of the United States, Britain, and Russia is precisely a union of three juridically equal but otherwise unequal states. In an alliance of juridically equal members the voice of Russia or Britain would weigh as much as the voice of the United States; this means that the decisive superiority of American power over Britain or Russia in industrial production, in armored ships of land, sea, and air, in potential allies, and in an unassailable strategic position, would be practically nullified.

I do not claim that the United States must necessarily have a final say in the world settlement, but I do claim that it would be to our decisive advantage to have a *free* say in order more effectively to support our own national interests and those of any other nation we choose. I also believe that to retain our freedom of action would be the most effective way of insuring the lasting friendship and co-operation of Britain and Russia.

Writing eloquent pages on the dangers of isolation, Mr. Lippmann says that the first concern of a statesman "must be to avoid isolation by becoming a member of an adequate combination." He fails to realize that to lock the United States in a power-politics triumvirate with Britain and Russia is the most effective means of isolating the United States from the rest of the world. It is also the most effective means of preparing new wars in which the United States will be neither Caesar nor Pompey but the rich uncle Crassus.

To bolster his arguments in favor of the alliance, Mr. Lippmann makes novel use of the technique of fear. He argues that unless we join an alliance with Britain and Russia they may become disgruntled and combine against us. The rule "If you cannot fight him you must join him" means, he explains ingenuously, "If you do not join him you will probably have to fight him." This is an extraordinary argument to follow his main thesis that Britain and Russia are indispensable to us for the future defense of the Western Hemisphere. However, let us carry Mr. Lippmann's reasoning through to its logical conclusion. Britain and Russia already have a twenty-year alliance. For the sake of argument let us assume that this alliance is directed against the United States. In that case we will be threatened in one of two ways: either Britain and Russia have combined to establish and maintain a world settlement best suited to their interests rather than to ours and other countries, or they have combined because we are the most powerful state in the world and they intend, for twenty years at least, to dispute our position in the world by building an anti-American bloc of which the Anglo-Russian bloc is a nucleus. If either of these two assumptions is true, what good would it do for us to enter into an alliance unless we were willing to sacrifice our own substantial national interests for their benefit? If, as Mr. Lippmann fears, we may be threatened by the Anglo-Russian bloc, then we must use our enormous power to make such a threat strategically and politically impossible. We must build our future security, not as equal partners with Britain and Russia for the domination of the world, but as equal partners under the law with all nations of the world. On the other hand, if neither of these two assumptions is true, and the Anglo-Russian bloc is *not* directed toward the power-politics domination of Europe, Africa, and Asia (which would be against our most vital interests), then, on Mr. Lippmann's own argument, we will not be threatened and our alliance with Britain and Russia becomes unnecessary.

What Mr. Lippmann recommends is, in effect, the worst kind of appeasement policy. Its result for us would be loss of all the potential allies we have in the world, in order to enter into an alliance with two states which, as he says, might become our potential enemies. Thus Mr. Lippmann's "Shield of the Republic" is but a broken shield.

THE TRIPLE ALLIANCE AS A NUCLEUS

Mr. Lippmann uses two sets of arguments in favor of the Triple Alliance, one derived from considerations of power politics, which I have discussed in the preceding pages, and the other set based upon the concept of the Triple Alliance as a nucleus for a system of collective security. He believes that such a nuclear alliance is the only "effective means by which collective security could be made to operate," and he reproaches Wilson for not having realized this basic fact. Mr. Lippmann was of a different opinion in the past. Now, however, he believes that "the precondition of a better world order is a nuclear alliance of the three powerful military states."

It is important to discuss this question, for it would be a catastrophe not only for the United States but for the world if such a fallacy were accepted as the basis of any system of collective security whatsoever. The fallacy lies in the very structure of Mr. Lippmann's nucleus, which is an alliance, and as such is an instrument of power politics, which is essentially an instrument of war.

If the nuclear alliance is to survive the enormous strains and stresses that will come, a very powerful common bond is indispensable. During a war such a bond exists in the presence of common danger from a terrifying enemy. In this war the United States, Britain, and Russia were somewhat in the situation of an owl, a snake, and a ground hog, driven into the same hole by fear of the German wolf. Once the common enemy is liquidated, what is there to keep these widely different states together?

Mr. Lippmann answers that the common bond is the necessity to keep militarist Germany and Japan from rising again. This is a neat way of staying in the hole and pulling it in after him. The fallacy here lies in the assumption that only an alliance of the Big Three could prevent Germany and Japan from again arming and attacking.

In spite of all the lessons of history, Mr. Lippmann retains an almost voodooistic faith in the magic word *alliance*. A few armored divisions would be more than adequate to keep a disarmed Germany and Japan from rearming for many years, provided Britain or Russia really desired to do so. Alliances notwithstanding, Germany or Japan will begin rearming as soon as any one great state decides that the danger from its own allies is more immediate than the danger from Germany or Japan. Besides, there will be other states willing to help in a thousand and one uncontrollable ways. The only permanent and effective way to keep Germany and Japan from rearming and attacking other nations is by keeping *all* nations from rearming and attacking each other. This can be done only through an international police authority.

Realizing that the need for pinning down a defeated Germany and Japan is not a strong enough bond to hold the Big Three together in a lasting alliance, Mr. Lippmann takes refuge in a noble generality:

What will keep the Big Three indissolubly linked, for better or for worse, is "the common desire for peace."

Desire for peace would have an enormous value if a real promise of lasting peace were offered to all the nations of the world through the instrumentality of a real collective defense with the United States, Britain, and Russia as founders. But here we are dealing only with a power-politics alliance of the three strongest nations, self-appointed protectors of the world, who are supposed to submerge their differences and renounce much of their freedom of action to preserve a peace that no one threatens except themselves.

No sooner is the pressure of the German and Japanese menaces removed than the old historic fears and ambitions will inspire new power-politics maneuvers and eventually wars. Each victorious great power will have its own idea of a "lasting peace" best suited to the promotion of its own national interests. The promise of lasting peace, so fervently distributed by Allied statesmen, will become another abstraction lost in the clouds.

As Mr. Lippmann says, it does not matter whether the nuclear alliance is written or unwritten, official or implicit. He fails to mention that an alliance of three sovereign states, each in control of its own armed forces and each swayed by its own national interests, cannot possibly last beyond a few years. Even during the war, difficulties have arisen between the three powers—one dominant during the nineteenth century, one dominant today, one expecting to be dominant tomorrow. Each has its own economy, ideology, and political structure; their national aspirations are fundamentally and widely divergent. Already Britain and Russia are taking positions to effect a world settlement suited to their purely national interests, which may not be the interests of the United States.

The only nuclear thing about such an alliance is that from it will come new and more disastrous wars—wars in which the United States will never again possess her present unique advantages.

For more than two decades Mr. Lippmann fought for the noble ideal of Wilson, and in the defeat of Wilson he suffered his own disillusion. Now he denies that a system of collective security, based on the co-operation of all states, would be more just and more effective than the paternalistic nuclear alliance of three dominant states.

The League of Nations, he maintains, "became impotent because the nuclear alliance of Britain, France, and America had been dissolved." One may answer that the League was not a true system of collective security precisely because it was built around the "nuclear alliance" of England and France, who were then the controlling powers of Europe. The United States, although not a party to this alliance, was deeply sympathetic to the League and certainly took no steps to prevent Britain and France from fortifying the principle of collective security. There were scores of opportunities offered for Britain and France to make the principle effective. The trouble was that the League was but a screen for an implicit power-politics alliance, an alliance already in its natural postwar stage of dissolution. The mutual fears and rivalries of Britain and France turned the League into a breeding place for the Second World War. And it will be the same story if Russia replaces France as a "natural and permanent" ally of the new nuclear alliance.

Mr. Lippmann asserts that "it is only around this strong nuclear alliance that a wider association of many nations can constitute itself." Let us see how this "wider association of many nations" will be constituted.

In effect, Mr. Lippmann's nuclear alliance divides the nations of the world into three classes: Class A, the master nations: United States, Britain, and Russia, who are the exclusive members of the nucleus; Class B, the remaining sovereign nations now members of the United Nations, and perhaps some neutrals; and Class C, the defeated nations and the scores of colonial peoples, whose permanent oppression will be sanctified by American participation in the alliance.

Thus the nuclear alliance is founded essentially upon the same disastrous ideology of protector states as the alliance of the Axis powers. What is the difference between Mr. Lippmann's division of the nations and Hitler's theory of master race? The only essential difference between the Axis alliance and the nuclear alliance is that the Axis powers sought to establish control of the world by conquest, while the three powers of the nuclear alliance, having conquered the enemy in the name of freedom, will seek to "consolidate and perpetuate their control." Hitler promised a new order that should last a thousand years, but Mr. Lippmann is more reserved. He promises only that "an order of this kind can endure, not forever in a changing world, but for a long and beneficent period of time."

Obviously a foreign policy that can be compared to Hitler's is not the kind of policy that Mr. Lippmann would like our country to adopt. There is no question of Mr. Lippmann's sincere devotion to democracy. But it is one thing to recognize the paramountcy of force in the existing relations between states so as best to defend our country, and it is another thing to have the United States participate, in the name of false collective security, in a system based upon the domination of a small group of states over the rest of the world.

Mr. Lippmann assures us that the three great powers will rule wisely and well because it is in their best interest to do so. "The order which they originate . . . can therefore be perpetuated only if they act so as to gain and to hold the good will of the other people." Perhaps they will, but the doctrine of great powers ruling the world wisely because it is to their selfish interests to do so is as valid as the doctrine that a king rules wisely over his subjects because it is to his selfish interest to do so.

But once this premise is accepted—that a group of strong nations may have the right to establish their control over the world, without a higher law to which all nations shall be equally subject—the parallel between the nuclear alliance and the Axis alliance is inescapable. If such a premise is accepted, the United States chose to fight on the wrong side.

Exactly how Mr. Lippmann intends to evolve a better world order out of the ever-recurring, ever-disastrous militarist alliance of sovereign powers remains a mystery.

If the United States, Britain, and Russia are to serve as the nucleus for a postwar world that makes sense, then their alliance must be based not on the anarchy of sovereign states, but on the supreme authority of law, embodied in the constitution of a true co-operative of nations and maintained by a true international police force. Only a separate international body politic, with well-defined but strictly limited powers, independent of the power politics of the sovereign states, has any chance of evolving into a higher organ of true world peace. If Britain or Russia, or both, should refuse for any reason to participate in such an international organization, the United States must then take the leadership into her own hands. She must set out with her enormous power and the good will of most nations to organize a true world order from which no nation will be excluded.

The real importance of this discussion lies in the fact that Mr. Lippmann is not alone with his fallacies. Many other leading Americans are troubled and are groping for solutions to the treacherous problems of the postwar world. Our real problem is to make sure that neither Mr. Lippmann nor others play the American grand slam for a part score.

CHAPTER THIRTEEN

Plans for Uniting Europe

WE SHALL HEAR MORE AND MORE about the movement for a United States of Europe. There are several variations of this plan, from Hitler's militarist plan for a United Europe to Count Coudenhove-Kalergi's plan for a democratic Union of Europe. Basically, all the variations propose a federated Europe in which the European states will preserve their internal and cultural independence but will be subject to a central European authority in control of foreign policy, armed forces and tariff regulations. This United States of Europe would be similar to the United States of America, except that it would be much less centralized.

This Pan-European movement finds supporters among both the democratic and the neo-feudalistic elements. The democratic elements look upon a united Europe as an important step toward the ideal of world unity. The neo-feudalistic elements, who are still the ruling class in most of the European countries, are beginning to realize that the centuries-old domination of the world by the Europeans is coming to an end, and that the principal reason for this is the disunion of Europe. Europe is like a country in a condition of continuous civil war. With its four hundred million highly civilized and highly industrialized people, Europe has not only lost its dominant position in the world (and the profits of that position for its ruling classes) but, because of its dissensions, is growing weaker; while the United States of America and the Soviet Union are growing stronger. Hence the increasing popularity among the Europeans of the movement for a United States of Europe, which a generation back was but an idle dream.

The question from the standpoint of American balance politics is, should we favor or oppose the movement for a United States of Europe?

We have already given our answer to Hitler's kind of a United Europe. It remains to decide whether we should favor a democratic or a semidemocratic United States of Europe, established by peaceful means.

To answer this question we must first answer the question: What is Europe? Geographically, Europe is a peninsula of the Eurasian Island, a tail that for centuries wagged the greatest body of land in the world. Geopolitically, Europe is but a name. There is not one Europe. There are many Europes—historically, economically, and psychologically irreconcilable. Like India, Europe forms a kind of blind alley, a cul-de-sac into which poured the peoples of the Asiatic and African continents. The innumerable nations that had crossed the steppes of Asia and the deserts of Africa into Europe found themselves at a dead end, with the Atlantic Ocean before them and behind them the relentless pressure of other nations. As with India, there was no retreat from this trap. As time went on, nations and cultures piled up, layer upon layer, in a pattern of millenarian hatreds.

Perhaps this very struggle for survival among different nations and cultures was the basic cause of the rise of ancient Indian and modern European civilizations. India thousands of years ago became the mother of civilizations, then found the static equilibrium for her overpopulated nations within the rigid mold of the caste system. Europe, overpopulated and fermented by the Industrial Revolution, is still at boiling point.

From the Greco-Roman civilization and anarchy of the feudal ages emerged three sharply distinct and separate Europes: Latin Europe in the southwest, Germanic Europe in the center, and Slav Europe in the east and southeast. The Latin Europe was molded in the psycho-economic pattern of the ancient Roman Empire, whose provinces became modern states. Although hostile to each other, France, Italy, Spain, Portugal, and Walloon Belgium have preserved through innumerable wars their common psychosocial pattern and Roman inheritance of language, law, and economy. The Germanic Europe emerged from the Holy Roman Empire of the Middle Ages, where the original German psychosocial pattern prevailed over the Latin elements. The Slav Europe is in turn divided into the Europe of the western Slavs, where Roman Catholic influence prevails, and of the eastern Slavs, where Greco-Byzantine influence prevails. However, the ties of the original Slavic psychosocial pattern are in the long run more powerful than the differences.

These three basic Europes—Latin, Germanic, and Slav—differ from each other more radically than, for instance, China and Japan. It is true that there is a cultural bond, an interchange of ideas common to all Europeans, but its power to hold them together is slight. It cannot overcome by itself the more fundamental differences in the psychosocial and economic make-up of the three Europes, or the conflicts of interest between nations, accumulated after centuries of wars and conquests.

It follows that a united Europe, like a united India, can be established only by one or at most two dominant powers, and can be maintained only by a common federal government in control of a common armed force. Any other type of European federation, such as a European League of Nations, would either break down under stress of its own diversity or be turned into a private racket for one or more dominant powers.

A federated Europe could be organized by Britain, with the assistance of France, and with the exclusion of Russia; or it could be organized by a postwar alliance of France with a revived Germany, excluding both Britain and Russia. In either event the United States would be endangered. If Britain is to be the nuclear power for a federalized Europe, it is well to remember that Britain is both a European and an oceanic power. Britain is a gigantic two-way state. Britain is a part of the continental system of European states and, at the same time, the dominant state of the British Empire across the oceans. If she should succeed in establishing permanent control over western Europe (perhaps in partnership with some European power), and at the same time should retain her dominant position in the British Empire, she would become, temporarily at least, the strongest nation in the world and a possible threat to us.

It might happen that France, in order to escape both Anglo-American and Russian domination, would be the spearhead in the organization of a United States of Europe. In that event France, who is not strong enough by herself, would have to help revive Germany, concluding a federal union both with her and with the Latin bloc, into which other European nations would be incorporated. France then would not need to fear Germany, who would be in the minority in this federalized Europe. But this United States of Europe would also automatically become a major threat to the United States of America. For we would be helpless against any hostile combination of powers in the world in which the United States of Europe participated.

There is a third, although much more remote, possibility of a United States of Europe—one organized by Soviet Russia as the nuclear power. The disastrous effect of a Soviet-dominated federation of European states on the American position in the world balance of power is self-evident.

These considerations and possibilities must determine our policy toward the project for a federal union of Europe. *So long as power politics prevails in the relations between sovereign states, the United States of America must oppose the formation of a United States of Europe.*

What we are actually fighting for today is to prevent Germany from forming a United States of Europe and Japan from forming a United States of Asia. And from the standpoint of American power politics, it does not matter whether a federated Europe is formed under democratic colors or by neo-feudalistic elements. Even an angelic, simon-pure, democratic United States of Europe (assuming it possible) would be a dreadful menace to us. For the European federal government would control the armed forces and command the vast resources of wealth, skills, and man power of three hundred and fifty million Europeans. The foreign and trade policies of a federalized Europe would be rigidly controlled. America would have to deal, in trade and politics, with a superstate more powerful than she, but desperately hungry for more food and raw materials and haunted by memories of its past domination of the world.

It would not be long before the unified political and economic forces of Europe would be directed against the United States of America in the Western Hemisphere. The Monroe Doctrine, which was never actually recognized by the European powers, would then be opposed by force. Latin America would become the new happy hunting ground for the power politics of the European federal government in search of new colonies. The slightest move that we might make anywhere in defense of our interests would be followed by "appropriate steps" of the now powerful Europe. After a few years of democratic bliss we would lose our world trade and influence and be driven out of both Asia and South America. White hordes, duly organized and militarized, would be trying to break from the overpopulated and exhausted lands of Europe into North and South America. Wars would come soon. And when they came they would not be waged by an American superstate of towering strength against a divided Europe, but by a united European superstate with three times the population and with industrial power at least equal to the United States of America.

A solid bloc—the American nation—has always faced a Europe whose great nations were usually hostile to the United States, but who were powerless to do us harm because of disunion among themselves. It is arrant nonsense to assert that the free growth of the United States after our liberation was due to "protection" by this or that European power acting as guardian angel. The same European disunity that saved bolshevism in its early days in Russia also saved the American revolutionists of 1776, and later did a yeoman's job against the designs of England and other European powers. It was largely the strife in Europe that enabled us to secure such unheard-of bargains as Louisiana and Florida, to spread out through the West, and to finish off, unimpeded, the decaying Spanish Empire.

In contrast, from the Atlantic to the Pacific coasts of the United States there were no tariff walls, no fortresses, no armies, and no separate governments with parasitic military castes. Except for a few brief moments in American history, there was profound peace. We have had only one Civil War, while Europe has had scores of civil wars. As a result we, although originally weak, were powerful; while Europe, though all-powerful if united, was weak. Europe was the victim of its own war lords fighting for the spoils of the world. In that disunion of Europe we found our strength.

A day may come on which all Americans can welcome the establishment of a United States of Europe as an advance toward higher integration of the European nations in world peace. But this day can come only after an adequate substitute for power politics establishes true collective security. Until that day any kind of federalized or semifederalized Europe must be viewed as a power-politics alliance fostered and controlled by one or two strong nations for the domination of Europe and of the world mechanism of balance of power.

This does not mean, however, that in the name of false power politics we must sow the seeds of discord and misery among the European nations. The peace of Europe is also, in future, the peace of America. But world peace cannot be achieved by a United States of Europe, however democratically conceived. For it would inevitably become, in the hands of European power politicians, an instrument of conquest and a mortal threat to the United States of America as well as to Soviet Russia and China.

European and Asiatic Leagues or Councils

Prime Minister Churchill said, in one of his recent speeches, "One can imagine that under a world institution embodying or representing the United Nations, and someday all nations, there should come into being a Council of Europe and a Council of Asia."

A basic rule for American balance politics is that the United States should refuse to participate in any international organization consisting of a separate European and a separate Asiatic League or Council of Nations.

The practical result of a European Council of Nations would be to exclude the United States, a non-European power, from Europe— thus leaving decisions in the hands of one or two dominant powers. The practical effect of an Asiatic Council of Nations would be to permit the United States, which is partly an Asiatic power, to participate in Asiatic affairs, but under conditions subordinating American interests to the interests of Britain, her Dominions, the Netherlands, and other Asiatic powers. In other words, the United States would be excluded from Europe and gagged in Asia, leaving the field wide open for the power politicians of Britain and other states. In exchange the American people would get the privilege of participating in a revived League of Nations, which Mr. Churchill calls "a world institution, embodying or representing the United Nations, and someday all nations." Someday.

Mr. Churchill, like other statesmen, is groping for some sort of world solution satisfactory to all. If such a solution is not available, there is nothing for him to do but fall back on consideration of British power politics. He would be a disloyal servant of his nation if he abandoned the tools of power politics when no other tools have been forged. Mr. Churchill is a loyal and brilliant servant of the British state, not the United States. He is also a loyal servant of the Conservative party, which is now guiding and is likely to guide after the war the foreign policy of Britain. Such foreign policy must necessarily be based upon consideration of British, not American, power politics.

If the European League becomes, as is quite likely, a stooge for the power politics of Britain and her friends, then American participation become a farce. If the European League of Nations succeeds in establishing some sort of federalized union among the European nations, then it becomes an embryonic United States of Europe and a threat to us.

Whether Mr. Churchill's suggestion for the European and Asiatic councils came as an echo of Nicholas Spykman's similar proposal is difficult to determine, since Mr. Churchill did not elaborate. But there is no doubt that another Tory plan, supported by some misguided liberals in Britain and the United States, would establish a military and economic control of western Europe under British domination. Professor Edward H. Carr, for a number of years adviser to the British Foreign Office, is one of the best British exponents of this British neo-imperialism. His book, *Conditions of Peace,* was well received in America. A number of liberals who dote on the "economic approach," forgetting that modern economic jargon is ideally suited to disguise totalitarian designs, were particularly impressed. The first two thirds of Professor Carr's book contains an excellent analysis of some of the economic causes and consequences of the war. But it becomes apparent in the last third of the book that this analysis was but a convenient premise on which to build a refurbished and revitalized version of British imperialism. Only this time it is recommended that Britain assume the white man's burden in western Europe as well.

Stripped of its economic jargon and noble generalities, the European Planning Authority proposed by Mr. Carr is Hitler's Nazi planning in reverse English. As with Hitler, the "liberated nations of western Europe will not be permitted to retain their full sovereign status." Western Europe will be turned into a gigantic trust, controlled by Britain with the "assistance" of the United States and Russia. The best features of Hitler's economic plans will be taken over. Professor Carr writes: "The European Planning Authority will in practice find itself the heir of two going concerns; the centralized economic machinery of Hitler's New Order and the machinery of Allied wartime controls . . . The rough foundations of an effective European Planning Authority will have already been laid before the end of hostilities. We must build on them . . ." On excellent economic grounds, Professor Carr condones the rape of Europe. "Hitler has, through his very ruthlessness, established some sort of centralized European authority, and has created bonds some of which might well prove difficult to destroy even if we wished." Instead of Nazi *gauleiters,* there will be in every country British-controlled "commissions" or British-nominated conservative governments, all supported by the bayonets of Allied troops of occupation. This will be a bigger, if not better, British Empire. Every nation will contribute according to its capacity and receive according to its needs. The whole will be interlocked with a world-wide scheme of economic controls, with the United States playing her just and glorious role in financing the rehabilitation of the world.

In British private and official circles there is a division of opinion as to the respective merits of the European League of Nations and Professor Carr's European Planning Authority for the purpose of dominating western Europe. Those who are politically inclined believe that the technique of a League of Nations is better suited for the purpose of British control. Others, who majored in economics, prefer Professor Carr's approach. Besides, they argue, it will help win over an important group of liberals in Britain and America who worship the goddess of "planned economy" above all else.

Fantastic as it may seem, either the plan for a European League of Nations or Professor Carr's plan for a European Planning Authority is perfectly capable of realization, unless the United States opposes. Russia cannot do much, since her first and principal preoccupation is to break down the impending danger of a world coalition—political or economic—against her, under the guidance of Anglo-American imperialists. With France and Germany prostrate and Russia partly neutralized, the only power left to oppose these schemes for British control of western Europe is the United States.

Britain tried the policy of European balance of power, and it failed. She then tried, although halfheartedly, the policy of collective security through the League of Nations; it failed also. There remains a third policy, not attempted since the days of Jeanne d'Arc. This is the policy of direct military and economic control of parts of Europe. Combined with a policy of balance of power between Russia and the United States, this is the postwar plan of certain British groups.

It may well be argued that even from the British standpoint such a policy cannot but end in new disasters. Already Britain is forced to accomplish feats of heroism and acrobatics in order to maintain the inverted pyramid of the British Empire. If, in addition, this tight little island should assume the even more gigantic task of balancing tumultuous Europe, a collapse within a few years is more than probable. However, it is not a question of whether such a policy will succeed in the long run. In the world of power politics the likeliest policy follows the line of least resistance and greatest immediate profits. And so far the least resistance has come from the United States.

But the domination of western Europe by Britain is only half the story. We shall now see that Britain's attempt to dominate western Europe necessarily involves the partition of all Europe between Britain and Russia.

THE ZONING OF EUROPE

A proposal for the partition of Europe in two zones of influence between Britain and Russia has never been made and never will be made officially. It is implicit, however, in the Anglo-Russian Alliance, and especially in the British preparations to retain postwar military and economic controls over western Europe.

For the first time in centuries a power vacuum has been created in Europe. After the defeat of Germany there will remain only two strong European powers—Britain and Russia, at opposite ends of a European land space stretching more than a thousand miles. It is only natural that Britain and Russia should seek to fill this power vacuum. Britain cannot maintain her postwar domination over western Europe without the support of either Russia or the United States. And Russia is the logical partner, as far as Europe is concerned.

Even if Russia did not wish to enter into this partition, there is not much she could do about it. The only effective way in which she could oppose Britain's domination of western Europe would be by occupying Germany. But if she did that, the rest of the world might organize against her. Therefore the only way in which Russia could maintain her relative power standing with Britain would be to enter into an agreement with her, dividing Europe into two zones of influence—the British and the Russian.

There will, of course, be a basic difficulty over Germany. Without controlling Germany, Russia's "zone of influence" in Poland and the Balkans would be relatively puny compared to Britain's magnificent inheritance in the West. Reasons of power politics may compel Russia to insist on the almost immediate re-establishment of a democratic (not communist) Germany. Russia may even seek to preserve, in part at least, the German armed strength. Once Hitlerite Germany is defeated, a strong, non-fascist Germany is necessary to Russia as an added weight in her balance of power against the dominant Anglo-Americans. On the other hand, the British and American governments are heavily committed to the unconditional surrender and total disarmament of Germany. They will insist on a weak Germany. The issue of a strong or weak Germany might well become a dominant issue of postwar Europe. But if these difficulties could be solved at least temporarily, then the power vacuum of Europe would be filled, with Russia in control of the eastern area and Britain of the western. Thus the British step toward the domination of western Europe leads necessarily to the Russian step toward the domination of eastern Europe. And both steps synchronize in the zoning of Europe.

The *Times* of London, in a significant editorial of July 28, 1943, suggests that "in certain areas of Europe where British interests are regarded as predominant, the ultimate decisions will rest with Britain, acting in close concert with the United States but independently of Russia, and that in certain other areas of special concern to Russia, notably eastern and central Europe, the ultimate decisions will rest with Russia, acting independently of the United States and Britain."

We may dismiss, as mere courtesy, the phrase "acting in close concert with the United States." Obviously a "close concert" with us is not necessary in "areas of Europe where British interests are regarded as predominant."

The point of this quotation is the same as the main point behind the various proposals for European leagues, councils, or planning authorities: In effect, Europe is to become a gigantic Persia or Poland, with Britain in working control of the western part and Russia of the eastern part. And the United States will be placed before the following dilemma, from which there is no issue except war:

Either Britain and Russia will be successful in organizing their controls over western and eastern Europe or they will not. If they are successful, then the United States will be confronted within less than two decades with two extremely powerful blocs—the British western European and the Russian eastern European. Each bloc will be at least as strong as the United States, and, combined, they might control the world. If, as is more likely to happen, Britain and Russia quarrel between themselves and fail to maintain their domination over Europe, then once again we will be dragged into wars which are not of our own making but which vitally affect the world's balance of power and therefore our existence. These wars will come either from revived Germany and the Latin bloc or from the struggle for European hegemony between Britain and Russia. In either event we will be facing a third world war complicated by events in Asia.

It may be argued that neither Britain nor Russia will seek really to integrate their respective zones of influence in Europe, and that both nations will relinquish their control over the liberated or defeated nations once Europe is reorganized and the passions "cool off." But in power politics one must be prepared for all contingencies.

Regardless of what Britain and Russia may or may not do, it must be the policy of the United States *to fill the power vacuum in Europe, not by helping to extend the domination of Britain and Russia beyond their agreed frontiers, but by restoring as soon as possible to the liberated countries their sovereign status and by remaining in Germany until the German people also are restored to a position of independence from the power politics of either Britain or Russia.*

The United States must neither withdraw from Europe into isolation nor participate in any European scheme of false internationalism. And she must oppose the establishment of any kind of British or Russian "zone of influence" in Europe.

In Asia the United States must follow a parallel policy of balance politics.

In both Europe and Asia the United States can carry out this policy by insisting on strict and full observance of the Atlantic Charter and particularly Article Three, which advocates restoration of sovereign rights and self-government to those who have been forcibly deprived of them. It is to be expected that some of the leading powers, once they become victorious, may seek to reinterpret, amend, or drop the Atlantic Charter. They may claim that since it was not ratified by the United States Senate it is not a treaty. That need not disturb us too much. In the eyes of the American people, at least, the Atlantic Charter is much more than a treaty. It is a great moral commitment. It so happens that the purely selfish interests of American balance politics coincide with the broader interests of the nations of the world. And since the reality back of any treaty is the desire and the power to support its provisions, the United States can securely anchor the Atlantic Charter in the abundance of her economic power, military strength, and the confidence of the world.

In the previous pages we have established new yardsticks for American balance politics and applied them to the United States of Europe, European League of Nations, European Planning Authority, and European "zones of influence."

It remains now to see how the same yardsticks of American balance politics apply in the relation of the United States to the individual nations—how much territory and rights we can concede to each in the coming world settlement, and at what point we should call a halt to their attempts at expansion.

CHAPTER FOURTEEN

Britain: Our Tie with the Past

FROM TIME TO TIME it is necessary to return to certain truths so obvious and so elemental that they often are ignored. One of these truths is that the American people are not only English-speaking and English-cultured, but essentially Anglo-Saxon. Anyone but a Hitlerite fool can see that this country's vital functions and its very blood stream are governed not by the Jewish or the Irish elements, not by the Teuton, the Latin, or the Slav, but by the Anglo-Saxon. Other nations have been made welcome here and their cultures have been learned. But these nations were not merely grafted on the Anglo-Saxon branch; they were, for the most part, dissolved and obliterated within the Anglo-Saxon stream.

This is the rusty, old-fashioned key which opens many of the secrets of British-American relations. Without this invisible magnetic force of a common psychosocial pattern, Anglo-American relations are unexplainable. Time and time again we have acted against our best interests and against all the usual rules of power politics. Hitler and Tojo, considering only rational procedure from purely egotistical motives, found their cleverest plans foundering on these invisible rocks of unconscious affinity. Goebbels, in complaining of the success of British propaganda in the United States, in spite of its insincerity and ill-disguised smugness, failed to take into account the fact that it began more than three centuries ago with the first English settlement in Virginia.

Whether or not the same psychosocial forces are operating on the British side is another matter. Past history shows the contrary. But then we have never been in real distress, and the British have not had a chance to prove the extent of their attachment.

It is true that, in general, the American people neither like nor particularly admire the British ruling class. There are, also, millions of Americans, especially of German and Irish descent, who are anti-British. Thus a strong anti-British current is always present in the United States, increasing or decreasing according to events. This partly explains why the American nation repeatedly comes to the help of the British Commonwealth in moments of supreme danger and yet fails to collaborate politically with Britain when the danger is over.

BRITAIN THROUGH TWO WORLD WARS

The three great sea empires of history—Minoan Crete, Carthage, and Britain—owe their rise principally to their sheltered position against the attacks of land powers combined with easy access to the seas.

For centuries Britain was immune to the attacks of the great continental powers. Only twenty-one miles separate England from the continent. Yet that moat was enough to create a fortress island from which spread tentacles of an empire circumnavigating the globe. For centuries the European land powers were stronger and wealthier than the island of England. But their wealth and strength had to be spent on land armies in continuous wars; meanwhile England's excess of wealth went into sea trade and ships of war to protect it. As the trade increased, so increased Britain's sea power and wealth. Enough wealth was left to equip small land armies for two purposes: to throw a decisive weight in the balance of land powers on the European continent, and secondly to conquer and to hold a vast living space across the oceans.

By the early nineteenth century Britain was mighty enough to defeat Napoleon in Europe and at the same time to conquer India and other vast possessions in the Far East. Her only loss was the

American colonies, to people of her own stock. Late in the eighteenth century a new and extraordinary formula was added to the ancient formula of world sea power and world trade. This new formula was steam and coal. This was the formula of the Industrial Revolution which enthroned her as the greatest empire of all time. During the nineteenth century Britain rolled on the wheels of the Industrial Revolution to the zenith of her power.

Although often she lost battles on land, she was never defeated. For the only access to her vital nerve centers was through the seas. And while the land powers fought exhaustive wars, staggering under the burden of vast armies, England sailed and traded.

The sun never set on the British Empire. But toward the end of the nineteenth century the British industrial sun began to set very rapidly. The first ominous symptoms came from the revolution in land communications. Better roads could be built, and much faster. The railroad threatened to outflank the British sea power. Since ancient times an army marching on foot was always slower than an army brought by ships. Strategically, the outer lines of communications, which were the sea lanes, dominated the inner land lines of communications. A sea power could always choose the point of attack, withdraw if need be, and attack elsewhere at will. Now, with the growing network of railroads, the faster land lines of communications began to dominate the slower sea lines. The Bagdad railroad and its branches threatened the solar plexus of the British Empire at Suez and the Persian Gulf. The Siberian railroad, with its branches running toward the frontiers of India and to the China Sea, threatened the British Far East. Economical, tight little expeditionary corps were no longer sufficient. To the already difficult task of maintaining her sea supremacy Britain was forced to add the backbreaking task of maintaining large mass armies. This was but a harbinger of the industrial cyclone that was soon to break over the gigantic, loosely integrated British Empire, sprawling over the five continents.

Powerful industrialized states arose—the United States, Germany, France, Russia, Japan, Italy—and took from Britain control of the seas adjoining their territories. The United States and Germany became rivals in world trade. In the First World War Germany made a formidable bid for the hegemony of Europe, and only the help of the United States staved off disaster threatening England and France.

After the First World War England's difficulties progressively increased. Her five hundred million people and thirteen million square miles of territory made the Empire look impressive. But, reduced to practical military value, the whole topheavy structure rested on forty-five million Britishers and less than twenty-five million in the Dominions. A tight little island, thousands of miles removed from its sources of food and raw materials, held the main nerve centers of the Empire. Only a few score miles away England faced a formidable bloc of seventy million Germans, with a superior military and industrial production. On the Mediterranean there were more than forty-five million land-starved Italians. In Central Asia another bloc of more than one hundred and fifty million Russians had it in their power to move against the feebly defended frontiers of India and countries adjoining the Persian Gulf. In the Far East was another formidable bloc of eighty million Japanese, not to count the vast potential forces of awakening China and revolutionary India. And the new, better organized industrial machine of the United States, with three times the population of Britain, was spreading over the world.

In the face of these tremendous new forces that threatened to tear to pieces the whole fabric of the British Empire, what did successive British governments do? After the First World War they reverted to their antiquated methods of balance of power, appeasement, and diplomatic intrigues. In the Orient they sought to appease the irrevocably imperialistic Japan. As a result, Japan was encouraged in her aggressive policies against China even though it was apparent to all but the blind that the inevitable result of such policies would be a formidable threat to Australia and to all the British interests in Asia, which only the United States could effectively defend. And Britain clung to her fleet as France clung to her Maginot Line.

As with most European countries, England was divided internally between the financier-aristocrats who controlled foreign policy and the democratic classes who sought control. But there was another split peculiar to England. An Englishman, especially of the upper and middle classes, is essentially a European. He breathes the air of Europe, partakes of the food and culture of Europe, and is inextricably tied to the events of Europe. At the same time an Englishman is a citizen of his empire across the seas. The political result is a nation with a "split personality," oscillating between a European policy and an oceanic policy. English pocketbooks were in the Empire, but English hearts belonged to Europe.

Traditionally, however, the British policy was first and foremost a policy of European alliances and balance of power; for centuries European events had determined world events. Britain's policy was an oceanic policy only secondarily; she wanted to draw as much profit as she could from across all the seas.

This was a logical policy before the twentieth century but tragically erroneous after. England's diplomats, missing completely the implications of the accelerating tempo of the Industrial Revolution, were still more excited about some obscure palace revolution in a minuscule Balkan state than about the tremendous vistas opened up for her overpopulated island. There were the vast tablelands of Africa to be colonized, enough for fifty million Britishers; Australia to be industrialized for the markets of the Orient; Canada to be brought into bigger play; India to be liberated, helped, and reorganized as a powerful friend and an equal member of the Empire. But England never wholeheartedly gave up the petty eighteenth-century mercantilistic policy that lost her the American colonies. Throughout the Empire the dominating policy was not to create strong, healthy communities but immediate dividends for the City of London. English business interests feared industrialization of the Empire as they now fear the rivalry of the United States.

In spite of Pilgrims' dinners, England looked upon America first as a colonial upstart and later as an unwelcome and somewhat gauche intruder into her vested "zones of interest" in Europe, in the Orient, and in South America. Even though she relied more and more upon America's help and feared alienating her oceanic-minded Dominions, she still clung with anguish to the European half of her soul. For a long time after the First World War she nurtured the flickering flames of her alliance with France, while appeasing Germany and reviling Russia. Even during the days of June 1940, when a deadly betrayal of England was being consummated by the French fascist politicians, Churchill made a stirring and deeply pathetic appeal to France, inviting her to form a union with England and to share alike the good and the bad. And only after the betrayal at Compiègne, with the Empire in mortal danger, did Churchill and the ruling class of England give up with a sigh the attempt to save their European face, and turn to America.

It was then that England, temporarily at least, hitched her imperial wagon to the rising star of the American superstate.

The vital interests of balance politics and traditional ties of kinship should have been sufficient for the United States to throw her might at once on the side of Britain in her greatest hour of crisis when Paris fell. But this time the American people did not move. Many felt that much of the needless suffering of the British people, perhaps even the war itself, could be laid at the door of successive British governments. Many Americans—and, for that matter, many English—saw little to admire in neglect of armaments to protect dividends, stupid appeasement of war lords intent on world conquest, blind ideological hatreds, and childish, antiquated dealings with the French politicians to betray or undermine every potential ally.

That this feeling may be wholly unjustified is beside the point. Its persistent and continued existence will have an important bearing on the postwar settlement. So long as a powerful anti-British current exists in the psychopolitical make-up of the American nation, it will be very difficult, if not impossible, for the American government to underwrite the security of the British Empire against future aggressions. In that event the British will be forced again to look to themselves for their future security, which might easily result in British neo-imperialism.

It is true that much for which the British Tories are reproached has been due not to their selfishness or greed, but to the necessities of a sovereign state whose faithful servants they were. These same necessities will play their role in the postwar settlement. There is little doubt that the British Tories, with Mr. Churchill or his successor at their head, will represent Britain in writing the victorious treaty of peace. In England today there are powerful political forces, centered in the Labor party and outside it, which oppose Tory control of the Empire. But after the Second World War the Empire will be threatened more than ever from within and from without. There will be a need for hard, realistic men to do a hard, realistic, imperial job.

And the Tories, whatever their defects, can do an imperial job better than the Liberals.

Labor and the Liberals, of course, have their dreams of a new socialist order. They have vague hopes about the returning soldiers, and youth. There is much talk about a profound spiritual revolution that is taking place today in England. All that is true, but the spiritual revolution is built around the core of the British Empire, preservation of which is dear to almost every Englishman, and is indispensable for the proud survival of England herself.

The progressive influence is responsible for the fact that the Tories, whose adaptability is far greater than that of our die-hards, long ago put through social legislation that surpasses, in many respects, the New Deal. The British ruling class may go so far as to support many measures of state socialism dictated, in England, by the economic necessity of a small, overpopulated island. This does not mean that the ruling class intends to give up any of its essential privileges.

In the present Long Parliament the Conservative party has an overwhelming majority. This is the same Tory parliament which so vociferously acclaimed the economical budgets of Baldwin and the fascist appeasement of Chamberlain. And this parliament is sitting at a time of British history when power politics dictates that only new and more relentless imperialism can preserve what the old imperialism gained.

BRITAIN AFTER THE VICTORY

Following the Axis defeat a victorious England will be at the peak of her power. Her Empire will be reassembled and probably will be increased by the Italian Empire. Her second "invisible" empire will also be reassembled and reorganized under the Netherlands' dominion. Her third "invisible" empire will be reorganized under Portuguese dominion.

In western Europe, France, Germany, and Italy will lie prostrate and disarmed. The smaller nations too will be militarily and economically mortgaged to the British tanks and armored planes. A mighty English navy supported by more planes will control the ocean approaches, and the Mediterranean once again will become a British lake.

Never in history has England been so mighty as she will be after this war, yet never has the might of England been so superficial and so fleeting. Almost as soon as the war is won, the basic facts about the position of England as a world power will make it evident that the world has to deal, not with the decline of the British Empire, but with its fall. The facts are these:

1. England, though retaining command of the seas around Europe, has lost command of the oceans to the United States. This throws England back to the days before the destruction of the Spanish Armada. True, control of the ocean remains in friendly, even kindred hands. But the United States is a sovereign state subject to its own pressures and political shifts. England depends for her food, raw materials, and trade upon the oceans. In these vital matters she must now depend upon the good will of another, stronger state.

2. England's military control of the Middle East and India can be exercised only through the continued good will of Russia. The overwhelming power of the United States on the seas and in the air is matched by the overwhelming predominance of the Soviet Union over England on the land approaches to the Middle East and India. Even if England succeeds in re-establishing the balance of power between western Europe and the Soviet Union, she will be gravely threatened within a decade by the rising land power of China.

3. The internal structure of the British Empire, under strain, cannot long survive. From India to South Africa the peoples of the Empire are in turmoil or on the verge of rebellion, which progressive industrialization will increase.

In the case of the English-speaking commonwealths, Australasia and Canada, England has, in addition, severed the most important tie that holds a free nation to a stronger nation—the tie of protection against the foreign aggressor. When Australasia was placed in grave jeopardy, only the power of the United States could adequately defend her from the Japanese. That this was not entirely the fault of beleaguered Britain is beside the point; the fact remains that the government failed in the fundamental function of any government, that of adequate defense against a foreign enemy.

4. The small English island is grossly overpopulated. Millions of English depend for their food, and the whole of England depends

for its high standard of living, on overseas export of its industrial products; yet the English industrial machine is antiquated and costly.

From these facts it is only too clear that England cannot simultaneously maintain the largest navy, the largest air force, and powerful land armies; nor can she at the same time keep order within her seething Empire, engage in world-wide trade to feed her overpopulated island, and hold off the continental powers of Europe and Asia. It was the British who coined an apt phrase for another empire, that of the Ottoman Turks, whose remnants Britain gathered after the First World War: "The Sick Man of Europe." The British Empire is the sick man of the world. Because the overpopulated island cannot get rid of the Empire without condemning half its people to slow starvation, England will be denied even the happy transitional stage when it could seek to become the first among the smaller powers rather than the last among the great. It is well that this point be kept in mind by those American liberals who imagine that a victorious England could easily be parted from the Empire in exchange for economic internationalism.

It is evident that the fundamental problem of postwar England will be how to preserve the Empire. There are many proposed solutions. Some seek collective security under a revived League of Nations, this time with the participation of the United States. British Tories never had faith in collective security as promised by the old League; quite realistically they looked upon the League as a convenient screen behind which the old and tried machinery of power politics could be operated. This time they certainly will favor all kinds of Leagues of Nations, and especially a European and an Asiatic League of Nations, provided they remain British-controlled.

Others see the solution in socialist economic planning. But it would be impossible for Britain to compete against the more fortunate nations without the strong protection of an empire tariff wall. In dire need of food, raw materials, capital, and new industrial equipment, no sensible Briton is going to entrust the destiny of his country to international economic experiment. Here again the British Tories will have no objection to all kinds of economic planning boards and especially to a European Planning Board, always provided that such boards serve as a convenient instrument for the play of British power politics.

Failing to solve the security problem through a refurbished League or in economic internationalism, England will be back where she started from, along with her threatened Empire. She will sorely need the services of a powerful ally, a friend to help her rebuild herself and preserve the Empire. Britain will turn to the United States.

American Postwar Policy with Britain

At first glance it might seem that, through the trials of war, Britain had found her ideal partner in the United States.

But the first and most important question asked by the British will be: "Will you Americans guarantee the territorial integrity and the security of the British Empire against foreign aggressors in exchange for our guarantee of your territorial integrity and security?" The United States must regretfully answer "No." Such a blanket guarantee would be an act of folly. The United States cannot guarantee the existence of another sovereign state whose foreign policy it does not control.

Nor can the United States by such an alliance condone the oppression of nations, which, however necessary from the standpoint of the British interests, does not set well on the stomach of the American people.

For their part, British interests even now are looking forward to world-wide trade competition with the United States after the war. Desperate need to repair the ravages of war suggests a bitter competition. Where can Britain obtain the new, vast resources necessary except in world-wide competition with American industry in Europe, in Africa, in Russia, in China, in the Netherlands East Indies, and in Latin America? But such competition will require as its basis of operations the closed economy of the British Empire and a reorganized western Europe, with the Netherlands and Portuguese colonial empires under British control.

After the Second World War the position of England will be exactly the same as that of France after the last war. Britain's loss of status as a world power follows that of France, which was preceded in turn by Spain, Holland, and Sweden. Like France, Britain will look to the new leading power of the world for security; but the United States cannot underwrite the British Empire after this war any more than she could guarantee French security after the last war.

Only an effective system of collective defense of which both Britain and the United States are a part could justify, politically and psychologically, mutual guarantees against any aggressor. So long as there is no such system, the necessities of power politics will drive England into a postwar policy of aggressive preservation of the British Empire.

We must make it absolutely clear that we ourselves have no designs whatsoever upon any part of the British Empire. The propaganda carried on by certain elements in America in favor of the "acquisition" of Canada or Australia is best calculated to drive Britain into permanent alignment against us. In the first place, neither the Canadians nor the Australians, who are free people, are anxious to join us; and if they were, we should be more anxious for basic stability in our relations with Britain than for new territorial acquisitions. We don't want to "inherit" the British Empire.

We may hope Britain will keep her promise to free India and thus gain a great new friend for both Britain and the United States. We may hope that Hong Kong will be returned to China and the crazy quilt of Africa will be straightened out. But we cannot interfere in the affairs of the British Empire.

In the same way that the British Empire is outside the realm of American power politics, the American strategic zone must be outside the realm of British power politics. In exchange for our amity and co-operation, we should expect that Britain renounce once and for all the exercise of power politics in the Western Hemisphere and in the Malaysian region. This stipulation does not mean that we intend to infringe upon the sovereignty of our Latin-American neighbors or upon the just rights of the Netherlands in the East Indies and of France in Indo-China. But it does mean that Britain must recognize the paramount importance to us of strategic approaches to the American continents.

American balance politics favors a free, healthy British Empire under Britain's guidance. But American balance politics must oppose any material increase of British power outside of her empire. In

Europe or elsewhere there must not be new, substantial "areas of predominant British interests" based on imperialistic control. It is here
that we must draw the line.

The British Commonwealth comes first not only in our affection
and admiration but as a keystone in American foreign policy. Certainly any feeling man is indignant over the many iniquities of British
imperialism. And thinking men know that the British Empire is
paved with good intentions. There is many a slip between the cup
of freedom and the lip service of the British Tories. But behind the
ugly façade of the British Empire we must not lose sight of the British
Commonwealth of Nations, which is obviously one of the most vital
civilizing forces of today and tomorrow. Certainly this great commonwealth must be preserved. But the only lasting guarantee of its
preservation lies in a system of collective security for the world.

CHAPTER FIFTEEN

Russia: Current Contentions

MOST AMERICANS have heard too much about Russian ideology and
not enough about Russian geography. Communist ideology has
shaped the life of the Russian people during this generation only.
Geography, or geopolitics, has shaped the body and the soul of this
Nordic-Slav race for thousands of years.

A look at the map of Europe and Asia will show how arbitrary
is the division between these continents, which are separated only
by the swellings called the Ural Mountains. Geopolitically there is
only one great continent of Asia, with Europe as its peninsula, and
with the British Isles, originally part of Europe, hugging its coast.
The southern part of this great Eurasian continent, with its European
peninsula, is filled with chains of mountains—they run from the Alps
through the Caucasus to the Himalayas—broken by warm seas and
deserts. In the far north are vast forests, lakes, marshes, and frozen
tundras tapering off into the Arctic Ocean. Sandwiched between the
mountains of the south and the subarctic lands there lies a continu-

ous plain of enormous width; it starts at the European shores of the Atlantic and ends at the Asiatic shores of the Pacific. In length it is seven thousand miles across, and in width between one and two thousand miles. This vast, enormously rich plain is broken only by a few outcroppings of mountains, marshes, or forests. The largest network of rivers in the world flows into its northern or southern water basins.

More than three fourths of this great plain is Russia. Geopolitically Russia is a gigantic irregular saucer with a large wedge, the one facing Europe, chipped off. Russian history is three interwoven epics: the struggle to fill up the heartland of the Eurasian world island, the struggle to dam the broken edge against invaders from the west, and the struggle to climb up the southern rim of the saucer.

This Russian epic of the plain surpasses in magnitude and duration even the American epic, although they have much in common. It began about fifteen hundred years ago, with obscure tribes of Slavs, a hundred thousand families at most, driven to the barren vastness of the Carpathian Mountains. They were left there, alone and unnoticed, by successive waves of invaders in the great migration of nations that broke up the Roman Empire.

About the time that William the Conqueror was invading England the Ukrainians (border people) had spread from their ancient habitat in Carpathian Russia to the valley of the Dnieper. By the tenth century their settlement at Kiev had prospered enough for the Russo-Ukrainians to descend the Dnieper, cross the Black Sea, and threaten to pillage Constantinople. Russian soldiers became the favorite palace guard of the Byzantine emperors. Kiev and the whole Russian Ukraine were converted to Greek Orthodox Christianity by the Byzantines, who transferred much of their civilization to the Slavs.

In the same way that a branch of the Anglo-Saxons, thrown off across the Atlantic from England, grew into the United States, a branch of the Ukrainians, thrown off into the forests of the north and the steppes of the east, formed the Great Russia of today. Moscow was the capital of the Great Russians, but Kiev, the capital of the Little Russians, was and still is the holy city.

To occupy their plains, the Americans had to displace a few hundred thousand Indians. The Russians fought against scores of nomadic kingdoms and empires, all of which they destroyed or absorbed. Early in their history they obliterated the vast empire of the Nordic Finns, who spoke a Mongolian language, and left only a broken fragment of Finland.

Thus one part of the rim of the great saucer, north of Moscow, was conquered and filled up with Russian social cells. At the time Columbus was discovering America, Russian farmers began to fill up the steppes from the great basin of the Don toward the gigantic basin of the Volga, conquering the Mongolian hordes who had previously held them in vassalage for two centuries. While the Americans were fighting the Revolutionary War the Russians reached the eastern rim of the saucer—the Pacific and Bering Strait. They overflowed into Alaska, and by 1811 there was a Russian settlement as far south as San Francisco.

Two generations before, while the American settlers were driving the Indians out of the Great Lakes region, Peter the Great in western Russia finally broke through the marshes and forests of the Russian great lakes into the Germanic Baltic Sea and founded St. Petersburg, a window toward Europe. The Poles and the Teutons were liquidated after centuries-long struggles, and with the destruction of the Swedish military power under Charles XII, the gap in the western rim was temporarily closed.

There remained the southern rim—the Balkans in the southwest, the Crimea directly south, and the Caucasus, with the lands behind the Caspian, in the southeast. The last two centuries of Russian history record peripheral wars to climb the mountainous rim of the great Russian saucer and to reach, over this southern rim, the warm seas—the Black Sea and, through the Dardanelles, the Mediterranean. To save the Russian bear his long winter hibernation the Ottoman Empire was mangled, and Persia.

By the early twentieth century Russia had completed most of her gigantic task. The vast Eurasian plain was filling up peacefully at the rate of thirty million every decade. The great mountains in the south, from the Black Sea to the Himalayas, were securely in her possession and she was edging her way through Turkestan to the frontiers of India. In the Pacific, Manchuria and Port Arthur were annexed. There remained only Constantinople to be taken, and the Russian Colossus could stand fully astride both Europe and Asia.

But in Germany the Industrial Revolution was laying time bombs which were to explode the heartland of Russia in 1914 and again in 1941. In the year 1904 the Japanese militarists were coldly measuring the corruption and impotence of the Russian caste of nobles. In Russia itself a small group of unkempt idealists, driven by the Czar's police into secret basements to which conspiratorial nicknames were the passports, were passionately debating a system for the liberation of Russia and mankind.

THE "HEARTLAND" BEATS

In the year 1903 a group of Russian revolutionists gathered in a dingy smoke-filled flat in London. They sat nonchalantly around the table with its eternal samovar, bread, butter, and bologna, their favorite meal. One man seldom sat still. He would jump up, walk back and forth across the room, whisper in a corner with a friend, write little notes, sit down, jump up again. He laughed heartily, and his moods had a wide, subtly changing range. Yet through all this restlessness and agitation there filtered a sense of serene power and authority. He was smallish, stocky, with a beard cut like a Russian provincial aristocrat, dressed like a small bourgeois, and used the gestures of a professor explaining something forcefully to his pupils. The man was Lenin.

The experts of Scotland Yard knew that of all the different species of Russian revolutionists, with or without bombs, these were the least dangerous. In fact they were absolutely of a non-poisonous variety, since they strongly disapproved of individual terrorism and played their inoffensive game of revolution like a group of quiet, well-behaved children.

They were system-mongers, devoting their lives to the study of different economic and political systems for the defeat of tyranny and injustice. The group consisted of delegates of the Russian Socialist Democratic party, assembled in London to discuss a momentous question. The question seemed fantastically unreal and scholastic, like the Trinitarian controversy over which wars were waged in early Christendom, dividing the Greek Byzantine church from the church of Rome. But it developed later that the question discussed at this London conference of 1903 led to one of the greatest social upheavals in history, the Bolshevik revolution of October 1918. The momentous question on the agenda of the Russian Socialist Democratic party was: Must Russian Socialists adopt the revolutionary strategy proposed by Lenin?

Lenin was part Robespierre, part Loyola; there is remarkable similarity between Ignatius Loyola and Lenin in their tactics of seizing the means to achieve their noble ends. One wanted the kingdom of God on earth, the other the kingdom of man. One sought salvation in religion, the other thought that religion was the opium of the people. Both were dreamers and cold realists. Both were supreme political strategists. Both sought to implement an idea with political machinery and use it as a lever to lift the world.

The difference between Lenin and the orthodox "evolutionary Marxists" went deeper than tactics. Lenin maintained that even in industrially ripe countries a resort to force was indispensable in order to establish a proletarian state. He scorned the opposing socialist school who believed that a proletarian state would fall into their lap like a ripe fruit, in accordance with Marxian laws of economic evolution. He knew that a privileged class, whatever its nature, would resort to violence before parting with its privileges, and he advocated organized violence in order to establish and maintain the proletarian dictatorship. While orthodox Marxists leaned heavily upon parliamentary procedure and peaceful democratic methods of evolution, Lenin realized that, in the last analysis, force must dominate a national organism. He believed that even in a backward state like Russia an organized minority of workers and peasants, led by a group of intellectuals, could seize by force the levers of the state. When this momentous question was put to vote in London a majority of the Russian Socialist Democratic party voted for Lenin. In Russian the word *bolshe* means "majority"; Lenin thus founded the Bolshevik party.

Within the same year, and in the same city of London, the British geographer, Sir Halford Mackinder, expounded the basic principles of geopolitics, proclaiming his theory of the world island, which is a single supercontinent formed from the three continents of Europe, Asia, and Africa. He spoke of Russia as occupying in Europe and Asia the heartland of the world island, which is the geographical pivot of history. And he wrote: "Who rules eastern Europe commands the heartland. Who rules the heartland commands the world island. Who commands the world island rules the world." Twenty years later the father of German geopolitics, Major General and Professor Karl Haushofer, was to implant this idea in the febrile mind of Hitler, who would make it the basis of the German foreign policy of *lebensraum* and world conquest. And Lenin's successor Stalin would clash with Hitler in the greatest battles of history, in the heartland of Russia.

Russia Prepares

For the sake of victory in the struggle to come, ruthless circumstances forced Soviet Russia to pursue a ruthless policy, which often the friends of Russia failed to understand.

I have been opposed to the Marxian economic state since early youth, and still am opposed. I am opposed to any state when totally controlled by a minority of class, ideology, or creed. Such a minority, be it ever so idealistic, will inevitably degenerate into a tyrannical clique if it stays long enough in power. A clique can maintain its control only by opposition to freedom, and the destruction of freedom means the paralysis and stagnation of social organisms. To me the ideal of democracy is an unstable equilibrium of pressure groups, in which no single minority succeeds in parasitically subverting the common purpose of the nation for the common purpose of its clique.

But I realized long ago that forces more powerful than the forces of ideology were operating in Russia, as everywhere else. They were the forces of power politics and the struggle for survival among states.

Much that is of a tyrannical, ruthless, and dictatorial nature in the Russia of today has been brought about by the continuous threat of capitalist aggression from outside and of ideological threats from within. There was the iron necessity of preparation for defense in a war that seemed inevitable. Stalin met the threat from the outside by a tremendously intensified militarization and industrialization of Russia. A nation of peasants became a nation of mechanics. The Russian Army was first to be really mechanized, and its leaders were first to realize the implications of the fact that the industrial potential had become equal to the military potential. Those who followed the evolution of Russia under Stalin were not surprised at the caliber of Russia's resistance to Hitler. As early as the late 1930s the Russian High Command had planned the military defense of Russia not only against Germany, but also against an assumed coalition of entire Europe against Russia. Even then they were preparing to withdraw, if need be, behind the Volga, where new industries were being developed. In their plans it was going to be a very long war, until Europe should be worn out and dissensions should break up the coalition.

Within Russia, Stalin and his group could carry their program to its logical conclusion only by a relentless policy of extermination of all subversive elements. Battle for the existence of the new Soviet state was complicated by jealousies and rivalries among the old Bolsheviks and by profound differences of opinion as to the role of the Russian nation in Marxian dialectics. The battle against Trotskyism was one of isolationist nationalism vs. internationalism. It was the more logical contention of Trotsky that since the best hope of the Communist International lay with the industrially advanced and "ripe" countries, poorly industrialized Russia should be used merely as a base of operation to promote the proletarian revolution in western Europe and in the United States. It was the more realistic contention of Stalin that a world communist millennium was not around the corner and that it was possible to accelerate enormously the industrialization of Russia, first establishing there a great socialist state which would then become a model for the world.

The Communist International, originally conceived in the feverish wild hopes of the revolutionary millennium that right after the First World War seemed to be just around the corner, became in Stalin's hands a powerful weapon of military defense against the constant threat of a capitalist coalition. In every country the local Communist party, behind its broad ideological façade, was an advance legion of militant scouts and guerrilla workers. It did not take Stalin long to discover that even if the Bolshevik millennium was still a millennium off, the strikes, dissensions, and armed outbreaks were a powerful weapon to use inside any potential enemy country. During the Second World War the Communist International ceased to be useful and, in fact, then hampered the power politics of the Russian state. It was abandoned.

Stalin became the greatest isolationist in history. His concept of the Russian state as a model socialist state did not rule out concern for the rest of the world, but it did make preservation of the Soviet Union the primary aim for communism not only in Russia but over the world.

Not ideology but power politics has been the key to Stalin's extremely brilliant military-political activities of the last twenty years. Stalin was defending Russia first and foremost, in spite of the jeers, groans, and vituperation of both the feudalists and many liberals.

For instance, power politics was stronger than ideology when a professedly pacifist Soviet state attacked little Finland in November 1939. This attack was motivated by the strategic considerations of a great state in need of space to defend its own space. Soviet Russia, very wisely, anticipated the inevitable onslaught by Germany. It also anticipated that Finland would be one of the important bases for the German attack. Finland was practically in the suburbs of Leningrad, and the Gulf of Finland, which is the sea entrance to Leningrad, was under control of the Finnish guns. Under the circumstances, it would be difficult to defend Leningrad, and the loss of Leningrad might easily have meant the loss of Moscow, turned from the north by the Germans. Accordingly, Stalin requested Finland to cede an unimportant part of Finnish territory near Leningrad, together with a fortified base in the Finnish Gulf, offering in exchange full compensation elsewhere. The German power politicians naturally opposed such a step, and Hitler secretly encouraged Finland's Mannerheim, with his feudalistic clique, to resist Russian demands. Soviet Russia then attacked Finland in spite of the grave danger that this attack might cause a resurgence of British-French appeasers and Nazi militarists in coalition. Hence the Russo-Finnish War, in which hundreds of thousands of innocent Finns and Russians were mangled and trapped by the inexorable conflicts of power politics.

HITLER ATTACKS

The greatest mystery of the Second World War is "Why did Hitler attack Russia?"

The complete explanation of this mystery is buried deep in the archives of Berlin and Moscow. But no matter how well diplomatic secrets are guarded, there are clues available for the historical sleuth. These subtle and elusive clues are to be sought between the lines of the official releases, behind the speeches of the statesmen, in the silent language of geopolitics, and in the psychology of power politics. In the case of the Hitler-Stalin mystery there are clues to be traced all the way from Dunkirk to Iraq, and only one explanation fits them all.

Hitler certainly expected to attack Russia at some future time. In fact his whole political and military strategy before and during the war revolved around the fundamental problem of eliminating the great western European powers so that he could deal with Russia, where lay his main ambition and hope for booty. But it was a vital necessity to avoid getting involved in the depths of Russia until he liquidated England. Otherwise he would face the historical nightmare of a two-front war.

From the moment Hitler realized that he could not invade and conquer England, he had one principal goal: failing to paralyze the nerve centers of England, he must, to win the war, paralyze the nerve centers of the British Empire, in Suez and India. Military considerations therefore drew him irresistibly toward Suez, toward India, perhaps deep into Africa. *But the only adequate road to Suez lay through the Dardanelles.* It was very difficult to launch a gigantic campaign against Egypt, Suez, and India by way of Spain, northern Africa, and Libya. The enormously long line of communications across several deserts must collapse under the attacks of bombers, armies, and the British fleet. Only a straight road across the Dardanelles, through Turkey, and down the Mediterranean coast—the immemorial road of all the conquerors from Europe—could serve the gigantic purpose.

When Nazi-inspired rebellion in Iraq broke out, *Hitler was ready to move across the Dardanelles,* and confidently expected to do so. Then what stopped him? The answer is: Stalin.

Stalin knew, of course, of Hitler's plans for the future of Russia. Hitler knew that Stalin knew. And Stalin knew that Hitler knew that he knew. Still Stalin scrupulously stuck to the Non-Aggression Pact with Germany of August 1939. Throughout the war he sought to be impeccably correct. He did not want to give the slightest excuse to Hitler. He knew his Russia was still unprepared, and another year or two of peace might make the difference between survival or destruction. Therefore Stalin was willing to do *almost* anything to satisfy Hitler. But he could not let Hitler move through the Dardanelles. He did not care about Syria or Suez or Spain or Egypt. But he had to draw the line on the Dardanelles and Turkey. There he must stand up and slug it out.

Why? Because, if he let Hitler's legions into Turkey and later into Iran, not only would the Caucasus be immediately threatened, but, what is more important, Hitler's armies would, when they chose, *appear behind the Caspian and the Volga.* A glance at the map suffices to show how easily Hitler's tanks and planes could overrun Iran and, moving along the eastern shores of the Caspian Sea through the ideal tank territory, plant their banners behind both the Volga and the Ural Mountains. In this manner the Germans could have turned all the magnificent defenses of European Russia. In history's most gigantic pincer movement, one end based upon the Carpathian Mountains and the other upon the Urals, the Germans would have crushed European Russia. In another gigantic pincer movement, one end based upon the Urals and the other upon the Japanese moving from Manchukuo, the Germano-Japanese would have crushed Asiatic Russia.

That is why Stalin had to say No to Hitler's demand that Stalin permit him to cross the Dardanelles for the attack against the British Empire. Hitler knew, of course, that Stalin massed vast armies both on the Rumanian border and in the Caucasus. We must infer that Stalin refused to budge. The irresistible Nazi force had met the immovable Communist objection.

Had Hitler moved across the Dardanelles and down the Mediterranean coast, he would have, sooner or later, found himself in an impossible strategical situation. The danger would have come, not from the British in front of him (who were still weak), but from the Russians behind him in Rumania and on his flank in the Caucasus and Iraq. The deeper Hitler advanced, the more extended his line of communications would have become, and the greater the danger. Stalin might not have attacked him immediately. He might have waited a year or even longer. But when Stalin did attack him, Hitler would lose the war.

Only effective guarantees by Stalin, in the shape of withdrawal of the bulk of troops from the borders of Rumania and elsewhere, could have warranted Hitler's moving across the Dardanelles. No such guarantees could be given. There remained but one thing for Hitler to do: to attack Russia and thus remove or at least nullify the formidable obstacle to the Dardanelles and the Middle East.

Today a war with Russia has only confirmed what the German High Command feared—that Russia cannot be crushed or conquered unless the hands of England (and therefore of America) are tied. The nightmare of the war on two fronts is back in Germany.

U.S.S.R. AND U.S.A.—IDEOLOGY

The history of the remainder of the twentieth century will be written around Russia and the United States. Never before have two nations with such widely divergent cultures been so much alike. Both are pioneer nations, children of the wide open spaces. Racially akin, both are the melting pots of history, but with the big, blond, raw-boned Nordic element predominant. Both hold vast, immensely rich continents, bathed by the oceans and lying in three climatic zones.

The Russian people are on the small list of nations which Americans have never had cause to dislike.

Although Russia and the United States come within a few miles of having a common frontier, and although both countries face the Pacific Ocean, there is not a single point of possible friction between them, except their different ideologies. The only other danger to the United States is the trade rivalry that will come with the greater industrialization of Russia. Even here the enormous possibilities of mutual trade, to the extent of several billion dollars yearly, far surpass any losses from trade rivalry.

Is it, then, possible for the American state to conduct its policy toward Russia on the basis of a lasting, sincere, and intimate collaboration? The answer is yes, because a foreign policy should be based not on considerations of creed or ideology, but on the permanent realities of history and geopolitics.

Here we have the two most astounding countries in the world, each conducting an experiment that may well revolutionize all the age-old social systems of the world. For the great American experiment we can still claim that, in spite of the contradictions and the glaring defects of the industrial-capitalist system, more scientific progress has been made and more happiness acquired for a greater number of people in the last hundred years than in five thousand years before. During the next two or three generations, if the United States can continue to develop in relative freedom from wars, it is possible that the American nation will begin to approach Himalayan heights of civilization. The horrible abuses of capitalism will become mere annoyances; there will be fewer and fewer really forgotten men, and the purely material problems of food, shelter, and clothing for all will be solved.

Therefore it would be dangerous not only to the United States but to the welfare of humanity to terminate this experiment in favor of some other system which, however good it looks, has not had time to prove itself. The great American experiment, based on democratic capitalism, must go on.

The great Russian experiment starts from totally different premises —those of collective economy. It is based not on constant remodeling and adaptation of the old system, but on pulling down and building something new. It will take another generation or two before we can answer definitely as to the success of the experiment. Meanwhile America can afford grateful and generous support of the great laboratory in Russia, where conditions for a new type of social experiment exist. In a vast, self-sufficient country a nucleus of highly intelligent Russians who have little to unlearn are blending with other Russian nationalities from lower cultural levels. The experiment was cruelly interrupted by militarist aggression, but with the aggression removed it should be continued, undisturbed by other states.

If the Communists' dream comes true, to convert the world they will not need bullets but only facts and figures. Glad tidings travel fast. But if the Communist experiment results only in failure, terminating in the dictatorship of a new ruling class, with vast masses of humanity condemned to an anthill existence, then the world will turn to the American experiment. Or perhaps, meanwhile, a new social experiment may be taking place elsewhere. The Russian people will have been put on the vivisection table of history, but they (and the world) will not have experimented in vain.

It follows that while we Americans should support the great Communist Laboratory *in Russia,* and not try to destroy it, the Russian Communists should also seek to preserve the great American Laboratory *in the United States,* and not try to undermine it. This is the only solution when an ideological conflict exists between two sovereign, non-aggressor states. For one country to sabotage a social experiment of another would be as barbaric as for Harvard scientists to bomb a Princeton laboratory because they were both working on the same problem but from different hypotheses.

U.S.S.R. AND U.SA.—GEOPOLITICS

Throughout the world there is no single point of friction between Russia and the United States in trade, economic expansion, or territorial ambitions. Instead, from the standpoint of purely selfish interest, Russia and America have much in common to defend. The geopolitical patterns of the two countries are strikingly similar, and the pages of this book dealing with the American superstate and the new principles and methods of American power politics could apply as well, with slight modifications, to the Soviet Union. Russia is the heartland of the great Eurasian island; the United States is the heartland of the Western Hemisphere. Russia lies at the continental crossroads of Europe and Asia; the United States lies at the oceanic crossroads of the Atlantic and Pacific.

The two countries are surrounded by the same enemies and threatened by the same dangers, and as time passes these common dangers will grow. Like the United States, Russia is threatened by the Europeans and the Asiatics; and, similarly, the vital nerve centers of Russia are thousands of miles away from the European and Asiatic powers. The future of Russia, like that of America, is under a heavy cloud from the industrial awakening of the vastly populated nations in Asia, or from a United Europe. Like the United States, Russia is seeking a workable system of collective defense in order to perpetuate possession of her magnificent share of the world.

Russian geopolitics accounts for the tremendous difference between the basic goals of Russian foreign policy and those of Germany and Japan. The psychological basis of German and Japanese militarism is hunger for living space; morbid pride and twisted, fantastic dreams of world conquest accompany profound national inferiority complexes. Because the Russian geopolitical situation is different, Russian national psychology and political activities are bound to be different also.

Strategically, with reference to Russia, there is a situation curiously favorable to us. Russia, in the long run, will be of decisive military value to the United States as a bulwark in the heart of the Eurasian continent, and we will be of great value to her. If, for instance, Russia is attacked in the future by an industrialized China or by Japan, the Mongolians must fight not only against the Russians but also against Americans in the rear. Similarly, if Russia is attacked from the West by Germany leading western Europe, the aggressor will have once more a war on two gigantic fronts, the Atlantic and the Russian. But should Russia choose to launch herself upon the conquest of the world, she must face alone not only a two-front war—on her western front against Europe and on her southeastern front against the Mongolians—but a third and decisive front, the Anglo-American, from Alaska and the oceans. Thus, while Russia's power is greatly increased when operating with the United States, it is greatly reduced when operating alone or against the United States.

U.S.S.R. and U.S.A.—Politics

Russia's relations with other states during the postwar period will oscillate between two mutually repellent poles:

1. The fear of the world lest Soviet Russia convert it to communism by fire and sword.

2. The fear of Soviet Russia lest the world destroy its socialist state by fire and sword.

After the destruction of Nazism, Russia remains the only great state in the world whose activities might threaten not only the national security of other states but their social structure as well. Since the Bolshevik revolution Soviet Russia has been, like the emblem of the Russian eagle, a two-headed state—one an ideological head and the other a sovereign head. Although the size and importance of the ideological head of the Russian state is rapidly diminishing, there still remains an air of menace. Soviet Russia is feared because she is a powerful sovereign state, and she is hated because her mere existence threatens the social structure of other states. Soviet Russia, in spite of the efforts of her government, sends out messianic waves of socialism and receives waves of hatred from all those who fear her, to which she reacts in turn.

Russian leaders fear that immediately after the war Russia, with her devastated lands and urgent need for a breathing spell, and in spite of her gigantic armies, might be in danger of being throttled by a new Anglo-American-European coalition. She could hardly resist an iron blockade on the seas combined with relentless bombings from the scores of thousands of planes at the disposition of possible enemies. A defeated and subservient Germany would be anxious to regain the favor of victorious Anglo-American powers by joining an anti-Russian coalition. The same would be true of Japan in the west. It would be a splendid opportunity for neo-feudalist elements throughout the world to destroy the very source and breeding place of socialism. At the same time, another partial partition of Russian peripheral lands in the west and in the Caucasus might be effected, to the satisfaction of others concerned. All this could be disguised by magnifying Russia's "threat to the world" through whooped-up propaganda calling the world to unite against the Russian monster.

What, then, is the real danger to the world from a powerful victorious Russian state? To answer this question we must distinguish sharply between the danger from Russia during the next few years and a long-term danger fifteen or twenty years later.

Will a victorious and irresistible Russia roll on to establish a communist German state as the first step in the bolshevization of Europe? I will answer, without reservation, no. The specter of a communist Germany or Europe in the wake of the Second World War is one of the great delusions of some of our leading statesmen and public figures.

Sporadic communist outbreaks will take place in Germany and elsewhere in Europe. But the rise of communist states, as after the First World War, will not take place. There are weighty reasons for this. The weightiest of them is Stalin himself. Stalin's dominant fear is a coalition of the world under Anglo-American leadership. Stalin is a realist. He must clearly realize that a communist Germany would be the most effective way to bring about the very coalition he fears. That would be the one issue around which most of the world could unite against Soviet Russia.

It follows, then, that however much the Soviet leaders may wish for a communist Germany, they will be compelled by the realities of power politics to work against their own ideal. Having destroyed Nazism, they will seek therefore to establish not a communist Germany, but a democratic one, with full safeguards of property and capitalistic structure. Such is the irony of history. Exactly the same line will be followed by Soviet Russia in her relations with all other states, including Poland—except perhaps the smaller states, such as Bulgaria, within her immediate zone of influence.

The Nazis, it is true, have said that they would rather throw Germany into the arms of Communist Russia than surrender to England. But this threat is a bluff, pure and simple. The Nazis would be the very first to be liquidated by either the German or the Russian Communists, if in the meantime they were not torn to pieces by their own enraged people. Under less ruthless, capitalistic Anglo-American control, many of them would count on saving their lives and wealth.

In China there will be an almost certain liquidation of the Communist armies and party. Two governments and two armies cannot coexist within one state. Either the Chinese Communists will have to liquidate the government of Chiang Kai-shek or vice versa. When the liquidation of communism comes—and it may assume the proportions of a gigantic purge—Stalin, whatever his indignation, cannot interfere.

This self-imposed line of democratic policy by the Soviet government in the affairs of Europe does not mean that they will walk on tiptoe lest they awaken the dreaded beast of coalition. Quite the contrary. The same logic of power politics that will force them to continue the defense of the democracies in the postwar world will also force them to a vigorous policy of building, everywhere in Europe, a counterweight to the crushing weight of Anglo-American power. That is why one may expect that Soviet Russia will insist on a strong Germany and on the restoration of sovereign rights to at least those states which she has reason to believe will not be too favorable to the Anglo-Americans.

It follows that for many years there will be no danger of a communist Germany, a communist Europe, or a communist Asia. So long as Stalin and his group are leading the Russian state there will be no danger.

It might be quite different, however, in fifteen or twenty years, when Stalin is gone and when Soviet Russia, recovered from her wounds and become a superstate, might fall prey to the tyranny of a clique. Lenin, in his carefully drawn blueprint for action, calculated everything perfectly except for one fundamental factor that is yet to be resolved in the future history of Russia. This factor is the inexorable law of cliques. If the members of a clique *can* implant themselves in power and seize the levers of the state, and if they *can,* by fair means or foul, retain this control, they inevitably *will.* No clique or ruling class has ever relinquished its power over any society unless it was forced to do so. Lenin realized this fact when he adopted the strategy of violence to wrest the control of the Russian state from the clutches of the thousand-year-old Russian nobility. He led a group of brilliant and devoted idealists. But he did not foresee that by this very violence a new privileged class could arise to oppress the people with a new tyranny and thus defeat his fundamental purpose. After the idealists come the opportunists. Russia might become an antidemocratic, totalitarian state ruled by a greedy militarist clique. This threat will not come from Stalin and his group of intellectuals; it could come from some other group that might replace Stalin. There is always the danger that the idealist intellectuals will be replaced by a new aristocracy—the politicians, the bureaucrats, the greedy and the violent ones, and the new doctrinaires. Two and a half times the size of the United States, with far greater man power, larger material resources, and the technical skills of ravaged Europe, a victorious Russia will emerge as a new superstate. With Stalin eliminated, a highly industrialized Russia in the control of a privileged clique could be in truth the menace that many thought they saw in Stalin's Soviet Union.

RUSSIA IN THE POSTWAR WORLD

The coalition of capitalistic countries is the ever-recurring nightmare that has brought so many sleepless nights to the Muscovite rulers since 1918, and will not end until past 1955. This is also the key to Russian power politics of the next decade. It ties up such wide-ranging events as the Anglo-Russian treaty of alliance signed in 1942, the historic dissolution of the Comintern in 1943, and Russian determination to help establish a postwar democratic (not communist) Germany.

The leaders of Soviet Russia believe that if she can survive the next tumultuous decade she will then be free from the incubus of hostile coalitions that has haunted her ever since 1918. In the years immediately following the war Russian power politics will therefore have four goals:

First, to prevent isolation of Russia and possible crystallization of a hostile world under Anglo-American leadership.

Second, to prevent domination of Europe and especially of Germany by Britain and the United States.

Third, to secure in the coming world settlement better strategic foundations for the Russian state.

Fourth, to help establish, if possible, a system of true collective security as a further protection.

The first of these aims corresponds to the basic principle of American power politics, according to which we must renounce wars of aggression against any state. It would be criminal folly for our statesmen to become involved in ideological adventures, which would be the sole excuse for war with Russia, in defiance of true national interests and security. Ideology and power politics do not mix. Ideology becomes a vital factor in international relations only when, as in the case of Nazism, it is used as a battering-ram for conquest and loot, or, as in the case of early messianic communism, for the conquest of society from below. Far from seeking to isolate Russia, it is to our great advantage in the long and in the short run to convince Russia that under no circumstances will we participate in ideological or imperialistic aggression against her.

The second goal of Russian power politics, to prevent domination of Europe by Britain acting alone or with other Western powers, is also our goal. Together, the United States and Russia could easily block attempts by British neo-imperialists to control western Europe, in the same way that Britain and the United States could block attempts by Russia to control eastern and central Europe. The main struggle will take place around the issue of postwar Germany.

As for the third aim of Russian power politics, the best proof of our friendship and understanding of the Russian position would be in not opposing establishment of a proper strategic zone for Russia, and restoration of some of her historic possessions lost after the First World War.

This is a crucial point. Any great nation has certain indispensable minimum requirements for its strategic defense, requirements which have nothing to do with economic imperialism or profits. This is the case with the American strategic zone; it is also the case with the Russian strategic zone.

Russian territorial demands so far published in *Pravda* and mentioned in official speeches have been exceedingly modest, considering the tremendous services rendered by Russia to the cause of the Allies, the loss of the territory she suffered in 1918, and her widely exposed frontiers. In the north Finland was established practically in the suburbs of Leningrad. The Russians will demand a better strategic frontier with Finland, as they demanded before their first war with Finland. Had there been an imperialistic tinge to the Russian demands, they would have insisted on possession of the Bay of Petsamo and on occupation of the priceless Finnish nickel mines not far from the bay. So far they haven't.

In the west the Russians demand Estonia, Latvia, and Lithuania.

From the time of Peter the Great until 1918 Estonia and Latvia were part of the Russian Empire. It is strategically very difficult to defend Leningrad without control of Riga and surrounding territories. Had Russia lost Leningrad during this war (and she was very close to losing it) Moscow could have been taken by the Germans from the north, and in addition Russia would have been cut off from her allies. This might have led, in turn, to the conquest of the heart of Russia and the collapse of Russian defense. This illustrates the importance of securing strategic approaches to the vital nerve centers of a great state. The Estonians and the Latvians are proud peoples, and they have made good use of their short-lived sovereignty. But there is no power that could wrest Estonia and Latvia from victorious Russia, and certainly the United States is not going to war over this issue when the Russians have both history and strategy on their side.

The case of Lithuania, however, is open for discussion. Lithuania is not indispensable for the strategic defense of Leningrad. Economically, Lithuania belongs more to central Europe than to Russia, and historically she is closer to Poland, with whom she had a union. A sovereign Lithuania with a customs union with Poland could very well solve the thorny problem of Baltic outlets for landlocked Poland, Czechoslovakia, and other central European countries. At the same time an arrangement could be made permitting Russia to have direct and unhindered land communications with Germany.

In Poland, Russia will demand the territories containing a majority population of White Russians and Ukrainians. This is both a strategic and an ethnographic necessity for Russia. The Ukrainians in Poland number several millions, and they have been exploited for generations by the Polish landlords and bureaucrats. In recent times no people has been more cruelly persecuted than these ever-patient Ukrainians. The attempts to suppress the Ukrainian language in schools, the jails, and the Polish Gestapo that flourished almost to the day of Germany's invasion of Poland, are the blackest pages in the history of the Poland that Wilson reconstructed. It is obvious that the Ukrainian people in former Poland would much prefer, after this war, to join the forty million Ukrainians in Russia. This is the contention between Soviet Russia and the Polish government in exile; the Polish people, who neither wanted nor profited by the exploitation, are not involved.

There is another side to the story, of course, and the Polish side unquestionably has some merits. However, it would be futile to go into a detailed discussion, because the conjunction of postwar powers will be such as to make it virtually hopeless for the Polish government to retain control over large parts of the Polish Ukraine. Here again only war could stop victorious Russia from unifying the Ukraines, and neither Britain nor the United States would be willing to go to war on the issue.

From Rumania, Russia will demand the return of Bessarabia, won from Turkey in 1812, and certain minor strategic readjustments of the frontier. In Turkey, Russia has apparently given up the millenarian dream of the czars for possession of Constantinople and the Dardanelles. In the Far East there may be some difficulties with China over parts of Mohammedan Sinkiang and Mongolia, but there is nothing that could not be settled to the mutual satisfaction of Russia and China.

These probable territorial demands have been reviewed in detail because the territorial settlement is the acid test of relations between states. China, for instance, will judge Britain not by the solemn assurances of British statesmen, but by what they do with the crown colony of Hong Kong. Russia will measure our friendship and intentions by whether or not we are willing to grant her reasonable territorial demands. And since her demands will not constitute a material increase of her power, we should not oppose them. Finally, we should at once rectify the psychopolitical blunder of not dealing with Russia as the great world power that she is. Russia, like the United States, is a world power whose interests are importantly affected by events everywhere, and she should always be consulted and listened to as an equal. By helping Britain exclude Russia from the affairs of western Europe, we enable Britain eventually to exclude us from affairs where our interests are vital.

The fourth and fundamental goal of Russian foreign policy—to help establish a system of true collective security—also corresponds to the American foreign policy.

It follows that, whatever differences may arise between Russia and the United States during the years immediately after the war (and they will be many), the long-term interests of both countries are identical unless one or the other country launches upon the road of imperialistic domination, upsetting the world mechanism of power balance. The present identical interests should be furthered now, through intensive trade, cultural exchange, and strategic preparations of mutual advantage. A railroad connecting the vast, virginal regions of Alaska and northern Siberia with Moscow and New York would be the best strategic insurance for both Russia and the United States against the future onslaughts from Europe and from Asia. I hope to see the fulfillment of my private dream of a railroad tunnel under the Bering Straits connecting Moscow with New York. This, with the intensive development of Alaskan territories, should be among the great postwar public-works projects. Alaska without a network of roads and settlers will be practically indefensible, two or three decades hence, against either Russia or a strong Asiatic power. With good fast roads the United States and Canada could bring to bear an overwhelming force against the enemy. As for the argument that development of roads might facilitate invasion, Britain, in refusing to build a tunnel to France and roads to Burma, paid a heavy price for this fallacy. The proposed Bering tunnel could, in case of necessity, be destroyed; meanwhile it will be a long time before aviation supplants freight cars, and locomotives can use coal or wood instead of oil. Besides changing the strategic situation in favor of both countries, a New York–Moscow rail line should prove a profitable business investment.[1]

Thus American balance politics requires lasting friendship with Russia, like lasting friendship with Britain, as a safeguard of our security. But American power politics also requires that beyond a certain point friendship must cease. Much as we must grant to Russia in the interests of intelligent balance politics, we must be prepared, as in the case of Britain, to draw a line beyond which the increase of Russian power over other states becomes dangerous.

The limit of the expansion of any great state is the resistance of other great states. In the postwar world the United States will be the one state that could effectively oppose the expansion of Russia in Europe and in Asia. It is only natural that Russia, like any other

[1] A similar railroad, for similar economic and strategic reasons, should connect New York and southern Argentina or Chile.

strong state, might seek to fill a power void; and if we should rely on appeasement or verbal bombs charged with sawdust, then in a decade or two we might find ourselves before an all-powerful Russia which we could neither defeat nor resist.

It behooves us, therefore, to be prepared, like Russia, for all contingencies. If we know what we want, if we are guided by what is essentially just to Russia and to her neighbors, and if we are firm in our policy, we need not fear Russia.

CHAPTER SIXTEEN

China: Power Problem of the Future

DURING THOUSANDS OF YEARS there were on this globe two distinct human worlds with two distinct histories: the world of China and the Atlanto-Mediterranean world. These two worlds existed oblivious of each other.

There were deep, slow-swelling subterranean channels of interchange in basic cultural elements. I believe that both the ancient Chinese and the ancient Mediterranean civilizations fell heir to an even more ancient common civilization which originated perhaps in India. In this hemisphere the remarkable Toltec-Inca civilizations may have originated from the same very ancient mother lode. But in recorded history the Chinese and the Mediterranean worlds did not shape each other's civilizations, except very faintly, through indirect cycles of migration. They did not trade except sporadically and through remote intermediaries.

Nature built around China a wall more impassable than any man-built walls: impenetrable jungles and mountains in the south, the seas in the east, the Siberian tundra in the north, and the Himalayas shouldering vast deserts in the west. Her frontiers kept China in a strait jacket, shaping her isolated destiny.

We can only guess at the thousands-of-years-old history of the Chinese. To a greater extent even than on the other great plains of the world, Chinese history probably revolved around the task of filling up with agricultural cells first the great plain of the Yangtze and then the great plain of the Yellow River. This task alone must have required at least five thousand years. By the first century it is probable that China already contained a larger population than the Roman world of that era with its fifty or sixty millions. As the farmers multiplied and moved northward and westward, they squeezed out the Mongolian and white nomads. The Mongolian nomads, who formed an inner belt, were pushed north; the white nomads, who formed an outer belt, were driven across the deserts west of China, never to return. This inexorable growth of Chinese families probably accounts for the great waves of migrations of peoples across the plateau of Iran and the steppes of southern Russia.

Marco Polo's historic discovery of the world of China was as startling and less credible than the geographical discovery of Columbus. In the same thirteenth century Genghis Khan unified by blood and iron the nomadic Mongolian tribes whose habitat was the lush grazing lands around Lake Baikal, the western limits of the dream empire proclaimed by Japanese militarists today. He developed a small but irresistible force of blitz cavalry and infantry at least equal to the Greek phalanx or the Roman legion. The strategic position of Genghis Khan between the two worlds was ideal. Striking west, across Russia to the banks of the Dnieper, he threatened Christendom. Genghis Khan was the only conqueror in history to hold large parts of both the European and the Chinese worlds. Both Russia and China fell under the Tartar yoke, while a branch of the Mongolian conquerors installed themselves in India.

The fine network of roads built by the Mongol invaders established for the first time a permanent interchange of trade and culture between the East and the West. But with the sinking of the Mongolian empire, China again became a world apart from our world. Only a few small streams flowed from this vast ethnical continent; one watered the trade of New England and helped launch the first ships of the United States.

But fundamentally the nomadic conquests were as unimportant as all conquests when the only change is that of the top rulers and the tax collectors. The Russian, Chinese, and the Indian peasants, artisans, and tradesmen remained in effective possession of their lands and towns. The processes of filling the Russian and Chinese plains continued, as the farmers conquered more and more of the virgin forests and the prairies. These were the conquests that counted. After a few generations the multiplying millions of peasants threw off the yoke of foreign conquest with its social organisms as easily as a healthy peasant throws off lice.

THE NEW CHINA EMERGES

The powerful ferments of industrial revolution were needed to connect indissolubly the world of China and the world of Europe and America. Now for the first time in history these different worlds move closer and merge or threaten to conflict.

The Middle Kingdom of China, ruled by Chiang Kai-shek and his party, might well become the middle kingdom of a world ruled by some future dictator.

China already has two prerequisites of a superstate: a continental living space and a gigantic homogeneous mass of people. It is well on the way to the third prerequisite: industrial skills and organization. In the midst of paralyzing struggle with the Japanese octopus, China is developing good embryonic plants and other machine organisms. Schools and laboratories multiply, turning out technicians by the thousand in almost every industrial field. Nothing will stop the future industrial development of China; after the defeat of Japan, a liberated and reassembled China will grow industrially as fast as Russia after the First World War. Perhaps even faster, for she possesses what no other single nation in the world possesses—the enormous mass of four and a half million people, intelligent and ever-patient, molded in the same image by a psychosocial pattern five thousand years old.

It was stupid of Japan to try to stop with bullets the inevitable growth of machines on the soil of China. It was too late. The China of 1937 was vastly different from the China of 1927, and with every year China grows much stronger. No longer does a country without a machine shop, without modern guns, and without modern organizations lie prostrate before a few foreign regiments.

Today China is like a powerful giant, still on his knees but about to rise for a leap into destiny. What will this destiny be?

THE MYTH OF CHINESE PACIFISM

As counterforces in the wake of industrial might, many experts point to the "inherent" pacifism of the Chinese nation and to the "natural" democracy of the Chinese people. But no great nation is "inherently" pacifist.

A nation may be pacifist at one period of its history; at other periods its basic pattern will be warlike. This will depend on whether the national economy is inward-expanding or outward-expanding, and on whether expansion has been brought to a stop by insurmountable obstacles of mountains, waters, or deserts. The traditional pacifism of China grew largely from the physical obstacles of the jungles, the Himalayas, the Gobi Desert, the Siberian tundra, and the Pacific. The Chinese reached their natural frontiers long before the Christian Era. There were no other great nations near by to threaten their destruction, and except for frontier defense and an occasional civil war there was little practice for the Chinese warrior. The trade of the soldier fell into disuse and disrepute; the pacifist virtues were exalted.

But that the Chinese are as warlike as other people is shown by their marvelous fight, almost barehanded, against the Japanese. The driving social forces of a great nation can turn the individual into a warrior as easily as into a pacifist.

China may become the largest of the "have-not" nations. Her living space, though large enough to build a gigantic war machine, is already too small to support her vast population. Many millions of the overpopulation will be absorbed by rapidly developing industries, but an even more rapid increase in population is usual in the early stages of industrialization. Then will come population pressure and social turmoil which might lead to dictatorships and wars of expansion.

The distances and the physical obstacles which for thousands of years contained China within natural limits have been practically eliminated by the Industrial Revolution. There will be nothing to stop the fighting machines of Chinese fascists except the fighting machines of other nations.

China, like any oriental country, is essentially a hierarchic state. It has not the feudal nobles of the Japanese, but it has a powerful ruling class made up of landed proprietors, petty war lords, bureaucrats, tradesmen, and merchants. The people themselves are democratic, and there is a highly progressive and idealistic intelligentsia devoted to the precepts of Sun Yat-sen. However, the idealists face a colossal task in view of the forces of rapacity and traditional privilege. It is to the credit of the new leaders of China that they resisted not only the Japanese feudalists outside, but their own feudalists within.

But Chinese imperialism is already rampant in certain militaristic cliques. Claims are being put forth to Thailand and to Indo-China as "Chinese lands." Chiang Kai-shek was forced to deny these claims officially. Most of the Chinese look upon their war with Japan as a war of liberation from Japanese enslavement. Others look upon this war as one of liberation both from Japan and from the Western powers. But a number of Chinese look upon the war as a struggle to decide the future leadership of the Mongolian race in a war against the whites for world dominion. In such a future conflict there is little doubt that it would be the Chinese and not the Japanese imperialists who, having learned the Japanese military technique and borrowed the propaganda of "Asia for the Asiatics," would take the lead. Above all it will be clear that the new factor of China's vast industrialized mass will upset possible combinations for the balance of power among the great nations. Whichever side China chooses to throw her weight upon must be victorious. Since no balance of power would be possible with China in it, power politics will sooner or later demand a balance of power with all great states united against China.

Against such a threat the promise of a postwar democratic China is no guarantee. Statesmen will argue that the Chinese democratic government may be upset or that it may in reality be a fascist government under false colors of democracy. The thing that will count is the fact of the power of the Chinese superstate and its potentiality for harm under future war lords. The more industrialized she becomes, the greater will be the threat to the nations of the world; the greater the threat, the more certain is partition and even enslavement of the Chinese nation by a coalition of powers. Once China was partitioned because she was too weak; in another generation she may be partitioned because she is too strong.

Thus, of all the great peoples on earth, China's future is darkest. When this war ends, China's long travail will still be beginning. She will be freed from her Japanese oppressor and her dismembered people will be reunited. For a few years China will live her historic dream—the world of One China described in the Chinese national hymn as "a similarity of structure under heaven."

But these years of breathing spell will be short, not because China will be confronted with tremendous problems of internal order and industrial development, which China can solve as well as, if not better than, other nations. The question is not what the Chinese will do to China but what the powerful white men will do to the Chinese in order to keep them from becoming too strong and too dangerous.

During the first intoxicating years of United Nations victory the question may not arise, although some of the power politicians of Britain, whose Far Eastern possessions are most exposed, will already be playing down the Chinese victory. But as convalescent China regains her strength, and her heart begins to pump the new economic blood stream brought by rapid industrialization, the question will loom larger.

If China is to be saved, she must solve one of the greatest dilemmas of power politics in history—the Chinese power theorem. If Chinese statesmen can solve and prove this theorem, China will be finally liberated; if not, Free China will be partitioned. I use the word *theorem* advisedly to emphasize the fact that this basic problem cannot be approached with emotional or ethical yardsticks. The problem involves not only the survival of China, but that of other great sovereign states and perhaps of modern civilization.

The Chinese Power Theorem

From the standpoint of power politics, there is no adequate assurance that some future Chinese Hitler will not arise to threaten domination of the world, once China becomes industrialized. Therefore efforts will be made by one or more foreign powers to keep China divided and backward, and if this proves ineffective, China will be partitioned before she becomes too strong.

This is a problem of utmost difficulty for Chinese statesmen: how to become industrialized and yet avoid being enslaved.

But why single out China? Other nations have become industrialized without threat of partition.

The emergence of the new China will be an event of world-shaking importance, comparable to the birth of Soviet Russia and the growth of the American superstate. We must remember that Russia after Munich had a narrow escape from being partitioned by Germany with the connivance of the western European powers, and the history of Russia's next twenty years is yet to be written. In the case of China the danger to other powers from her industrialization is enormously greater because of the crushing weight of her man power. The rise of a nation made up of a half billion people will play havoc with the world power mechanism, heretofore balanced by blocs of forty, seventy, one hundred and thirty, or two hundred million people. When China is industrialized and the Mongolian world unites, it will be necessary to throw on the balance scale the weight of all remaining world powers.

An industrialized China will possess man power four times that of the United States, and considerably larger than that of the United States and Russia together. Fifteen million American soldiers—ten per cent of the estimated population in 1960—would face sixty million Chinese soldiers; forty million American workers would be matched by one hundred and sixty million Chinese.

With her enormous man power under militarist control, even a partly industrialized China would offer a sinister threat to the rest of the world. We have seen what Japan could do with less than seven per cent of American industrial capacity and without the advantage of China's continental hinterland. Had China today been as far industrialized as Japan, and fighting as the ally of Germany and Japan, it would have been virtually impossible for the Anglo-American-Russian alliance to defeat the Axis. Russia and India would have been conquered. How much greater would be the danger from a fascist Chinese superstate?

Strategically, China can operate on interior lines surrounded by three widely separated powers—British India, Russia, and the United States. Burma, India, Netherlands East Indies, and Australia could not be defended against the might of a Chinese superstate, either by the United States and Britain thousands of miles away or by the Russians separated by ocean-size deserts.

With the central government seized by violent and fanatic Chinese fascists it would hardly be possible to stop the march of a Chinese military machine. The Japanese fascists would, of course, join with the Chinese, and to the staggering mass of four hundred and fifty million Chinese must be added the Japanese bloc of seventy million people. Spykman is naïve in his assumption that the Chinese and Japanese nations will keep on cutting each other's throats to the secret delight of the Western power politicians. After this war a defeated and hopeless Japan will probably find her greatest profit and security in joining China for the common purpose of struggle against the Western powers who will threaten both China and Japan with subjugation.

This threat from a postwar China will not come, of course, from the present leaders of China, who have repeatedly shown a greater sincerity and a deeper concern for the world as a whole than is being shown by many statesmen of their allies.

Nor will the threat come from the Chinese people, who, like all peoples, seek only to live and to work in peace. The danger is that the people of China will be as helpless as the peoples of other nations before the armored fighting machines, the propaganda, and a Chinese Gestapo. The threat will come from future Chinese military cliques, seeking to rise on the foundation of Chinese industrial might to dominate the world for themselves and their followers.

These, then, are the reasons for which the Western powers will view China as the greatest threat to them all and will take steps to remove this threat.

What is the answer to this Chinese power theorem?

Humanists in China and outside argue that if injustices toward China are removed, and if China is treated as an equal, there will be no reason to fear her. This thesis is brilliantly presented by Lin Yutang in his recent book *Between Tears and Laughter*. Lin Yutang is one of the true humanists of today, steeped in both occidental and oriental cultures and speaking for occidental and oriental humanists with equal authority. If I disagree with certain aspects of his humanism which are not realistic, it is only because I am a humanist myself and feel deeply that Lin Yutang is not a realist as well.

Among other proposals for world peace he analyzes the World Federation Plan, and particularly my solution of the problem of an international police force. He pays me the compliment of praising the plan highly: "If Euclid or Pythagoras could save us, Culbertson will." The trouble is, he says, that the world cannot be saved by mathematics alone—a belief which I share. Where we differ is in our concepts of humanism and psychology.

Lin Yutang writes, "There will be peace in the world only when the English, French, and Dutch empires collapse. I know this war is not big enough to reverse the process and wipe out the empires, and I hope World War III will do it."

In the World Federation Plan I provide for eventual freeing of the oppressed peoples; but this war is not being fought because of the iniquities of the British, French, and Dutch imperialists. It is being fought largely because militarist cliques, using modern techniques of enslavement, captured the peoples of Germany and Japan together with their vast resources and decisive heavy weapons. When they accumulated enough fighting machines, and the leadership of other great powers was paralyzed, they attacked. It was the mathematics and psychology of sheer force. If they miscalculated it was not because they were too mathematical, but because they did not know how to measure all the social forces, and especially the vast industrial potential of the United States. What did the three empires have to do with all this?

As for Lin Yutang's hope that World War III will destroy the three empires, World War III will do much more than that. It will probably partition China. It might destroy civilization.

In calling the problem of peace "a problem of the psychology of the big powers," Lin Yutang tends to confuse the psychology of the individual, a horse of one color, with the psychology of a social organism, a herd of a different color. Any reader of *Moment in Peking* will gladly concede Lin Yutang's deep insight into individual psychology; readers of *Between Tears and Laughter* must reluctantly decide that brilliantly turned phrases, often true and always beautiful, are not enough to change the hearts of men grouped into nations. Suppose we could, by waving a magic wand, abolish all the trouble-making states—Dr. Lin's "three or four big powers . . . upsetting the peace of the world"—and start a new life with peaceful states. How long before the ever-present cliques of ambitious rulers and parasitic hangers-on would rise again, to prey upon their neighbors? Not ethics or philosophy, but force alone, can restrain the evil that is found, not in the heart of individual man, but in the heart of the human herd.

Admitting that "Mr. Culbertson is well disposed toward China," Dr. Lin goes on to say, "the inverted reasoning he employs—one set of reasoning for China, another for America and Great Britain—is purely unconscious and profoundly human." I don't know about its being profoundly human, but it is purely conscious. There is no question that China should be treated with honor as an equal member of the family of nations; the sham and arrogant stupidity of so-called white supremacy must be abandoned once for all. But the cultural, juridical, or political equality of a sovereign state is one thing, and the equality of the same state *in terms of power* is quite another thing.

The object of power politics is to preserve or increase favorable inequality. The strength of states is seldom equal: China, after many centuries, has emerged as a relatively weak state; the United States, justly or not, has emerged after three centuries as a powerful state. To demand equality of power is like asking a well-armed man to divide weapons with a potential enemy. To expect foreign states to sterilize their power and permit China to arm her overwhelming mass of four hundred and fifty millions without guarantees that the nation will not fall under militarist control is the height of naïveté. It is also unjust to China, for so might her own people, as well as the rest of the world, be enslaved.

No nation has been treated more fairly and more justly than Japan since the disastrous visit of Commander Perry in 1853. But when Japan accumulated fighting strength she began her wars of aggression, and now only total conquest and disarmament will stop her. China, if she is to escape the operation of power politics, must first find means of escaping the tyranny of future war lords—a tyranny whereby the helpless Chinese people, like the helpless German people, could be used to flay the world.

Some economists may urge that an industrialized China, with a high standard of living, would have no reason to attack her neighbors or support a militarist clique. The fallacy here lies in the fact that militarist cliques enslave their own people and attack other nations largely because they are able to lay their hands upon the decisive weapons of war. Armored planes, tanks, and warships, whether for wars or dictators, can be produced only by nations with a fair degree of modern industrialization. It is precisely because Germany and Japan were able to produce the intricate engines of destruction that they were able to threaten the world.

A free and democratic China would make it more difficult for a dictator to plunge his country into war, and in the future China may become a great democracy. Today she is not. A democracy affords freedom for the individual within his family cell and in other social organisms. The suppression of the individual within the family cell and ancestor worship are still the dominant elements in the hierarchical structure of Chinese society. Although China today is led by great and unselfish leaders, it is still the leadership of a clique which under stress of events is rapidly crystallizing into a military caste.

Even a democratic postwar China is no assurance against wars of aggression; there was democracy in Weimar Germany, yet Hitler came. Also, democratic states can make wars of aggression, as proved by Britain and France.

So far I have discussed the Chinese power theorem from the standpoint of power politics as played by the dominant Western powers. How do the Chinese themselves propose to resolve this problem?

One Chinese group believes that the perennial rivalries and intrigues among the foreign powers will enable China to become highly industrialized without partition. They cite the rise of Hitler, which was made possible because of the rivalry between Britain and France for control of Europe and their fear of Russia.

But China's future industrial rise and consequent military threat present so many extraordinary and unique features that even the dullest of the Western power politicians cannot miss them. It will be impossible to hide under a bushel the mass of five hundred million industrializing people. The example of the rise of Hitler and the Japanese militarists will be a reminder to the Western powers that a small preventive war is infinitely cheaper than a large war postponed.

The second Chinese group, at the opposite pole from the first, is fully conscious of the future danger of partition of China and believes that the only way to avoid it is to limit her industrialization. A peaceful, dominantly agricultural China would not seriously disturb the world power balance and would allay the fears of Western states. This group accordingly advocates perpetuation of the Chinese agricultural way of life, with a small, strictly limited heavy industry and concentration on "harmless" industrialization in textile and other fields.

This in a way is, as Lin Yutang puts it, the "old rogue's Lao-tsean philosophy of the wisdom of appearing foolish, the advantage of lying low, the strength of gentility, and the victory that comes from not inviting the fear of the world." This solution, however, breaks down on the fundamental fact that industrialization can neither be stopped nor diverted to "harmless" fields. Industrialization is an inexorable world-wide process. It is based on textbook formulas and can no more be controlled than a table of logarithms. It would be as futile for the Chinese as for outside powers to attempt to turn back the million clocks of history; industrialization might be delayed a few years and that is all. After this war, capital will pour into China from all over the world, and with capital will come technicians, blueprints, and machines. Thousands of businessmen and promoters, once the Western world is made idle by peace, will seek in renascent China a happy hunting ground. Industrialization will come to China whether she seeks it or not, and with industrialization comes the great threat.

In a world dominated by power politics there is no way for China to escape the tragic conflict between inevitable industrialization and/or inevitable partition. This is not because China or the Western powers are inherently evil. It is because, in the organized anarchy of sovereign states, the most peaceful of nations and the best of governments have no choice but to resort to violence in order to survive the violence, actual or potential, of other nations. It is because no industrialized nation is immune from seizure of power by parasitic cliques, able to build up large armies equipped with intricate fighting machines.

The only hope for China lies outside the realm of power politics. It is the hope of a system of collective defense, a World Federation in which each nation may live in peace and freedom because no nation need fear aggression.

This was the hope of China during more than twenty-five centuries, when she sought to assemble the fragments of a feudal country into a united world, which was called a "Similarity of Structure under Heaven."

Since then the world that the Chinese sages knew has been greatly enlarged by the addition of our own world, but now the world has become small again. Today a world united under a higher law is the hope of all nations.

But until this hope is realized there is no law governing the relations of sovereign states except the law of force, and no method of applying it except power politics.

It is therefore necessary to examine the Chinese power theorem in the light of American balance politics.

American Postwar Policy with China

Traditionally, our policy toward China is one of friendship and economic co-operation. We are the only great power consistently to oppose the infringement of Chinese territories and sovereignty by other powers. Should we give up this traditional friendship and join other nations in attempts to weaken China?

The answer is no. Such attempts are false power politics. Quite apart from the traditional friendship between the Chinese and the American people, a friendship sealed by this war, there is the fact that for fifteen or twenty years China cannot possibly offer any threat to us.

If after twenty years we fail to establish some satisfactory system of world collective security, then we must re-examine our policy with China. Meanwhile our postwar policy for the next fifteen or twenty years is clear:

1. We must become immediate neighbors of China on the Asiatic continent, through occupation of a chain of fortified places leased on a non-imperialistic basis in Indo-China and Thailand. This move is not directed against China, but is part of a general strategic scheme for defense of the Pacific approach to the American continent.

2. We must strongly support Chinese claims to a fully reunited China, including Formosa and Manchuria. We should seek to persuade Britain to give up Hong Kong, in exchange for compensation elsewhere in Italian Africa. Nothing is better calculated to exasperate nationalistic feelings and promote militaristic spirit than a festering wound left in the body politic of a great nation.

3. We must oppose attempts of our war allies to establish, directly or indirectly, new "zones of influence" in Chinese territory or otherwise infringe upon Chinese sovereignty. We must give China an opportunity to work out in freedom the solutions to her problems.

4. We must unstintingly assist China in recovery from devastation, and co-operate in rebuilding her economy. We should open new and direct channels of trade with China. China will prove as good a financial risk for our government and private capital as Russia.

5. We should co-operate as much as possible in establishing a truly democratic China. One way is by helping to raise her economic standard. Another way is by sending our teachers, missionaries, technicians, and businessmen—provided the Chinese welcome them—and by making it easy for Chinese students to be educated in the United States.

China today is necessarily ruled by a very small minority. If China is to become truly democratic, this narrow basis must be greatly enlarged so that the leadership structure is not concentrated in the elite, but includes intermediate and lower group leaders from a strong middle class and a well-developed working class. This is an important added protection against militarists.

In turn, the United States should expect from the leaders of China a sincere and wholehearted effort to build a democratic China strong in science, culture, and trade. China today is at the crossroads of history. She may contribute enormously to civilization or she may destroy it. If postwar China is to be a nation of military dictators, of secret imperialistic dreams, of scheming, corrupt bureaucrats, and of a thinly disguised totalitarianism, then our ways must part. If it is to be a true New China, we must go a long way together. And China will find the friendly co-operation of the United States an enormous asset, perhaps a salvation.

From the standpoint of American balance politics, close co-operation with China immediately after the war has many advantages. One is a grateful China. Another is a well-integrated, democratic China. But the most decisive and vital advantage is that China and the United States together may be able to lay the foundation for an effective system of collective security, whether or not other nations choose to co-operate.

Together, China and the United States are invincible, on the American and Asiatic continents, against any combination of foreign powers. The Western Hemisphere, with its two hundred and sixty million people, the Malaysian region, with one hundred and twenty million, and China will form a continuous bloc of almost a billion people. Running from the Straits of Magellan to the steppes of Mongolia, this bloc will contain unlimited man power, unlimited raw materials, unlimited transportation, and two thirds of the world's industrial production.

The United States is the most threatened nation in the world because she is the most powerful and the wealthiest. China, next to the United States, is the most threatened nation in the world because she is the most populous and potentially the most powerful. Their only hope of lasting security is in establishing, now, an international organization open to all nations, with an international police force. The United States and China, together with other nations who will come in, undoubtedly have the power to establish and maintain such an international organization. In this way both the Chinese power theorem and the problem of the American superstate can be solved.

It may happen that in this country, during the postwar period, the will of the nation will be paralyzed by political dissensions and the struggle between nationalists and internationalists. Men with minds of yesterday and not tomorrow may try to dictate the peace. China then can offer a supreme proof of her love of peace by urging the American people to join China in establishing, on the basis of a comprehensive and specific plan, a system of collective defense. If her offer is not accepted, then at least the world will know that China is not seeking to conceal her designs behind vaporous generalities but is in earnest about finding a way to lasting peace. If her proposal is accepted, then it may well be that the Chinese power theorem will be resolved and the ideals of both the ancient Chinese statesmen and Wilson will be fulfilled.

CHAPTER SEVENTEEN

The Smaller Nations

IN THE PAST, smaller states survived mainly for two reasons: They were a by-product of the balance-of-power mechanism, since any attempt by a great power to absorb a smaller state would meet with the opposition of other great powers. At the same time the smaller states possessed a substantial capacity of their own to resist aggression. Their people, armed only with rifles and small guns, conducted stubborn guerrilla warfare and made it costly for a greater state to maintain control.

Today the revolution in military weapons has practically disarmed the smaller states, reducing their resisting capacity against the planes and tanks of great powers to but a few weeks' struggle. The only hope that remains for the smaller states is, therefore, the rivalries among greater states inherent in the balance-of-power mechanism. But even here the power of the small states grows more and more precarious. The number of leading powers is being gradually reduced, and the world power mechanism approaches an era of a few superstates with satellite smaller states revolving in their economic orbit around their political protector.

In postwar Europe the balance of power will no longer be distributed among four or five leading states, but might be reduced to Britain and Russia with their respective "zones of influence." The smaller states, in self-defense, may seek to imitate their bigger brothers by concluding among themselves various defensive alliances. But such alliances will be worth even less than the power-politics alliances of the bigger powers. It will be equally futile for the smaller states to organize themselves into regional federations, Danubian, Poland-Balkan, or Baltic-Scandinavian. The great European powers, for reasons of power politics, could not permit formation of independent power blocs by the smaller states. Nor could a large number of smaller states ever get together on any federation principle involving reasonable limitation of their sovereignties and a common armed force, without which common action and a joint defense is impossible.

The difficulty is that the governments of many of the smaller states are controlled by cliques constitutionally unable to see beyond the petty day-to-day interests of the clique, ideology (usually much to the right), or class. Their generals will not give up their grip over their Lilliputian armies, while their diplomats will not give up their minuscule power politics. These cliques and local caciques would rather die than sacrifice a particle of their precious sovereignty for the salvation of all smaller states.

Even now many of the smaller states are but satellites, poor relatives at the table of the diplomatic conferences. Unless new solutions are found, all of them will eventually be doomed. This would be a great loss to civilization.

The smaller states' loss of capacity to resist aggression is already having important effects on the concept of sovereignty. It must be revised if the principle of collective defense is to prevail. A nation must retain a healthy concept of sovereignty, but refusal, in the name of *absolute* sovereignty, to participate in common defense against aggressors will in future be considered a pathological extension of that concept.

In the ultimate analysis, the juridical concept of absolute sovereignty is based on the capacity of a state to defend itself and thus contribute to the common defense against aggressors. From the standpoint of power politics, a sovereign state which cannot defend itself against an aggressor for more than a few days or weeks, and which at the same time insists on scrupulous observance of "absolute sovereign rights," is like a bankrupt who insists on exclusive management of his properties even though this management may affect the interests of others. All sovereign states have a common stake in defense against aggressors. And when a small state isolates itself behind the magic circle of "absolute sovereignty," that state will be simply profiting by the sacrifice of others against an enemy who, if victorious, would have destroyed all. I speak, of course, of the future trend in the concept of sovereignty. As for the past, one may impeach the judgment of the smaller states who allowed themselves to be destroyed one by one by Germany, but not their moral and legal right to remain neutral under the existing international law.

The interests of civilization in the perpetuation of the smaller states everywhere coincide with the selfish interests of American balance politics. We must respect the sovereignty of our neighbors in Latin America and in the Malaysian region. We must support the principle of freedom and sovereignty of the smaller states in Europe and the Middle East, opposing possible attempts by either Britain or Russia to increase their power by encroaching on the sovereignty of other states.

But in addition to this purely negative policy of American balance politics, we have a unique historical opportunity to organize most of the smaller states of Europe and the Middle East as part of an integrated system for collective defense. The collective power of these states, when added to the collective power of the United States, the Latin-American sovereign states, and the Malaysian region, would insure the lasting security of the United States and her co-members against any foreseeable combination of powers.

No state would be coerced into joining this system of collective defense and no state would be excluded from joining it. I consider the idea of collective organization of small nations of the world with the United States, for common defense, to be of tremendous importance to our future security. A collective force of small nations is a powerful force for peace and must form part of any effective system of collective defense with the participation of the United States and other great powers. But, in the highly improbable event that no other great nation chooses to join the United States in such a collective-defense system, it is entirely practicable for the United States *alone* to integrate this perpetual alliance with the smaller states of Europe and the Middle East. This can be accomplished by means of a special government of trustees with powers strictly limited to common defense, a special court to settle disputes, and a special armed force made up on a quota basis from the small nations and the United States. Elsewhere I explain just how simply such an international perpetual alliance can be established and maintained for mutual defense and co-operation.

At first glance it might seem paradoxical that the most powerful state in the world should seek to ally itself with a group of weak states. But there are adequate reasons for this course.

A large number of these small states are highly industrialized. Most of them are well-to-do or possess considerable natural resources. With few exceptions, these states have reason to fear either Britain or Russia, not to count Germany, Italy, and even France. None of these states has any reason whatever to fear the United States. We and they seek to survive, not to conquer. We seek to survive because we are the strongest; they seek to survive because they are the weakest. Thus the largest state in the world has a fundamental common interest with the smaller states—the interest of security against future aggressors.

But, it may be asked, what help can these smaller states be in the event of aggression? The answer lies in the tremendous difference between individual and collective power.

Individually, each of these small states is weak and helpless as an ally. *Collectively,* all of them, when integrated into a system of world organization, become a tremendous power. And when the collective power of the European and the Middle Eastern states is added to the twenty sovereign Latin-American republics (integrated in the Pan-American Federation) and to the four sovereign Malaysian states in our strategic zone (integrated in the Malaysian Federation), we have a collective force of the smaller nations of the world which will surpass the force of any other great state and equal that of the United States. This actually doubles the power of the United States in defense against future aggressors.

The smaller nations have between four and five hundred million people. It is feasible to create, from the contingents of the smaller states and from the United States, an irresistible international police force under the command of an international organization for collective defense. Such an international police force would have unlimited numbers of military bases. It could be equipped from the vast accumulation of American armaments and maintained by joint contributions. It would not interfere in the internal affairs of any state. It would prohibit wars of aggression between member states. And whenever a member state was attacked by a non-member, all would be ordered by the trustees of the international organization to move against the aggressor.

Since the very purpose of such an organization is collective defense against any aggression, it will in no way affect the vital interests of non-member states. And since any state is free to join this system of collective defense, only those states having secret designs on the territory or freedom of other states will object.

The great error in the British balance-of-power policy lies in the fact that it was purely negative, never positive or creative. Britain always sought to prevent her rivals from growing too strong. This must be done too in American balance politics. But the policy of prevention must be supplemented by a creative policy, an integrated system for collective defense, with our immediate neighbors as well as with nations outside.

VI. AMERICAN SPACE POLITICS

CHAPTER EIGHTEEN

Geopolitics: Made in Germany

BALANCE POLITICS, which seeks to prevent by force, if need be, the military expansion of other states, is not enough to secure the safety of the United States in a world of tooth-and-claw struggle among the nations. A state must either grow or decline; it cannot stand still. If attacked, it must present to the enemy a maximum of strategic obstacles arranged in great depth and based on space controlled by fortified places. Therefore the negative policy which opposes the expansion of other states must be supplemented by a positive policy designed to increase the power of the state and insure its maximum strategic security. The goal of balance politics is to prevent other states from becoming too strong; the goal of space politics is to enable a state to become stronger and strategically more secure.

Balance politics and space politics are two sides of the same coin, which is power politics, since in both cases the goals must be backed up by armed force when necessary. Another point to remember is that balance politics deals essentially with the relation of the United States to foreign powers *outside* the Western Hemisphere and the Malaysian region, while space politics deals essentially with our strategic problems and with our relations with other nations *within* the Western Hemisphere and the Malaysian region.

The kind of space that a people lives on and the amount of space it possesses shape its destiny. The ideal space for a people is a large area of rich land *well adapted for defense against all outside enemies*. For the law of survival comes before abundancy. Space not only maintains life but also defends it. Cities, villages, castles were built, as a rule, not on the richest but on the least accessible space. Shangri-las are hard to reach. Nations have risen because strategically their space sheltered them against invaders; other nations have fallen because their space exposed them to the enemy. The history of Egypt was written as much by the sheltering desert sands defending the lower Nile as by the Nile herself. Great civilizations rose when bounteous lands and trade routes combined with sheltering space. The history of China in her millenarian isolation is wrapped up in the Himalayas, the Gobi Desert, the jungles, and the seas. The history of the United States would be incomprehensible without the protective blanket of the oceans around the American continent, which are now disappearing. The immense depth of Russia's space saved her again and again.

Space not only defends but builds and molds the physical and mental characteristics of a people living on the space. According to political geography, in the same way that a man is largely a creature of his physical environment, a nation or a state is largely shaped by the extent of and the kind of space it occupies. Area, topography, climate, and the kind of food people eat are all vital factors, besides the geographical security from aggressors, in the evolution and characteristics of a people or a state.

That there is a great deal of truth in this intimate relation of space to societies few will deny. Four centuries before Christ, Aristotle pointed out that Crete seemed destined, by its geographical position, to be the mistress of Greece. Aristotle was a greater space expert than he knew, since he lacked the information that Crete had been an ancient mistress of the Mediterranean a thousand years before. And three thousand years later, in 1943, Crete's air bases would still dominate Greece.

Space, so used, means a large area of land and seas with the goods and peoples contained in the area. Space politics may be defined as *the study of the relations between space and a state from the standpoint of power and strategic security.*

There are three subdivisions in the study of space politics:

1. The study of space from the standpoint of distances, natural obstacles, and fortified places (strategic space politics).

2. The study of space from the standpoint of the goods in the space, particularly strategic raw materials (economic space politics).

3. The study of space from the standpoint of the peoples inhabiting the space (psychosocial space politics).

The revolution in communications and military weapons, by reducing distances and physical obstacles, has revolutionized the state and space relationship and made it necessary to establish new concepts of the space required for defense. The new concepts of space politics, as developed here, refer particularly to the United States, although the general principles are applicable to other states. Furthermore, these new concepts differ considerably from the original German concepts of geopolitics, many of which were already antiquated before the Second World War.

The term space politics is here used, instead of geopolitics, to avoid the Germanic distortions which have given to the science of geopolitics a sense of pseudoscientific wish fulfillment rather than scientific accuracy. Space politics as treated here is not only different, but more inclusive and more exact.[1] The teachings of German geopolitics were the basis of the Nazi doctrine of *lebensraum* and of Nazi foreign policy. Only a few of its principles are scientifically sound. Unfortunately much that is unsound has crept into our higher seats of learning, our diplomacy, and the command of our armed forces. We must know how to separate the wheat from the chaff.

GERMAN GEOPOLITICS

In 1917 Rudolph Kjellen, a Swedish pan-Germanist, first used the much-discussed term *geopolitics* to describe the study of the influence of geographical factors on the destiny of the state. But Kjellen went beyond political geography to hitch his wagon to the star of the German state. His predecessor, Friedrich Ratzel, laid the foundation of the science Kjellen named. Ratzel's basic concepts of geopolitics were space (*raum*), a virile state, and living space (*lebensraum*). He believed that the decline of every state may be traced to complacency and satisfaction with a small space: "A nation pressed into too narrow a space faces national extinction." He tied this geographical concept

[1]The adjective "geopolitical" in the original sense, introduced by Rudolph Kjellen to denote the relation of political geography to the state, is retained.

of space to the political concept of state, creating the science of geopolitics.

According to Ratzel, all virile states obey the inexorable law of expansion at the expense of states which lack the "space instinct." A great state feeds upon its conquests, and the more space it conquers the more rapid is the process of "amalgamation" of further territories. Thus the function of *lebensraum* is more space in order to conquer still more space. There is no limit to this "law" of expansion because, according to Ratzel, "There is on this small planet sufficient space for only one great state." Ratzel's teachings were meat for the German imperialists and poison for other nations.

It was left to Rudolph Kjellen to identify geopolitics with enthronement of the German state. Kjellen's work, like Ratzel's, abounds in glib biological analogies to human society. In Kjellen's system the living state manifests itself in five aspects: territory or space, people, economy, society, and government. The territory is the "body" of the state. Like any other biological organism, the state must grow and have organs, and the best way to acquire a better body is by conquest: "Vitally strong states possessing only limited space owe it to themselves to enlarge their space by colonization, amalgamation, or conquest." Germany, with small space, yet vitally strong, is such a state. Can German expansion be called the lust for conquest? Decidedly not, says Kjellen: "It is clearly a case not of the lust for conquest but of natural and necessary growth. . . ."

Hegel had already taught that the state can do no wrong, is godlike, and is not subject to the moral laws of humanity. Nor is there question of the rights of other states whose *lebensraum* the German state so urgently needs. This is due to the fact that of the many nations who are called upon the stage of history, only the Germans, with their "superior culture," are the chosen people. Fichte, another great German philosopher, taught that "Only the German can be patriotic, for he alone can embrace humanity in the task of his nation. . . . In every other nation patriotism is egoistic, sordid, and hostile to the rest of humanity. . . . Thus are you, of all modern peoples, the one in whom the seed of human perfection most unmistakably lies, and to whom the lead in its development is committed." Not only the German state but the individual is beyond good and evil. Nietzsche called on the herds of German "blond beasts of prey," unburdened by morals, to exalt in their power as supermen. The latter-day Nazi saints distorted Nietzsche's poetical outbursts to proclaim every German a superman. Thus German metaphysics combined with pseudo Darwinism to produce this geopolitical hybrid, the concept of the German state in its new *lebensraum*.

The frontiers of the new *lebensraum* were mapped out by Kjellen, who anticipated a German victory in the First World War. They ran from Dunkirk to Riga to Kharkov and Bagdad. That was enough to start with. Nor did this house of geopolitical maps crash with the collapse of Germany in 1918; on the contrary, it was enlarged and improved. When the time came, the geopolitics of Ratzel and Kjellen was taken over, body and soul, by Hitler and Nazi Germany.

It was Major General and Professor Dr. Karl Haushofer who presided at the rebirth of geopolitics after the First World War and guided its steps into the thundering blitzkrieg. Haushofer was more than a prophet of *lebensraum*. He took the geopolitical philosophy of Ratzel and Kjellen and, nicely rounding it out with the teachings of the British Mackinder and the American Mahan, made geopolitics a doctrine of military action.

Himself a geographer and teacher, Haushofer settled down with a thousand research students to his patient, relentless lifework—preaching to the German elite the geopolitical destiny of the German state. Under Haushofer's direction, geopolitics was enriched by the famous "World Island" theory borrowed from Sir Halford Mackinder, who first presented it to the Royal Geographical Society, London, in his lecture "The Geographical Pivot of History." Haushofer called his theory "a grandiose description of world policy compressed in a few pages." During the peace negotiations in 1919 Mackinder, in his book *Democratic Ideals and Realities,* reaffirmed and broadened his geopolitical concept of the Russian plains as a pivot of history and warned the Allies of the dangers of a possible Russo-German alliance or the conquest of Russia by a revived Germany. Here is Mackinder's theory of the World Island in geopolitics which he had not modified as late as 1942:

Geographically and historically, the joint continents of Europe, Asia, and Africa form an island—the World Island. This great island is the largest land mass in the world. Nine twelfths of the surface of the globe, Mackinder wrote, is covered by the sea; of the remaining three twelfths, the World Island covers two. America and Australia together occupy less than one twelfth. They are merely smaller islands detached from the World Island. The World Island can outbuild and outfight any or all powers based on the satellite continents of America and Australia.

Strategically, the World Island consists of a core which is landlocked and inaccessible to sea power, and marginal regions which are accessible to ships. The core is the "heartland" of the World Island, and it stretches from the Volga to the Yangtze and from the Himalayas to the Arctic Ocean. The bulk of this heartland, measuring some nine million square miles, or more than twice the area of Europe, is occupied by Russia.

To the east, south, and west of the heartland are marginal regions of the World Island arranged in a vast crescent. Germany, Turkey, India, and China have access to the seas, and all are part of this crescent and of the World Island. But outside of this inner crescent there is an outer strategic crescent consisting of Britain, South Africa, the United States, Canada, and Japan. The maritime powers occupying this outer crescent are further removed from the heartland and suffer, in relation to the World Island, from the strategic disadvantage of operating on the outer line and of being unable to reach the heartland with their sea power.

Such is the structure of the World Island, with its heartland, inner crescent, and outside crescent of satellite islands and continents. What is the strategic significance of this structure? Mackinder believes, with Mahan and Haushofer, that conflicts of world history have largely been struggles between seafaring and land peoples, maritime and continental powers. Mackinder also holds that world history has always been made and always will be made by the pressure of great landlocked peoples of the plains of eastern Europe and western and Central Asia upon the peoples settled on the coastal areas. He writes: "As we consider the broader currents of history, does not a certain persistence of geographical relationship become evident? Is not the pivot region of the world's polity that vast area of Euro-Asia (heartland) which is inaccessible to ships, but in antiquity lay open to the horse-riding nomads, and is today about to be covered with a network of railways? Russia replaces the Mongol Empire. Her pressure on Finland, on Scandinavia, on Poland, on Turkey, on Persia, on India, and on China replaces the centrifugal raids of the steppemen." Russia's land power is adequately balanced by the outside maritime powers. But what would happen if this balance of power were upset? "The oversetting of the balance of power in favor of the pivot state (Russia), resulting in its expansion over the marginal lands of Euro-Asia, would permit the use of vast continental resources for fleet building, and the empire of the world would then be in sight."

This balance of power between Russia, who controls the heartland of the World Island, and the maritime powers who control its littorals can be upset either by a German-Russian alliance or by German domination of Russia. "In the world at large, Russia occupies the central strategical position held by Germany in Europe." Germany, once in possession of the heartland together with her own oceanic frontage, could undertake the conquest of the world by sea power. A similar combination of heartland with ocean frontage, secured through a Russian-German alliance, could also dominate the world.

Mackinder observes that "substitution of some new control of the inland area (heartland) for that of Russia would not tend to reduce the geographical significance of the pivot position. Were the Chinese, for instance, organized by the Japanese to conquer the Russian heartland, they might constitute the Yellow Peril to the world's freedom just because they would add an oceanic frontage to the resources of the great continent."

During the Second World War Mackinder republished his study, *Democratic Ideals and Realities,* in the United States. Without any change, his famous warning of future peril to the world from joint domination of the heartland of the World Island by Germany and Russia or by Germany alone was repeated. "When our statesmen are in conversation with the defeated enemy," he wrote of Germany, "some airy cherub should whisper to them, from time to time, this saying: 'Who rules east Europe commands the heartland; who rules the heartland commands the World Island; who rules the World Island commands the world."

Haushofer, delighted, took over Mackinder's theorem lock, stock, and barrel for his own system of geopolitics. Only, of course, he played Mackinder's globe in reverse English. The great fears of Mackinder became the great hopes of Haushofer. For was it not the manifest destiny of the German state to find at last its *lebensraum* in the heart of the World Island? The German strategic position in the heart of Europe was ideal. She could operate from interior lines across the plains of Poland and Russia without fear of the sea power of the already decaying British Empire. Soviet Russia, which was but an "agglomeration of many racial minorities," could oppose with only a halfhearted resistance. During the years after the First World War, while German strength was being rebuilt, there could be a German-Russo-Japanese alliance. After that Germany could strike with all her power against the decaying democracies in the West and the Russian giant in the East. The Soviet Union would be broken up before it had time to become fully industrialized. On its ruins would be created a Ukrainian national state, a Baltic-German state, a rump Russian-Volga state, and lesser national states in the Caucasus and eastern Europe. These satellized states, together with the Russian possessions in Asia, would become part of Greater Germany, mere parcels of her imperial *lebensraum*—"the heartland, reaching from the Elbe to the Amur." Besides this West-East empire, there could perhaps be a North-South empire from Narvik to Dakar. It was a grandiose dream with the stuff of blood and reality.

And how about the United States? The United States troubles Haushofer a great deal. It fulfills all the requirements of the purest geopolitical ideals. In this New World, heartland and sea power are one. The United States is endowed with all the geographic depth, material wealth, and strategic position that is an indispensable condition for a truly great state. Her home base is the vast American continent. This self-contained continental space, backed up by Latin America, gives the United States a massiveness unsurpassed even by Haushofer's Utopia, the German-controlled heartland.

No wonder that Haushofer, when he considers the United States, is torn by mixed emotions. On one side he fears that the United States might become a gigantic fly in the German ointment. He predicts that "the future struggle for world power and the fate of National Socialism will be decided in America." One of his principal collaborators, the geopolitical journalist, Colin Ross, went further, to write in 1938: "Potentially the United States is the world's foremost political and economic power, predestined to dominate the world once it puts its heart into power politics."

On the other side, Haushofer hopes that the United States will follow her "true" geopolitical interests, which lie in using the blocks from a broken British Empire to build an American empire in the Pan-American as well as in what he calls the Indo-Pacific space. Germany would be quite willing to help. Britain, he argues, is already heavily mortgaged to the very power, the United States, which has the strongest geopolitical interest in liquidating the British Empire; in the Indo-Pacific space the United States has a vital stake. There, according to Haushofer, she faces enormous conflicts with Britain, Japan, and Russia; he sees the Pacific area as the theater of a gigantic struggle between these four world powers. Here again Germany would be willing to help, at a price.

The secret dream of the German geopoliticians is division of the world between the German state and the United States. But in view of the "immaturity" of the American nation with regard to the true teachings of geopolitics, Haushofer supports the Japanese geopoliticians in their claim for hegemony over a Greater East Asia. Unperturbed by the contradiction between his avowed support of the Japanese and his hints to the United States about her mission in the Pacific, he argues that the United States should be content with the Western Hemisphere and parts of the British Empire. Remarkably enough he misses the even more important role of China, with both a continent and an ocean frontage and lacking only the technical skills for her overwhelming man power.

Fluidity and adaptation are the characteristics of Haushofer's geopolitical technique. Decisions of world policy, he says, are "set against a background of infinite variety." In the same way that the frontiers of the future *lebensraum* expand and contract as the power of Germany expands and contracts, Haushofer's geopolitical concepts expand, contract, are modified and readapted to the fluctuations of political events. What matters is that the future belongs to the giant Germanic state, the only state possessing a superior culture, superior strategic position, and a superior "space instinct." It is therefore this state that must and will be the master. Even a world divided between the Germanic state and some other giant state will be but an intermediate step, for "the heartland dominates the World Island and the World Island rules the world."

Such are the principles of Haushofer's New World Order so crudely expressed by Hitler and so amateurishly carried out by the Nazis and their Japanese imitators. Today Haushofer is still alive to witness, after brief moments of exaltation equaled only by Hitler, the second and more tragic collapse of his map dreams.

What malevolent fates of history pursue the German state, in defiance of all the laws of German science? Is it possible that only Hitler's intuition and the blunders of the high command are responsible? Or is there something fundamentally wrong with German geopolitics, some invisible leak, some inner crack in this science of sciences which has twice betrayed the German people? Doubtless Haushofer and the German *geopolitiker* will re-examine the principles and methods of geopolitics, to rid it of its fatal defects. Let us help them in this critique.

Most fallacies in German geopolitics involve two fundamental mistakes: one an exaggerated, semimystic concept of geographical space and *lebensraum,* the other an oversimplified, naïvely brutish concept of the force needed to achieve this *lebensraum.*

THE EXAGGERATED CONCEPT OF SPACE

The *geopolitiker* took sound political geography and endowed the concept of space with mystic qualities it does not possess. Forgetting that peoples inhabiting the space, not the space itself, are the dominant factor, the *geopolitiker* formulated pseudoscientific laws of space to which every state is "inexorably" bound. Before the immensity of space they lost sight of the infinity of man.

Space shapes the man, but man also reshapes space, shortening distances and changing the face of the earth. No state can be measured merely on the scale of space. A nation is a social organism resting on a human as well as a geographical basis. Geography is of vital importance in shaping the characteristics of a nation and the policy of a state, but even more important are psychosocial and other forces which determine the patterns of societies and nations. There are human heights and valleys not mapped on the charts. No one who understands history can overlook the relation between the politics of a state and the facts of geography, the dynamic relation between space and power. But, as the French insist, it is man, not space, that makes history.

Haushofer himself was quite aware of the influence of psychosocial forces in world politics. He stated that the geographical factor of space in geopolitics accounts for "about one quarter." But in practice Haushofer, like his predecessors, was a geographic hundred-percenter, and stretched the twenty-five per cent of geography to cover one hundred per cent of geopolitics.

Like Karl Marx, Haushofer created a system of political philosophy and sought to explain all political events from one set premise. Geopolitics, like Marxism, is a revolutionary doctrine that has developed a dialectic. What the class struggle is to the Marxists the struggle for space is to the *geopolitiker*. With Haushofer, economic determinism has been transformed into geographic determinism. The union of the proletariat under a proletarian dictatorship has become the union of Germany with the heartland under the German *geopolitiker*. For the economic materialism of Marx the *geopolitiker* substitute the geographic materialism of Haushofer. In Marxism history is interpreted in terms of economic factors; in geopolitics it is interpreted in terms of the political struggle for space. The state, a "geographic organism," is the sole reality of geopolitics; the German state is its ultimate expression.

But the geopolitical state, unlike the Marxist state, does not promise economic and social equality for all as the reward of struggle. It promises only a colossal physical space—heartland today and to-morrow the world—dominated by the master race. Thus it is the political philosophy behind geopolitics and not its scientific method that turns geopolitics into an instrument of war.

Much of the scientific residue in geopolitics is further weakened by fallacies in Mackinder's heartland theorem which Haushofer took over. Both Mackinder and Haushofer are so hypnotized by geopolitical space curves that they ignore the dominant factor of any modern space—the curve of industrialization.

By the industrialization of the world, time and space, which for thousands of years remained static, measured by the pace of the horse and the speed of sailing ships, have become fluid. The *volume* of space has remained the same, but its *distance* has been drastically reduced. Sea power which was about to be turned on land by the railroads was suddenly turned from the air by warplanes, and Mackinder's inner and outer crescents around the World Island look pretty on a map but have lost their strategic meaning.

Mackinder built his theorem of the heartland upon a concept of exclusive sea power that was valid before but is no longer valid today. He saw the strength of the heartland largely in the fact that it was inaccessible to sea power. He feared a conquering land power, ensconced in the heart of Eurasia, building irresistible fleets to destroy Britain and other maritime powers.

What Mackinder did not see was the basic fact that sea power today, like any other form of military power, depends more upon the degree of industrialization of a state than upon distance or inaccessibility. Britain lost control of the oceans to the United States not in shipyards but on the assembly lines of American mass production. The United States in turn may lose control to an industrialized China without Mackinder's heartland, or to Russia alone without the German oceanic frontage. Space has not lost its importance as a source of raw materials and bases for defense in depth; sea power will long remain a vital factor in the modern three-dimensional war equation of air-sea-land. But both space and sea power have become integrated within a highly complex network of industry. Mackinder's heartland is still important, but more important is the rising tide of industrialization from China to Brazil.

The centers of heavy industry have become also the centers of war power. Industrial centers will develop fastest where space conditions are most favorable, but whatever the importance to industry of space, the primary condition is man power. The mass of four hundred and fifty million Chinese, when even partly industrialized, is of greater and more immediate importance to the world's balance mechanism than the Russian heartland which contains, from the Urals to the Pacific, less than forty million people. These landlocked "horsemen of the steppes" can no longer overrun even a province. An industrialized Brazil will play a more decisive role in the balance of power on the African continent than the perennially agricultural Egypt or the underpopulated Union of South Africa. Yet China and Brazil, according to the precepts of geopolitics, are barely in the race.

Mackinder's equation, space-to-sea-power-to-world-power, no longer holds. What does hold is a far more complex equation, space-to-man-power-to-industrialization-to-world-power. There have been no drastic changes of frontier in the last century, yet the world balance of power has been profoundly changed by the Industrial Revolution and will be changed even more.

The heartland is but one of many fundamental issues of world polity, and after the defeat of Germany and Japan it will become the least urgent of them. Similarly, the proposals of Mackinder and other British geopoliticians for a series of buffer states between Germany and Russia influenced the Versailles Peace Conference, but the buffer states were swept away like straws in the wind.

Whatever the faults of Mackinder's theorem, he has never gone so far as Haushofer and other *geopolitiker* in the contortions of space to suit antiquated concepts of military strategy—concepts still timing distance by a foot soldier or a ship. They persuaded themselves and some American students of geopolitics that South America below the "hump" of Brazil was strategically indefensible by the United States because it was nearer to Europe than it was to the United States. Spykman wrote many pages on this question.

There is a double fallacy in this view. First, it is no longer space but the centers of industrial production on the space which are important. Latin America south of the Brazilian hump possesses a considerable industrial potential which, properly developed, could become a valuable strategic asset in its and our defense.

Second, the strategic value of distance, overwhelming in the past, is less and less important. We have shifted millions of American soldiers all over the world, a task which would have been impossible a generation back. Strategically the matter of five hundred, a thousand, or two thousand miles is less important than the possession of a strong and continuous chain of air and naval bases. California could be defended adequately against future enemies only by a chain of such bases running across the Pacific up to and including Indo-China and Thailand, nine thousand miles away. The defense of Latin America depends upon our ability to defend the *approaches* to the Western Hemisphere from the Atlantic and the Pacific.

Similarly fallacious is the view that only the countries ranged around the North Pole are strategically and politically important. That leaves out Latin America, Africa, India, Netherlands East Indies, and China. This indeed is a shortsighted view when we consider that in this geopolitically "unimportant" space live more than a billion human beings, with inexhaustible resources, on the threshold of industrialization. Here again many experts in geopolitics repeat their basic fallacy of exaggerating a good idea, the concept of space, until it becomes a bad idea. It is not enough to plot strategic curves on maps. These curves, to be truly strategic, must be corrected and supplemented by the industrial and psychological curves of the vital and growing organisms which are the nations.

THE GERMAN FALLACY OF FORCE

It is not a paradox, but cause and effect, that the two military states, Germany and Japan, which have made the greatest use of force know least about it. Had they known more of the inherent limitations of force and of their own wholly inadequate power, they would not have used it with such cruelty or miscalculated its use so disastrously.

In the case of the Japanese militarists, their cold reptilian reflexes are understandable. They have been taught only the technique of force, not its philosophy and psychology; they learned to use the weapons of force without understanding all of its elements. In Japanese training camps and officers' schools any philosophy not directly related to the handling of weapons was taboo. Bushido code was a substitute for a truly scientific study of force. This is particularly true of the bulk of semi-ignorant Japanese officers who rose from the peasant class.

The Germans should have known better. Yet the Germans, who have written an encyclopedia on worms and three thousand books on geopolitics, have never studied the immensely complex problem of force. They filled libraries with volumes on the use of force in military tactics, without writing one book on its *nature*. Their science of force is the technique of *schreklichkeit*. Theirs was a world governed by a system of penalties, a naïvely savage, medieval world resembling Dante's Inferno. The entire German plan for the conquest of *lebensraum* is based upon that part of force which is least effective and least necessary—the department of terrorism. Force can be wielded as a surgeon's scalpel, as a rapier, or as an ax. The Axis powers were totally oblivious of the difficult art of force, with its vast possibilities when used properly and its grim limitations when abused.

Although, like the Japanese, the Germans were sedulous imitators, they never learned the Anglo-Saxon concept of force. In this concept the true strategy of force is how to avoid using it or how to reduce its use to a minimum. The true strategy of force is based on the inescapable fact that force always generates counterforce, and the more force is used, the greater are the counterforces. In a thousand subtle ways these counterforces wear down, exhaust, and eventually overwhelm the bully, be he a village or a world bully.

The Germans have no concept of the principle of *economy* of force. As a result they have missed thousands of opportunities to organize at least a part of the conquered peoples without creating bitter hatreds and miles of concentration camps. Even in local matters they do not know how to put law above force. Tolerance terrifies them. Sense of humor frustrates them. The Germans could have organized a New Order in Europe that would have had at least a semblance of sense, reducing resistances to a minimum. They still would have been hated, for they came as conquerors, but not so disastrously.

The Germans had definitions of military strategy galore; they understood perfectly that the object of military strategy is to create a positional situation where the minimum use of force will produce the maximum effect. And yet in the larger strategy of force, political and psychological, they were so clumsy that they invariably obtained the minimum effect from the maximum waste of force. Like poor bridge players, the Germans led out all their aces at once and never knew the enormous value of a deuce, or that "pass" is the most eloquent of all the bids.

Moving as though the German mailed fist were the biggest in the world, and as though a fist could do the trick, the German militarists and *geopolitiker* had no understanding of the insurmountable obsta-

cles between them and their *lebensraum*. They never stood a chance
to conquer the world or any substantial part of it, for there were other
and better mailed fists. Hitler might have conquered England and a
large part of Russia, while the Japanese might have spread like the
seven-year locusts over Asia, and still their conquests would have
been in vain. There was the industrial might of the United States in
the impregnable American island, and in addition the United States
possessed the enormous psychological superiority of having the support of the peoples of the world, aroused as counterforces opposing
conquest.

The industrial potentials of the United States, of Britain, and of
Russia were no secret to the geopoliticians and to the German High
Command. They also could have learned about the psychological
aspects of force and the powerful countercurrents generated by its
use. The catastrophe into which they plunged the German nation is
the price paid for ignorance of the true strategy of force. This is a
lesson to be pondered by American, British, Russian, and Chinese
would-be imperialists who may seek in future to strut the stage of
history.

The most striking feature of German failure is the disproportion
between the grandiose geopolitical plan and the means of achieving
it. The high command committed the colossal and amateurish blunder
of seeking to achieve unlimited goals with limited means, a blunder
equaled only by the Japanese High Command when it took upon
Japan's puny industrial shoulders the weight of China, Britain, the
United States, and even perhaps Russia. The mistake of the Japanese,
whose ignorance outside their own bailiwick is fantastic, may be
understandable. But the vaunted, superefficient German High Command also behaved like a Broadway angel who twice backed a losing
play.

Twice the German High Command failed to grasp the significance
of the United States as the world's greatest industrial, and therefore
military, power. In the First World War they excused their miscalcu-
lation as an error of timing; this was not true. Even if France and
Britain had been defeated by Ludendorff, Germany would have been
defeated by the United States, which was then in a position to control
the seas and the unlimited resources of the world.

In the Second World War the German High Command repeated the tragic blunder, failing once more to realize that the way to *lebensraum* in the heartland of Russia lay through New York, Chicago, and San Francisco. The greater were the German victories, the nearer was the inexorable hour of conflict with the United States. It is understandable that an exalted maniac like Hitler should disregard the military mathematics of industrial production, but the German military elite should know at least as much about the power and cohesiveness of the United States as any American high-school boy. And in counting on the remoteness of the United States and on the slowness of the American industrial machine to adapt itself to war, the German High Command stands convicted of ignorance of industrial fundamentals.

How is it possible that the military elite of Germany and Japan should make such stupendous blunders? The answer is psychological: their military science had a mystic core, a delusion of grandeur characteristic of all military cliques. The German High Command believed they were the elite of a master race; German youth was naïvely fanatic because the leaders were. The Japanese High Command were also elite, the chosen of a race of living gods, so Japanese soldiers died hopefully in fox holes.

The elite lived in a foggy climate of delusions, in which industrial statistics did not matter. The Japanese have a proverb: frogs live in a swamp and believe it is an ocean. The Russians have a fable: a bullfrog, green with envy at the size of a cow, began to swell and swell himself up until he exploded. This proverb and this fable picture the fate of the German and Japanese geopoliticians.

So intent were German and Japanese leaders on robbing other peoples of their *lebensraum* that they missed entirely a new kind of *lebensraum,* a vertical expansion through science and co-operation which gives solid promise of a true New Order for all. Had they devoted but a part of their tremendous driving force toward new conquests in the fields of science and industrial organization, Germany and Japan would have been well on the way toward the only *lebensraum* that can be lastingly conquered and they would be honored by humanity.

The price of their ignorance is the Second World War. The price of the ignorance of future war lords will be the Third World War. For there will always be wars and a philosophy of war until the decisive heavy fighting machines are segregated and a system of collective defense is established under which no government or military clique could with impunity attack another nation.

THE AMERICAN HIGH COMMAND

What of the future of our own high command? Will our officers, like the French High Command, be corrupted by politicians? And what will be the broad strategic goals of the American High Command in peacetime? Will they be perverted, like the German High Command, by insane geopolitical dreams of world conquest? On the answers to these questions depends much of the future of our country.

Among many profound changes brought about in the United States by our era of great wars and turmoil is permanent establishment of a very large American military class, consisting of commissioned and non-commissioned officers of army, navy, and air forces. This new military class will be led and largely controlled by its top-ranking officers—the American High Command. In the past the American High Command existed only embryonically. Today we possess the most powerful armed force in the world.

In the future the United States will or should continue to maintain large armed forces. Our shrunken oceans and the ever-present threats, potential or actual, from foreign powers will make it impossible for us to demobilize, as we did after the First World War, and return to the policy of a nuclear land or air force. We shall have to continue our system of conscription so as to build up large numbers of trained reserves, one of the principal factors in Russia's triumphant resistance against Germany, and lack of which largely accounts for the fact that both Britain and the United States lost from one to two precious years before decisive moves against Germany could be made.

Establishment of a system of collective defense will not affect the necessity of maintaining large American forces for many years. It will require years to test the efficiency of such a system, and in all events no system of collective security would be or should be acceptable to the United States unless it includes, as part of an international police force, an American armed force which is larger than that of any other nation, commanded by American officers and stationed in time of peace on the American Strategic Zone.

It follows that a large military class and the American High Command have come to stay. Few Americans would dispute the splendid achievements and management of our army and navy during this war. The remarkable fact in the gigantic job of creating the most powerful armed force in the world in less than three years is not that so many errors were not made but that many more errors were avoided. In all fields of weapons and in many fields of strategy we have surpassed the professional European and Asiatic armed forces organized during generations by military castes. We have proved that a militant democracy can equal and surpass the vaunted superefficiency of the feudalistic castes.

Our high command is democratic not only in form but in spirit. It begins its new role in history without two serious handicaps of the military castes that form the bulk of the European high commands: the handicap of a confused militarist ideology that sets conquest and increase of territories as its ultimate strategic goal, and the handicap of feudalistic castes who look upon themselves as the masters whose "duty" it is to rule the people for their own good.

Thus the American military people start with a clean slate. But the very structure and dynamics of any military organ is such that unless the American High Command fills the void with its own American concepts of long-term strategy and military ethics, there is a danger that a European militarist ideology of conquest and a European militarist caste and code of ethics will find lodging in the heart of the American armed forces. I have shown that our strategic and psychological conditions are so different that we cannot imitate either the European concepts of conquest and geopolitics or the code of ethics of their militarist caste. What is needed is an American concept of basic strategic goals and an American concept of the relation between the armed forces and the national government.

The concept of basic strategic goals will be outlined, at least in preliminary form, in the following chapters on space politics and the American Strategic Zone. The concept of the relations between the armed forces and the national government is contained in the Constitution of the United States, the letter and the spirit of which every responsible American officer is glad to obey. There are some exceptions among irresponsible officers whose heads are not only hot but swollen, and who talk privately about taking over the country and running it themselves. But these exceptions, inevitable in our vast armed forces, merely confirm the rule. What is needed to eliminate any possible exception is an elaboration of the code of ethics already contained within the framework of our Constitution.

The basic object of this general code of ethics should be to draw a sharp line of demarcation between the armed forces of the nation and its politics or civilian government. An army or a navy is an instrument of the will of the nation, as expressed through its constitutional government. It does not matter how good or how bad that government is, whether Democratic or Republican, reactionary or radical— the high command of the army and navy must remain rigidly isolated from the political life of the nation. Its sole concern should be the strategic and tactical defense of the nation against a foreign enemy, and maintenance of order within the country if so directed by the constitutional authority. Only under these conditions can the armed forces retain the confidence of the entire nation.

The greatest tragedy that might befall our future high command would be to be drawn into politics. In France many members of the high command became politicians, supporting this or that political party or group. As a result, numerous political cliques arose within the army itself, and France had Royalist-generals, Socialist-generals, democrat-generals, fascist-generals, and finance-generals. This led to a paralysis of the will of the French High Command that began years before 1939 and ended in the greatest disaster of French history. Such a paralysis of the will within the army and navy itself can be avoided only by a new, rigid code of ethics governing all the higher officers, a code that is based upon the concept of the army and navy as pure instruments of the will of the nation and nothing else. A similar rigid code ruling our Supreme Court preserved the Constitution of the United States.

This does not mean, of course, that an officer should not exercise his duties as a citizen or that a general may not run for president once he has resigned from the army. What I mean fundamentally is that by establishing an American doctrine of basic strategic goals and by maintaining a rigid code of isolation from our political life, the American High Command will achieve its higher purpose of serving as an instrument of the will of the nation.

CHAPTER NINETEEN

The American Strategic Zone

UNTIL A WORKABLE SYSTEM OF SECURITY relieves us from the vigilance necessary to national safety in the present world, we must consider American defense in terms of space politics. But we must establish strategic space requirements for the United States in accordance with the new relations between space and state imposed by the revolution in weapons and communications.

As we have seen, the science or art of space politics is concerned with space from the standpoint of distance and accessibility, with space as it affects resources of goods, particularly strategic raw materials, and as it contains people.

As new industrial techniques reduce distances the strategic value of space is altered; for example, our defensive ocean space may now be considered inferior to the Russian land space. Under modern conditions an ocean may become a highway for invasion; a few powerful air-naval bases in enemy hands can control vast areas. On land space, as the Russian defense in depth proved, every inch of territory can be defended and the advancing enemy becomes progressively weaker as his supply lines lengthen.

Industrialization thus ties up the three aspects of space politics —strategic space, goods, and people—into one. For instance, the tempo of Chinese industrialization will profoundly affect the strategic value of the Netherlands East Indies, and this in turn will profoundly affect strategic problems in the Pacific approaches to our own continent.

The study of space politics, important both to the foreign policy of a state and to the grand strategy of its high command, therefore involves higher military strategy and political geography, but also the structure and dynamics of a state, mass psychology, philosophy, history, and economics. Since the physical problems, the psychology, the history, and the economic structure of states are different, there is an American space politics, a British space politics, a Russian space politics, and so on. But as there are important similarities of situation or of psychology between the American, the British, and the Russian people, it follows that the general principles of American space politics apply also to Britain and Russia.

Despite differences between American and German concepts of the state, it is also possible for students of American space politics to learn from the German mistakes in geopolitics.

THE AMERICAN CONCEPT OF THE STATE

The American state, like the German, is an organism. It is not the crude biological organism of Ratzel, knowing no higher law than brute force; but neither is it the dream state of the humanitarians. The modern American state is a highly complex and deeply integrated social organism. It is subject to the laws of force, but it is also (and willingly) subject to the higher law of co-operation between states.

The American state is also conscious of its present enormous military power, aware that it is a superstate. But as the best means of preserving its great possessions and lasting freedom it must renounce expansion by force, for profit, over the space of other states. This is the basic difference between the American and the German states.

Although the American state renounces the imperialistic use of force, this does not mean that it will not use force, if necessary, to defend itself against the power politics of other states. The American state must take advantage of its immense power to establish just and lasting conditions of strategic security for itself and, if possible, for the world. As there is a time limit to the supremacy of the American state, we must create the best strategic conditions now, while we are powerful.

We must forge our security with the help, if possible, of other states; alone if need be. It is arrant nonsense to assert that the United States depends upon the good will of any great power or powers, such as Russia or Britain. Our concept of security is based first of all on the individual power of the American state and secondly on the power of collective defense with other states. The American state recognizes that other states are subject to the law of expansion and might seek its destruction, also that even peaceful states may fall victim to militarist cliques, which might combine against us. Under such conditions we would need not allies alone, but full use of our own power.

The American Concept of Space

The American concept of space retains the teachings of modern geography but rejects the German metaphysical overtones. Space feeds, shapes, and shelters nations, but it cannot, à la Haushofer, perform miracles.

American space politics is based upon the concept of a living space of continental dimensions. But it is a space which Americans truly possess because it has been cultivated and enriched by millions of American social organisms. The German concept of living space is one of vast lands—blooming valleys, rich mines, productive forests—cultivated and enriched by the labor of other peoples, and to be obtained by conquest.

This concept of conquered space, a driving compulsion behind the Axis powers, is the fundamental difference between American space politics and German geopolitics. American space politics is based on the fact that we have a vast *lebensraum* and seek only to defend it. From opposite concepts of space come opposite goals of strategy. The American goals are strictly limited to defense of the United States and of the strategic approaches to the American continents. American space politics studies the space of other nations only from the standpoint of American security. But German geopolitics considers every space as potentially its own and seeks to conquer space as a springboard for the conquest of still more space.

It is no mere coincidence that the principles of American space politics just outlined are but a continuation of the traditional policies established by Franklin, Jefferson, Hamilton, Monroe, and their successors. Their foreign policy was American space politics at its best. They were keenly conscious of the value of the vast living space that became the American heritage after liberation from England, and they sought to protect it for generations to come. Their whole foreign policy was based on a double concept: first, a common American heritage west of the Atlantic seaboard; second, a strategic space in North and South America, *outside* the living space of the United States, peopled by a friendly Canada and the free Latin-American republics. This outer space was strategic, not in any imperialist sense, but in the sense that these vast neighboring territories must be withdrawn from the pressures and encroachments of European power politics.

In other words, our founding fathers were not content with narrow isolationism. They not only sought to safeguard the United States on its frontiers, but they extended the strategic frontiers for thousands of miles.

This is the deeper meaning of the Monroe Doctrine, which Haushofer cites admiringly as a classic example of pure geopolitics. Because his European military mind was accustomed to consider space only in terms of conquest, to him the object of the Monroe Doctrine was to retain Latin America as a private hunting preserve of the United States, with a view to eventual absorption of the Latin-American continent. He misread the true significance of the Monroe Doctrine as a new and higher type of strategy designed to defend vital approaches to the United States without seeking to conquer peoples or their territories.

Politically, also, the Monroe Doctrine was a withdrawal of the American republics from the European balance-of-power mechanism. Its formulation was considerably influenced by the ideological considerations of the young, free republics, opposed to the reactionary monarchical structure of the European states.

It is true that certain purely imperialistic American adventures have corrupted and undermined the true value of the Monroe Doctrine. But the imperialism was either short-lived or, as in the case of the Mexican wars, it involved thinly settled and undeveloped territory into which waves of American settlers had penetrated in a people's conquest of the soil which, justifiable or not, was well-nigh irresistible. Subsequent American deviations were corrected, to the bewilderment of European space politicians who could not understand why we restored the independence of Cuba or the Philippines, merely reserving leased bases for our defense. Nor could they understand why we hadn't long ago gobbled up Latin America or why we should tolerate the "insolence" of Argentina when a few squadrons of warplanes would turn the trick.

To the "realistic" European politicians, American policy seems naïve and inexperienced. Yet it represents the highest strategic wisdom and a revolutionary innovation in the concept of space politics. Almost for the first time in history an all-powerful state, surrounded by helpless neighbors in possession of immense natural wealth, seeks not to absorb but to strengthen them.

Traditional American policy is characterized by bold imagination and realistic toughness. In 1803 Jefferson maneuvered Napoleon into "selling" Louisiana to the United States. New Orleans controlled the mouth of the Mississippi; this meant that any foreign country in control of New Orleans would indirectly control the whole of the Mississippi Valley and thwart American expansion westward. On this vital issue Jefferson was prepared to make war against America's French ally and to fight on the side of Britain, who only a few years before was America's enemy.

Another perfect, though unfinished, example of American space politics is furnished by Seward's purchase of Alaska and his plan to purchase Greenland. Alaska in the Pacific and Greenland in the Atlantic are like two enormous shoulders, strategically set on top of the American continent. Seward managed to purchase the Alaskan "icebox" but was unable to carry out his plan of acquiring Greenland from Denmark. American politicians in Congress, too immersed in local politics to understand even the rudiments of space politics, laughed him down. Later, too, there was much opposition from the local politicians to America's strategic expansion, but in spite of it the United States gradually projected a network of defensive bases into the far reaches of the Atlantic and Pacific oceans.

The one outstanding blunder of American space politics was Wilson's acquiescence in Japan's demands for the island mandates in the Pacific. Wilson's strategic error was in not realizing that a great nation cannot trust even a perfect system of world collective security—much less the imperfect machinery of the League of Nations—until such a system is tested in actual operation.

From the standpoint of American space politics, the United States has no lasting friendships, no true allies, and no unbreakable system of world security. The United States can count only upon her own strength and her own chain of strategic bases, established in the Atlantic and the Pacific in accordance with America's own requirements. Any system of collective security must include, as the first and indispensable condition of American participation, the essential requirements of American space politics.

Our New Strategic Needs

In the evolution of American space politics there are three stages or periods: the continental, the oceanic, and the transoceanic.

The continental period lasted from the founding of the United States to the Spanish-American War in 1898. Like Russia, we were then almost exclusively a continental power. We had a large oceanic trade but no substantial territorial possessions beyond our continent and no remote naval bases. From the middle of the nineteenth century our continental strength alone made us immune to invasion.

The oceanic period lasted from 1898 until the Second World War in 1939. During this period we rapidly expanded into the Caribbean and the Pacific, acquired important naval bases, dug the Panama Canal, and rivaled Britain as an ocean power. The American continent became a fortress impregnable to great powers from across the seas.

Today we are at the beginning of the transoceanic period. We have become the greatest land, sea, and air power in the world. But this transoceanic period is one of the greatest danger to us, requiring new concepts of strategy and politics for our security.

We are on the eve of losing both our industrial supremacy and our historical immunity to invasion from across the oceans. In another twenty or twenty-five years, unless we take strategic and political precautions now, both the Pacific and the Atlantic shores of the American continent will be exposed to powerful and eventually decisive drives from the combination of hostile industrialized states.

I call this period *transoceanic* because the only effective strategic precautions that we could take would be to maintain a powerful network of air-naval bases in the Atlantic Ocean near the African and European continents, and in the Pacific on all the non-British islands and on the mainland of Asia.

The strategic concept of American space, first continental and then oceanic, must be extended to an outer, transoceanic zone of defense near or on the shores opposite our continent. Only in this manner can we effectively lock and bolt the outer gates of the American continent in the Atlantic and Pacific oceans.

The transoceanic policy of strategic defense is paralleled in the field of balance politics by a transoceanic policy of active participation in European and Asiatic politics, in order to preserve a favorable world balance of power. A political policy of narrow isolationism is incompatible with transoceanic strategy.

The American continent is shaped like a gigantic ant, with its narrow waist at Panama. Strategically it will be as impossible to defend America without controlling distant air-naval bases as it would be for an ant to defend itself without its antennae. Without such bases as feelers, America is but a rump continent; we can be blockaded, isolated, and cut off from the world by future hostile powers. Then, with our activities limited to cross-continental bombing, our enemies can proceed methodically with preparations to invade the American continent. If they choose, they can stage a hundred "Pearl Harbors" over our vital industrial centers from their island bases in the oceans.

The greater the industrial development of the world, the farther away from the American continent must our defenses be located. We must anticipate the world's industrial development *now* and build our defenses accordingly. The beginning and the end of our strategic defense lie not somewhere in the middle Pacific, but across the oceans, near the shores of Europe, and on the mainland of Asia. And this defense must be entrusted not to "friendly foreign powers," but to our own army and air-naval forces. The articles of all American treaties of friendship with other great powers must be rooted in the American Strategic Zone.

The only effective defense in depth of the American continent is a network of fortified, unsinkable aircraft carriers, covering a vast area of ocean for thousands of miles. On this fortified network will be located new types of ships and super-fighting planes, capable of intercepting the flights of heavy bombers from continent to continent. In the Atlantic this network will girdle the shores of Europe and Africa from Iceland through the Azores to Cape Verde. In the Pacific it will form a bridge of fortified bases from Pearl Harbor and Truk, through the Philippines and the Netherlands East Indies, ending on the continent of Asia in Indo-China and Thailand. Practically all of this gigantic chain of bases has already been built, and most of it is already occupied by Americans, or soon will be.

With such a strategic zone the United States will be in a position not only to defend the approaches to the American continent, but to intervene quickly and effectively in either Europe or Asia whenever future Hitlers seize the resources of powerful nations for probable aggression against us. The American people have learned by bitter experience that it is cheaper to break up the political formations of war lords than the formations of their bombers.

There is another way, of course—the way of collective defense. The *most important* solution lies in a workable system of collective defense, but the *first* solution must lie in a new concept of the American Strategic Zone. Only when we have achieved a minimum security can we seriously turn our attention to the necessary task of helping to rebuild the world spiritually and materially.

Let us, however, consider the space of our American Strategic Zone from the standpoint of our relations with the peoples living on that space. For the military value of fortified bases can be drastically reduced or even destroyed by the psychological reactions of peoples living on that space if these peoples are hostile or undeveloped. We must therefore fortify ourselves not only in the strategic space, but in the hearts of the peoples.

The fundamental blunder of German and Japanese geopolitics was to ignore the enormous strategic value of the peoples. They saw no further than the range of their guns. They forgot that every individual is himself a miniature fortress and that this fortress can never be taken by storm. In the American concept of space politics, the relation of space to the peoples living in that space is as important strategically as the fortified bases.

What should be our relations to the one hundred and twenty million Latin Americans? And how can we best integrate the one hundred and twenty million peoples of Malaysian stock in the Pacific Islands, Indo-China, and Thailand, so that these peoples will become our free, loyal, and permanent allies?

CHAPTER TWENTY

First Step: Regional Federation

THE LATIN-AMERICAN PEOPLES do not doubt the sincerity of the American people in their wish to be good neighbors. Nor do they doubt the good intentions of the American government. Moreover, the Latin-American leaders are beginning to realize that we and they face common danger from enemies across the Atlantic and the Pacific, and that only the power of the United States will prevent the Latin-American republics, in the future as in the past, from becoming European colonies. There has existed, since Bolivar, a natural solidarity among all the American nations before Europe and Asia. The two great cultures—the Spanish-American and the North American—are supplementary to each other. Each can learn a great deal from the other. The two great economies can be made mutually supplementary; each can profit from the vast resources of the other and yet maintain individual ties with the rest of the world.

Why, then, are the Latin-American people so hesitant in grasping our hand, outstretched in sincere friendship? Why has our Good Neighbor policy produced so little of lasting value despite our extraordinary propaganda efforts?

The answer is that between the Latin-American nations and our own stands a wall of fear and suspicion a century high. Latin Americans cannot forget that in the past the foreign policy of the United States has been paved mainly with good intentions. Even today our

Good Neighbor policy consists largely of honeyed words, noble resolves, diplomatic speeches, blank checks, and behind-the-scenes deals with politicos.

"What guarantee is there," all but a few Latin Americans ask, "that the United States will not change its Good Neighbor policy into a tough neighbor policy after the first election? How can we trust our whole future to the shifting sands of American sentiment or to the kindness of one of many presidents of the United States, some of whom in the past plotted our destruction?"

Not only is there no protection whatsoever for the Latin-American republics against a change of heart or a change of policy by the United States, but the existing relations are those of an all-powerful sovereign state dealing separately with each of the twenty weak sovereign states, who can make no appeal higher than to the State Department of the United States. There is no separate "Pan-American Body Politic" with a constitution, however limited, and a higher court before which all American nations, including the United States, are equal. The present relations of the United States with its twenty divided neighbors are, in effect, the antiquated relations of a powerful protector who can back up his sovereignty by his military might and enormous wealth, dealing separately with satellized nations whose sovereignty is but a polite diplomatic fiction, since they have neither the physical nor the *constitutional* power to protect their sovereignty. Under these conditions the present Pan American Union is even more hollow than the League of Nations at its worst. For in the League of Nations there were at least two great powers, Britain and France, who served as mutual checks to each other's ambitions. In the present Pan American Union there is only one all-powerful state with twenty satellized "sovereignties," each suspicious of the other and all fearful of the big boss.

This is not the wish of the American people or the American government, but the reality of the situation. It is all very well to say that we are not going to abuse our power and that we are going to behave like a good big brother toward his little brothers if they are good. The point is that we *might* abuse our power, and we certainly did abuse it in the past. The Latin-American republics, proud of their own civilization and sensitive to the point of morbidity about the inferior position which history allotted them, naturally seek, by hook or crook, some means to improve their position. They certainly will not open their hearts or release their good will until some real solution is found that will insure to them Freedom from Fear to a far greater extent than the freedom now promised.

So great is the fear of the United States among even the progressive elements in Latin America that some hoped for a stalemate peace between the United Nations and Germany, though they strongly disapproved of Hitlerism. These considerations were fully confirmed during a recent journey I made to our nearest Latin-American neighbor, Mexico—a country which I learned to love nearly thirty years ago, though I was in a Mexican jail for having participated in the Zapatist revolution.

From the Latin-American viewpoint, two great calamities have taken place since the First World War. The first is the revolution in military weapons and communications which has completely and hopelessly disarmed them. In the past they could heroically defend their freedom by going into the mountains with their rifles. It would have required an enormous army and many years of costly effort for the United States to conquer even parts of Mexico, let alone South America. Today a few hundred tanks and planes would suffice to occupy and control all of the Latin-American states. The second calamity is the destruction of the European balance of power. With a victorious, all-powerful United States, the Latin Americans during the next fifteen or twenty years can no longer count on even a limited support of any of the great European powers to check possible aggression from the north.

Thus our Latin-American neighbors feel like a man completely disarmed who lives on an isolated island with a giant, the United States, who is armed to the teeth. Until we remove this fear of the "Yankee Colossus" by the Latin-American nations, we cannot count on them as true friends. Until we implement the Good Neighbor policy with an integrated system based on a higher law governing the relations of the United States and the sovereign Latin-American republics as equals, its noble words are futile.

Yet, without the good will of the Latin Americans and their cooperation in the common defense of the Western Hemisphere, our whole strategic zone will be dangerously weakened by the suppressed hostility of the twenty million Latin Americans, now being rapidly industrialized. We can, of course, conquer Latin America, assuming the people of the United States can stomach all the gore that such a conquest would entail. But if we were to conquer Latin America, this would only facilitate our defeat in future wars against European or Asiatic powers. One does not beat up one's younger brother repeatedly and then expect enthusiastic co-operation in a common enterprise.

How, then, can the United States achieve its goal of removing the wall of fear and perpetuating the co-operation with the Latin-American nations, who are our natural and necessary allies? The solution exists, and could be carried out immediately, with a little bit of imagination and intelligent planning. This solution is highly acceptable to our Latin-American neighbors, and at the same time is effective in insuring, on the basis of sovereignty for each state, our common interests in the Western Hemisphere. The roots of this solution are to be found in the great and practical vision of Simon Bolivar, who wrote in 1818:

"Nothing, I repeat, in all I have laid down is so important at the moment as the formation of a League of American States. It must not, however, be founded solely on the principles of mutual assistance in offense and defense. It must be closer than the Holy Alliance, which was founded merely to suppress national freedom. A council or congress of plenipotentiaries should meet at once to safeguard all American interests and settle all disputes. If there is no such organization, we shall find ourselves plunged into disastrous wars which have already destroyed other less fortunate nations."

Bolivar's contemporary, Thomas Jefferson, who learned to speak Spanish and thought all North Americans should, wrote: "I hope to see a cordial fraternization among all the American nations . . . and their coalescing in an American system of policy. . . . I should rejoice to see the fleets of Brazil and the United States riding together as brethren of the same family, pursuing the same objects."

Although the Monroe Doctrine was specifically formulated in 1823, Alexander Hamilton sought to popularize it as early as 1787, and went beyond the Monroe Doctrine. He maintained that the new

United States would strengthen the new world ". . . in erecting one great American system superior to the control of all trans-Atlantic force or influence . . ."

All these historic proposals for joint action support me when I propose that the United States government or the government of any leading Latin-American republic take steps immediately to establish an integrated regional system, to be called the Pan-American Federation. The basis of the system shall be a regional constitution or a Treaty of Collective Defense, to be adopted by the United States government and those of the Latin-American republics who voluntarily choose to become member states.

In order to implement and integrate this Treaty of Collective Defense, a government separate from the governments of the member states shall be established as a government of the Pan-American Federation. The powers of this government will be strictly limited to matters pertaining to the prohibition of wars of aggression, common defense against foreign powers, and the peaceful settlement of disputes with interpretation of treaties by a Regional Supreme Court.

Representation in the Pan-American Federation shall be based on two equal blocs: the bloc of the United States, with its one hundred and thirty million people, and the Latin-American bloc, with its one hundred and twenty million people. The Latin-American nations will arrange among themselves the selection of the representatives from the Latin-American bloc on the basis of population, except that Brazil, in order to equalize powers, shall not have a larger representation than Mexico, which is the next most populated state. For the purpose of regional representation, Guatemala, El Salvador, Nicaragua, Honduras, Costa Rica, and the Republic of Panama shall be considered as one state. Other smaller Latin-American nations may be likewise grouped. The structure of this Pan-American Federation is set forth in Book Two, the World Federation Plan.

But regardless of whether or not the World Federation is first established, the Pan-American Federation is of vital importance to the security of the American and Latin-American peoples.

One may argue, of course, that such a system of Pan-American Federation still cannot fully guarantee our Latin-American neighbors against aggression by the powerful United States, who may choose to violate the Treaty of Collective Defense. From an absolute standpoint, it is true. But I submit that there is a vast difference between our present power-politics Pan American Union and the proposed collective-defense Pan-American Federation. Quarrels and dissensions will not be settled in the heat of passion or by arbitrary decision of our State Department or of the foreign offices in the Latin-American republics, but by the highest court of the Western Hemisphere and on the basis of a constitution to which the people of the United States and the people of Latin America have pledged their solemn word. Once power politics, ever present among sovereign states, is eliminated, most of the quarrels bred by fears will also be eliminated. We will have announced, by action rather than by words, that as far as our neighbors in Latin America are concerned, the American people have thrown the gun away.

If we thus establish the Pan-American Federation now, on the basis of a higher law of nations, we will electrify the world and we will attach to us, as perpetual allies, the Latin-American peoples.

One may be certain that Bolivar and Jefferson, if they were alive today, would gladly underwrite the provisions of this Pan-American Federation as politically just and strategically sound. This or a better proposal for a Pan-American Federation should be strongly supported by public opinion in the United States and especially in Latin-American countries. Mexico, most of Central America, and some republics at least of South America would gladly join. Like us, they have everything to gain and nothing to lose. Those who did not join for any reason whatsoever would still remain our good neighbors, retaining security against aggression, but losing the enormous advantage of economic and cultural co-operation within the federation.

It has been said repeatedly by members of our government that we must avoid too concrete discussion of the problems of the world settlement with our European and Asiatic allies, lest "dissensions" jeopardize the united war front. I do not agree with this viewpoint, and in fact I believe that while such discussions could in no way have jeopardized the war front, the lack of preliminary concrete planning has already jeopardized the peace front. But in the case of the Pan-American Federation even such fallacious objections could not be raised. I am sure that neither Britain nor Russia nor China will find their interests unfavorably affected if we seek to establish a new, more just, and more lasting order in the Western Hemisphere. As for our Latin-American neighbors, there is little doubt but that they would be more united in any war effort and far more united in our peace effort if we follow the lines of policy as laid down by the liberator of Latin America, Simon Bolivar.

The Pan-American Federation will not only help mightily to insure the lasting security of the Western Hemisphere, but may well become the foundation for a larger system of world collective defense. Once the Pan-American Federation is established it will be necessary only to obtain the adherence of either the British Empire or Russia or China, in order to proclaim a new integrated system of world collective defense—a system already tested in an important area.

In the Malaysian region there are one hundred and twenty million people of the proud and gifted brown race, whose psychosocial pattern has been submerged through centuries of exploitation by the Mongolians, the Hindus, and the Europeans. The Mongolian is as much a hereditary enemy of the Malaysians as of the white. The Malaysians live on lands which, as has been pointed out, are of vital necessity to the strategic defense of the American continent. Our problem, therefore, is not only to build up a chain of fortified bases but to build up these Malaysian peoples on the basis of freedom as our strong and permanent allies. In so doing we must seek to preserve the legitimate historic interests of our allies, the Netherlands and France.

The United States seeks no imperialistic advantages in Malaysia. Our object is to do for the whole of Malaysia what we have done for the Philippines, and to win the friendship of the whole of Malaysia as we won the friendship, and help against a common enemy, of the Philippines.

The best way for us to accomplish this is by establishing a Malaysian Federation, composed of the Philippines (sovereign), the Netherlands East Indies (under Netherlands sovereignty), Indo-China (under French sovereignty), and the smaller Pacific islands of the Malaysian region. Although all the members of the Malaysian Regional Federation shall be either sovereign or fully autonomous, the Federation should be under the trusteeship of the United States until the economic and educational standards of the Malaysian peoples are sufficiently developed. The structure of the Malaysian Federation is set forth in Book Two, the World Federation Plan.

So established, the Malaysian Federation will be a natural bridge between the nations of Asia and the nations of the Americas, as well as a powerful anchor for the American strategic defense of the eastern Pacific Ocean. But only close co-operation between the United States and the Malaysian peoples, as with Latin America, on the basis of equality of peoples and freedom of states, can make possible the creation of this vast strategic zone of four hundred million people, which will serve as a mighty bulwark for their common defense against aggression.

CHAPTER TWENTY-ONE

The Unsolved Problems

As PREVIOUS CHAPTERS HAVE SHOWN, balance politics and space politics form the nationalist basis of our foreign policy. They seek the security of the United States against future aggressors in the power of the United States alone. They assume, correctly, that sovereign nations live in a world of force, and that the greater the nation, the greater the threats to her from other sovereign states.

But there remains a third principle of foreign policy, with its corollaries, here repeated: *The United States, as the strongest and therefore the most threatened state, must use its present power to establish an integrated system of effective collective defense against wars of aggression.*

This principle has to do with the internationalist basis of our policy. Its corollaries are two: first, *a system of collective defense acceptable to the United States must provide for all possible contingencies, such as future betrayals and coalitions of other powers, and must not deprive the United States either of its sovereign rights (except the right to wage wars of aggression) or of its own military power to defend itself.*

The second corollary is that *until a system of collective defense is fully established and thoroughly tested in actual operation, the United States must not abandon the first and second principles* (balance politics and space politics).

The reader will judge for himself, but I am convinced that principles and methods of foreign policy based on the use or threat of force alone cannot insure lasting security for the United States. In a world of force we have no choice save to use the methods of balance politics and space politics. In fact we must insist during the coming world settlement that our American Strategic Zone is included as an indispensable precaution, regardless of any alliance or system of collective defense in which we might participate. Still, if that is all we obtain from this war, we will have suffered a defeat in peace after our victory in war. We will have increased considerably our chance of victory in future wars, but that is all. We and our children will be condemned to carry the enormous load of armaments and to respond to preparation for war by any other power with new preparations for war. The cost, in the best of power-politics worlds, is staggering. Above all, even with our integrated strategic zone of four hundred million, and even with a ruthless policy of balance politics, we will be far from secure. We can hope for postponement of the sentence of execution, but we cannot assure for our grandchildren lasting survival as a nation.

Under these conditions it would be political folly not to seek, in addition to the tried methods of security based on the use or threat of national arms, new and as yet untried methods of collective defense. It would be criminal folly for the most powerful and least aggressive nation in the world to surrender the hope of generations because of the temporary defeat of the League of Nations, when the battle for collective security was fought with inadequate weapons under almost impossible conditions. Let simple and superficial minds babble about "human nature" and "the inevitability of war." If we have a spark of the divine or a particle of the scientific spirit, we must not leap to such a tragic conclusion until all hopes are exhausted. We must search for a specific cure for the social cancer of war because the only hope for America lies in lasting peace for the world.

Let us start the search by reviewing briefly various proposals for world peace now being put forth.

The democracies are today more tragically unprepared for peace than they were for war. They have no comprehensive and concrete peace plan, which may be the major tragedy of our time as it was of the last war.

The country is filled with planless planners; everyone is telling everyone else what should be done about our "peace aims" or the "postwar order." But no one offers a blueprint in the sense that a blueprint for a bomber or the German High Command's detailed plan for an attack on Norway is a plan; no one has a plan that compares in forethought, precision, and timing to any one of thousands of simple war plans prepared whenever an air squadron or a division attacks or even moves from one place to another. No one has anything even vaguely resembling a simple legal contract, such as must be prepared for thousands of business transactions. Yet the world order can be built only upon the foundation of social contracts (backed up by judges who in turn are backed up by policemen) between the citizens and the state, between sovereign states, and between all of these and the world organism.

What Happened to the League

It may be argued that the League of Nations was a world organism of sorts, superimposed upon the sovereign nations. If there were no better plan, I myself would gladly work for an improved League of Nations, imperfect though it must be, as the best plan available. Yet, as all the world knows, the League failed of acceptance in this country and failed again when faced with fascism and war.

Part of the trouble was with the contract; the articles of the League Covenant were clumsy and often contradictory. The covenant itself was a thin political wrapper, without economic content, and, in its naïve faith in world "public opinion," oblivious of the tremendous psychological and military forces raging in the world. Ill-suited to prevent disasters in the twentieth century, the League Covenant merely modified *Le projet de la paix perpetuelle* by l'Abbé de St. Pierre, who lived in eighteenth-century France and was himself inspired by Dubois, Sully, and still earlier thinkers of medieval Europe. Yet Wilson's bullet-riddled covenant is the nearest thing to a real peace plan I have seen so far.

It is possible that even a perfect League, under the then existing conditions, could not have staved off the new cycle of wars, since the age of planes and tanks was only dawning and segregation of the decisive heavy weapons would have been difficult. But by affording better organized defense against the feudo-militarists it might have limited the scope of their depredations. It is therefore tragic that, like a child with a beautiful soul but with defective bone and muscular structure, the League of Nations was fated to die in infancy.

Leadership in the League was paralyzed from the start by twoscore of sovereign voices ready to shout "No!" while seeking a concession for shouting "Yes!" The League assembly resembled too much the *Sejm* of the Polish nobles in the Middle-Ages, where a single shout of "I veto" by a small provincial noble was enough to paralyze the government in the midst of dangerous wars against the Turks, the Russians, and the Germans—a weakness responsible in part, at least, for the subsequent partition of Poland.

Above all, the League Covenant failed to solve the key problem of any government, the problem of effective use of force. The world social organism, if it is to survive, must have—in addition to a noble soul and superior brains—a quick and powerful muscular system. It must possess a military kick far stronger than that of any member state or combination of member states comprising it. Yet this powerful government must be of such a nature that except in the perpetual collective defense against aggression and the prohibition of war and other related matters, it cannot govern at all. Otherwise we risk substituting for a smaller tyranny of state governments (where escape or remedies might be found) the intolerable tyranny of a world government where no escape and no remedy will be available.

Today it is unnecessary to criticize the League of Nations except as it serves as an example of how we failed. In the light of what has happened, it is much easier to criticize than to formulate a workable plan; indeed, brilliant criticism of the League has already been made by Mr. Clarence Streit, whose "Federal Union" plan seems to me quite as impractical as Wilson's. At one with Mr. Streit in his analysis of what was wrong with the League, I must part from him before the politically unscalable heights of "Federal Union." But in justice to Mr. Streit's approach to the true solution, his proposals deserve careful consideration.

THE FALLACY OF "UNION NOW"

The basic idea of Federal Union is alluringly simple: The United States Constitution is a marvelous piece of work—let's use it broadly

as a model for a new Federal Union which will include the British
Empire and the remaining democracies of the world!

Originally Mr. Streit's plan included many democracies within the
same federal union. Since then France and most of the other democracies have disappeared, and Mr. Streit's "Union Now" of democracies has been reduced to union with Britain, Eire, and the four British
dominions, while the remaining democracies are invited to join later.

Mr. Streit has also revised, from time to time, some of the other
features of his system. It has not been decided whether the proposed
union congress will consist of one or two houses, whether there shall
be one or two chiefs of state of the union, operating simultaneously
or, as the Roman consuls, on alternate dates. Nor is the constitution
drawn, except for an "illustrative draft" taken almost entirely from
the United States Constitution with the substitution of a parliamentary board for the President, and discussion of the Canadian plan
for senate representation by population.

Future constitutional conventions of the union are to decide these
matters; meanwhile Mr. Streit proposes as the supreme government
of the union an intercontinental Congress, with each member democracy represented *in proportion to its population*. These representatives will be responsible directly to the people of each member state,
instead of to its government. There will also be set up executive and
judicial organs.

The colonies of Great Britain and of all other member states shall
be transferred to the government of the federal union. There will be
a common citizenship among all "self-governing" democracies, and
the government of the union shall have the sole power over war,
peace, foreign affairs, currency, trade, communications, admissions to
membership of other democratic states, and generally all the other
powers now possessed under the United States Constitution by our
Federal Government.

An important provision is that a member state can have any form
of government, including even monarchy, provided such a government is a "democracy." Mr. Streit excludes Russia and China until
they become "true democracies." However, Mr. Streit has recently
advocated a loose over-all organization, along the lines of the League

of Nations he criticized, in which other non-democratic nations can participate until they become of democratic age.

Regardless of theory, Mr. Streit's plan has only an infinitesimal chance of acceptance, still less of survival, for the following reasons:

It is psychologically impossible to obtain, at least for several years, the necessary two-thirds majority for amendments to the American Constitution which would be required. Federal union would require drastic revision of the constitutional setup, in order to build the larger and considerably different structure of Mr. Streit's union within the narrower structure of the United States. Analysis of pro- and anti-British forces in the psychological pattern of the American nation shows the "natural" anti-British elements count more than one third. To these elements the innate conservatism of the public will add opposition to any constitutional change.

England, under Mr. Streit's plan, loses her empire: Under Mr. Streit's plan the people's representatives from the democracies, comprising the supreme government of the union, are elected on the basis of population. As a result the country with the largest self-governing population will control the union.

To start with, the United States, with nearly one hundred and forty million, will have a great majority over the populations of England, Canada, Australia, South Africa, Eire, and New Zealand. It will therefore control the union. As the union expands with the development of democracies over the world, control will pass into new hands until it lodges finally with the Chinese and the Indians, whose politicians will then peacefully conquer the world without firing a shot.

If there be a senate, in addition to the union's single chamber, designed to check overwhelming control by the United States, then one of three things will happen: either (a) the senate will have a greater power than the lower chamber, in which case the union is of course unacceptable to the United States; or (b) the senate will have an equal power with the lower chamber, in which case there will be a series of disastrous deadlocks ending as a rule in favor of the stronger and more homogeneous United States; or (c) the senate will have less power than the lower chamber, in which case the control remains in the hands of the United States, with added acrimony.

Whichever way the cat jumps, there is the United States now—and China or India tomorrow.

As British colonies, under the plan, would be turned over to the union government, the United States would become the immediate possessor of all the colonies of the British Empire. The American people will have no objection against Mr. Streit's "Union Now" with Britain, provided Mr. Streit first secures the approval of the British government and of the majority of the British people. Such an approval will, I believe, be impossible to secure.

England herself becomes a poor-white dominion: In Mr. Streit's union no member state can impose tariffs or make treaties. These and other important sovereign functions are taken away from the member democracies and concentrated in the government of the union—i.e., controlled by the United States. The sovereign rights of member democracies are thus reduced to the rump sovereignty of the states of Rhode Island or Pennsylvania. The British dominions and Eire, with their homeopathic representation in the union congress, will be reduced to the role of political kibitzers.

Deprived of control of her own currency, and with no raw materials from her vast empire, industrial machinery, or man power to compete with those of the United States, England will be reduced to a status worse than that of a colony, or that of the Southern states after the Civil War.

Though this picture may seem exaggerated, it illustrates the logical end of a union in which one all-powerful party (in this case the United States) is in majority. It is true that some American representatives will side with England, as, before the Civil War, some American senators were in sympathy with the South. But on fundamental issues there will be no remedy save secession, which means dissolution or civil war. Thus the union, instead of achieving world peace, will add to already existing threats a new type of war—fratricidal conflicts between the Anglo-American commonwealths.

World democracy would wreck us: At first glance, the "Union Now" plan seems a splendid bargain for the United States. The catch is found in Mr. Streit's principle of representation by population (which first gives us majority control) and Mr. Streit's other principle of inviting non-English democracies to join the union, which loses us the majority. As long as England, Eire, and the four British dominions are the only member democracies, Mr. Streit's calculations give us twenty-seven votes out of forty-nine in the union congress. We might survive the addition of the Netherlands democracy, although it is highly dubious that Dutch burghers would be willing to join us and hand over the rights (whatever they may be worth) to the Dutch East Indies.

But after that our situation becomes more and more precarious. Italy goes wildly democratic—and the British Empire, under American sponsorship, is in jeopardy. Democratic Greece joins the union, and we must fear the Greeks bearing votes. France will come in, and a "re-educated" Germany will knock at the door—still the Anglo-Saxon nations might, by closing their ranks, outvote the newcomers.

Another democratic victory, and we are lost! Suppose that the long and naïvely expected democratic revolution breaks out in Russia? If democratic Russia and China are admitted, not only the United States but all the Anglo-American nations will become a permanent minority, their interests controlled by elections held a hemisphere away. In time American or British troops could be used by some Russian or Chinese Lincoln to put down the rebellions of American or British peoples.

That is, this could happen if the original member states proceeded, in accordance with Mr. Streit's plan, to admit new members according to their democratic deserts. But according to the constitution, admission of new democracies is rigidly controlled by the union congress; and this article strikes a deathblow to all hope for world order and world peace. Either the federal union will admit new members or not. If it does admit new democracies throughout the world, the Anglo-Americans lose control. If the Anglo-Americans wish to retain control they cannot admit new members, however democratic.

Political realists will see that it will always be easy to find a convenient definition of democracy to exclude applicants on the ground that they do not possess the proper degree of democratic ripeness. This means that "Union Now" is for all practical purposes an exclusive imperialist club, and that it is actually "union never" as far as the rest of the world is concerned.

I have no doubt that Mr. Streit, a sincere idealist, believes all he says about federal union as "the nucleus of a world government of, by, and for *you—the people*." He writes of "the United States of the World" and, more temptingly still, "the United States of Mankind," and would no doubt include the planet Venus if he could. But his followers who cherish visions of a peaceful world order should realize that the very structure of federal union creates an almost insurmountable obstacle to world peace.

For—the final objection—Mr. Streit's exclusive club will force the counterunion of all the powerful nations excluded from the Anglo-American federal union. The revived Latins and Germans, Soviet Russia, a rising China—none of these nations could for long tolerate the obvious threats to world dominion of two hundred million powerful, wealthy, and united Anglo-Saxons. The inevitable new wars would not be wars of the "have-nots" against the "haves," but of the "left-outs" against Mr. Streit's member states. Even the League of Nations, since it excluded no one and provided for all, offered a better theory.

These fatal contradictions in Mr. Streit's plan do not diminish the great service which he and his supporters have given to the noble ideal of Anglo-American accord, any more than the fatal contradictions in the League of Nations diminish the service of Wilson, and all who fought and lived for the League of Nations, to the even more noble ideal of world peace. Even though the methods of both plans were wrong, the ideals were right, necessary, and today feasible.

Both the proposed union and the League offered rickety political frameworks, without economic substance and without the enzymes of mass psychology. Their builders failed to calculate the tremendous strains and stresses of disruptive social forces that can crush political structures like cardboard. Thus both fail to solve the basic social problem, the problem of war.

The Economic Cure-Alls

Admirable plans for economic help in the postwar world have been outlined in the United States by Vice-President Wallace and others. But there is a serious danger that these generous plans will come to naught unless a powerful framework of world federation is established, meanwhile, to carry them out. No matter how generous the American people may be, their assistance will be at best but a salve, not a solution. The true solution can be worked out only by the nations concerned, and only under the powerful protection of a world federation able to provide adequate peace. Without that requisite, no international boards, no commissions of abundance, and no abundance of commissions can save the world.

Not only the collectivist groups but many important elements among the liberals are inclined toward the economic solution of the postwar world. When their faith in the League of Nations burned out, long ago, mistakenly they lost faith in a permanent world order. Today temporary, makeshift solutions are the limit of their horizon, with hope for an economic peace the pot of gold at the end of the rainbow. But we need not expect to find world order in the triumph of any politico-economic system, be it the communist, feudo-militarist, capitalist-democratic, or what have you. The world cannot wait until the communists and socialists unite the proletarians of the world in perpetual peace, or until the American collectivists, casting miraculous billions of American dollars upon the stormy waters, get them back in waves of abundance; until Anglo-American imperialists conquer the world under the flag of democracy and "with the consent of the governed," or even until the Republican party wins an election and lets the world once more stew in its own juice. The difficulty is not in determining the relative value of these solutions, but in the fact that none of them has the slightest chance of success for years or for decades over the whole world. World order can give the various economic plans a chance to work themselves out in peace. But world order cannot be established in a tumult of conflicting ideologies, interests, and sects, each claiming complete control.

The best way we can save the nations of the world is by helping them to save themselves from another conflict. If the American government attempts to impose heavy sacrifices upon the American people to save the world economically, having saved it militarily, it is certain to face serious trouble at home. If the American government limits its salvation projects to feeding, clothing, and temporarily assisting the "neediest cases," it will have trouble abroad. In either case, while suffering peoples are fed and economically assisted from American bounty, a prolonged period of foreign military occupation, following upon a devastating war, will inevitably mean violence, indescribable chaos, and revolutions throughout the world. The net result will be either an attempt to establish world-wide Anglo-American dictatorship, in which case Russia and other powers will be preparing for another series of even bloodier wars, or, after the withdrawal of British-American troops, a series of national dictatorships also preparing for war.

The Fallacy of the Long Armistice

One point of agreement with Mr. Streit is the vital importance for the United Nations of planning *now* for the peace to come. Otherwise there is danger of losing the war through a "rump" peace, or of making peace only to lose it in the storm of the postwar world.

This problem of *immediacy* is neglected by most of the peace planners, many of whom worry no more about the time factor in the battle of peace than did certain generals at the slow period of the war, or their industrial colleagues in the battle of production.

Indeed, many planners agree as to the advisability of postponing any real peace plan for a decade or so, after a "transitional" or "experimental" period. One important, nationally known peace organization seriously debated the advisability, after the defeat of Germany, of a "ten-year armistice." Other groups propose periods of three to ten years. They concede that it is small consolation to a very sick man if a doctor prescribes a cure to be applied a decade or two later. But they propose to keep the patient, meanwhile, in a strait jacket of military occupation, guarded by American and British soldiers. Lest he break his heart by straining in the strait jacket, he can be kept well doped with economic pills.

These period planners should consider that since the First World War there have been twenty-five special armistice periods, each of two minutes' duration, making fifty minutes altogether. A pause in the traffic at eleven o'clock on November eleven may be harmless or even beneficial, but postponement of peace plans to a more convenient season means lessening the chance of peace with every second lost. After the war the relative strength of the different states will undergo immediate change. National interests which were quiet, because dependent, will rise to impose new demands. Gaining strength, they will break old promises and make new alignments. In the midst of ideological jealousies and economic rivalries, claims of sovereignty and territorial grabs, power politics will once more mount its horse of war.

While each member of ten thousand peace commissions makes a speech, and the ambassadors of sovereign nations trade consent for concessions, the organization of the world will be left to international (meaning Anglo-American) "commissions" and "boards." The net result will be either an Anglo-American world-wide dictatorship, assuming that Russia and the other powers would stand for it, or— as happened after the last world war—a series of national dictatorships preparing for the new war.

Delay is actually the device of the planless planners who offer only "peace aims" or "points," and who, like the French strategists, bristle with negatives. The danger from some of these armchair planners of peace is far greater than from the military commanders, for we can lose our military battles, change moth-eaten generals, and still win the war. The battle of peace we can lose only once, as we lost it before when Wilson went to Paris armed only with his Fourteen Points. There for long, weary months the politicians and planners wrangled and worked on the Versailles Treaty while the people clamored for peace, *any* kind of peace. The practical British liberal, Lloyd George, kept asking Wilson, "How, how, how?" and the French cynic, Clemenceau, kept insisting, "With what?" Certainly Wilson made a thundering reply: "By and with the brotherhood of man." He was right; this is the point of the whole history of the world. But even the brotherhood of man needs power and machinery (and that means blueprints) for its operation.

A Conclusion and a Prophecy

Thus the democracies have reached an absurd situation: because no definite and satisfactory master plan for world settlement has been evolved, it is openly advocated that *the best plan is not to have any plan.* It is urged upon us that we do not hurry, but wait and shop around. As a result, the world is heading for a new postwar catastrophe which will dwarf the convulsions following the First World War.

One need not be a prophet to see clearly the sinister shadows of coming events in the postwar world. The time bombs are already being set to explode in future wars. Ostensibly, democracy will "triumph" everywhere, since the neo-feudalists everywhere will assume the protective coloration of a democratic front. But once the heavy blanket of this war has lifted, confused and violent struggles for power will be resumed by the political parties and ideologies within each of the democracies, weakening them; and among nations there will be no effective force other than nationalism—distilling, unchecked, the poisons of power politics for future wars.

A smiliar disastrous pattern of a coalition's victory and a victor's peace of revenge has been repeated many times in history, with practically identical speeches by the victorious statesmen, promising the identical lasting peace. Similar structures result in similar functions. The postwar political events will necessarily flow from the structure common to all coalitions and alliances, which by their very nature are but temporary unions of sovereign states. The United Nations is such a coalition. The general pattern of these events will be somewhat as follows:

There will be some kind of a "Holy Alliance," written or implicit, of Britain, Russia and the United States, with China as a side-kick. Or there may be an Anglo-American power-politics alliance, with both Russia and China as side-kicks. The same old war horse of the League of Nations will be trotted out, only this time with a new blue ribbon on its tail, gold lettered, "the League of United Nations." Or, to increase the confusion, there may be *two* Leagues of Nations, one European and one Asiatic, where the more skillful power politicians of the foreign leading states will prevail. In any event, a League plan will serve as a convenient screen for the power politics of its leading members. At the same time, it will serve conveniently to rationalize promises and hoax the people of the world in their yearning for lasting peace.

Soon, however, will come the inevitable quarrels between Britain, Russia, and the United States, each with the other and two against one. There will be, as in the past, power politics inspired by national interests, power grabs, diplomatic maneuvers and innumerable conferences leading nowhere. There being no longer the danger of a common enemy to cement the union of the allies, each of the allies will become a danger to the other. The United States being the most powerful (and the richest) will logically be considered the greatest danger of them all. However fearful of each other the other leading victorious powers may be, they will be united in attempts to effect a world settlement without too much interference from the United States.

The United States, torn by dissensions or perhaps turmoil at home, will sooner or later withdraw from the costly occupation in Europe, Africa and Asia, leaving to her allies numerous unfinished and costlier experiments in economic alchemy. Or, belatedly, she will seek to establish her own independent line of policy. In Europe, Britain and Russia will continue their precarious balance of "Zones of Influence" —Britain in control of western Europe and Russia in eastern Europe with Germany as a bone of contention or appeasement. There will be a struggle over the question of a "hard" Germany (favored by Russia) or a "soft" Germany (favored by the Anglo-Americans).

The guests temporarily absent from the banquet table of the victor's postwar settlement will soon return. France—for a thousand years the *enfant terrible* of Europe and for centuries the soul of the world— will rise again. Italy, purified by suffering, will also rise. The one hundred and twenty million Latins of the still fructifying Roman Empire cannot, without bloody future wars, be denied the historic place in Europe which is theirs. France will be rapidly rearming, probably seeking to establish a Latin-European bloc. Germany, even though condemned by the Anglo-Americans to become a pariah among the nations, will soon enough find new friends and abettors— if nowhere else, certainly in the inevitable rivalries of the victorious allies and in the semichaos of a long armistice. The Balkans once more will seethe in their miniature but tragic whirlpools of internecine warfare. The nations of the world will be seething either against the domination of the Unholy Alliance (and seeking favors of France and Germany) or against the domination of the Anglo-Americans (and seeking to rally around Russia). The leading powers, having liberated them from Hitler and still in search of "a permanent system of general security," may forget to restore to them their sovereignties and freedom.

Meanwhile, in the schools of Asia, from the Black Sea to the Blue Nile and the Pacific, and in new industrial plants, ready-made from the latest American and European blueprints, and financed by foreign capital, momentous events will be brewing. The new Long Armistice, during which the men of Asia will have learned to produce machines of peace, will be approaching its end. And we will be on the threshold of perhaps the last war of *our* era of great wars and revolutions.

The Machine of Peace

I have tried to show that even the most carefully calculated methods of American balance and space politics and the most powerful American Strategic Zone could not offer us lasting protection. Only lasting peace in the world can do that. And lasting peace can be achieved only through a new system of collective defense. Unless we find an adequate substitute for power politics, there is no hope for us except the hope that in the inevitable future wars we will be strong enough to survive.

Unless war is put into a merciless strait jacket, it will probably destroy free civilization in spite of anything we can do. It is not enough to defeat the war lords; either war itself must be conquered or it will finally conquer the world.

But war can be conquered only by creating a new machine of peace more powerful than the machine of war which holds the world in thrall.

Can such a machine of peace be built? Can the immemorial hatreds of the nations of the world be neutralized, and the forces of nationalism which now devastate the world be diverted and integrated into a new system of lasting world peace?

I say, Yes, because *new and unique circumstances have arisen as a result of the Industrial Revolution which make lasting peace not only theoretically possible, but feasible; and not in some remote future, but now. These new circumstances fall into three groups:*

One: *The revolution in military weapons.*

A just and lasting world peace must necessarily be enforced by a powerful international police force. This means effective disarmament of all the individual nations. In the past such world disarmament was an idle dream because military power was derived from troops armed with light weapons which could be easily procured or manufactured anywhere. Today, as a result of the revolution in military weapons, all but a few of the nations of the world have been virtually disarmed. They are not able to build vast industrial plants for planes, ships, and tanks; their rifles and most of their cannon have been made useless; their distances and physical obstacles have been practically obliterated.

The *effective monopoly* of decisive weapons (armored ships of land, sea, and air) has passed into the hands of only five industrial nations: the United States, Germany, Britain, Russia, and Japan. After the defeat of Germany and Japan the monopoly will be controlled by the three richest nations in the world, *none of which is land-hungry*. Since the world-controlling monopoly by these three nations will be temporary and will necessarily break down (either because of rivalry among themselves or because of new industrial rivals), it will be to their advantage to establish a system of collective security, *if such a system is possible.*

Two: *The emergence of the United States as the greatest industrial, and therefore military, power of all time.*

The same Industrial Revolution that made Germany the greatest military power of the old world, enslaving peaceful nations, has made the United States an even greater military power than Germany and the only hope of the enslaved nations. No nation in history has had the power to do so much good or so much evil. But, although America's opportunity is unique, her power will be limited to a few short years by the rapid growth of rival postwar powers.

It becomes imperative, therefore, that the American people seek to perpetuate their own security in co-operation with the nations of the world by establishing a system capable of maintaining the peace of the world against any aggressor.

Thus, during these all-precious moments of unrivaled American power, the American nation can do, almost alone, what no nation has ever done before: *declare lasting peace on the world.*

Three: *The development of solutions for the hitherto unsolvable* problems of collective defense, world government, and world economy.

There are four fundamental problems involved in building any system of world order—problems which in the past have baffled the architects of peace. Each of these fundamental problems contains an inner contradiction, the resolution of which is indispensable.

Dilemma No. 1: How to disarm effectively all the individual nations and create a powerful World Police Force—which is essential if wars of aggression are to be stopped—and at the same time avoid the risk of creating out of the World Police Force a Frankenstein's monster, a world military organization which may be turned into a world tyranny. The solution of this all-important problem, without which lasting world peace is impossible, is contained in the Quota Force Principle (see Book Two).

Dilemma No. 2: How to create a world government sufficiently strong to maintain order in the world, and at the same time avoid interference with the essential freedom of the sovereign nations. The solution of this problem is contained in a new system of regional federations, integrated into the World Federation, with strict limitation of powers. The preceding chapter describes how to form a Pan-American Federation as a possible first step in this solution.

Dilemma No. 3: How to create a world economy in which the so-called backward nations may be liberated and other nations may move toward a higher standard of living, without at the same time requiring a heavy sacrifice, involving a lowered standard of wealth and welfare, on the part of the industrially advanced nations. The general solutions of the problem of world economic reconstruction are contained throughout the World Federation Plan, particularly in the economic structure of the regional federations and in the provisions for economic organizations controlled by the Vocational Senate. In addition there are special economic solutions dealing with pooled colonies, priority treaties, two-way states, etc.

Dilemma No. 4: How to create a world-wide system of education, which is the most important line of defense in world peace. The

World Federation Plan provides the machinery for the solution of this dilemma.

Conclusion: If Dilemmas No. 1 and No. 2 can be resolved beyond doubt, and *if* Dilemmas No. 3 and No. 4 can be resolved in their essentials, then the reader must admit that it is possible to achieve lasting world peace.

These new solutions have been found and are embodied in a new system of world federation which, as will be demonstrated, will insure the permanent military security and freedom of each and every nation of the world.

BOOK TWO

HOW TO ORGANIZE PEACE:

The World Federation Plan

What Is the World Federation Plan?

THE TERM "World Federation" as used here does not denote a closely knit union of states under a powerful central government along the lines of the United States of America. Nothing is farther from my thoughts than to work for establishment of a world state with manifold sovereign powers. Under present conditions such a world state would be wholly unacceptable to the leading nations, and if it were acceptable it might well become a seat of world tyranny surpassing the militarist clique of the Roman Empire or even the depredations of Genghis Khan's world state.

The World Federation is a voluntary association of two or more leading sovereign states, open to all states, the object of which is to establish adequate machinery for collective defense of its members against aggression. The World Federation that I propose embodies the ideal of world citizenship, to be achieved eventually through gradual evolution. But it is not yet the brotherhood of man. It is not a guarantee of eternal peace. It is realistic, and it puts war into a strait jacket tighter than any yet devised.

The World Federation is a specific, detailed, and comprehensive blueprint for the coming peace settlement and for a new system of collective defense.

The actual work of taking the accumulated results of lifelong research on problems of societies and force, and from them building this new system for a co-operative of nations, began in 1939. Early in 1942 the first draft of the blueprint for the World Federation was completed. Then began a series of practical tests. The plan was submitted to a number of specialists in the fields of political, economic, psycho-social, and military sciences. Valuable criticisms and suggestions resulted from this. In the fall of 1942 an improved blueprint was submitted to much larger groups of intellectuals and specialists and later published as a *Summary of the World Federation Plan*. Persons in the governments of the United Nations were consulted unofficially. In addition various tests of mass reaction were made by means of lectures and group discussions.

Since then a year has passed, during which so many valuable suggestions and improvements were received from various parts of the world and incorporated in the plan that the World Federation Plan could no longer be called mine. Although the structure of the plan remains the same in all its essentials, there have been a number of changes in details, some of them important. It is to be expected that as time goes on further improvements will be made, thanks to the criticism and suggestions which I invite from all those who have at heart the interests of our country and of the world.

The Objects of the World Federation Plan

First: "To create appropriate international machinery with power adequate to establish and maintain a just and lasting peace." (Fulbright Resolution.)

Second: To implement without undue delay the provisions of the Atlantic Charter dealing with the territorial, political, and economic settlement of the world, as well as the solemn promise to establish "a wider and permanent system of general security."

Third: To establish without undue delay, and in accordance with the provisions of the Atlantic Charter, a territorial, political, and economic settlement just to all states, and to provide for the liberation of all peoples now oppressed.

Fourth: To establish without undue delay a workable international organization (the World Federation) separate from the governments of sovereign states, based on a higher law to which all states are equally subject, and supported by a separate World Police, so that all may be protected in collective defense and each may be protected even against all.

Fifth: To establish without undue delay just and adequate conditions of peace for the defeated states which, while making it impossible for evil militarism to rise again in the defeated countries, will provide for their admission as equal members into the World Federation upon fulfillment of the essential requirements of the Conditions of Peace.

Sixth: To provide through the World Federation an adequate framework, organs, and means for temporary postwar relief and reconstruction measures, and for permanent world-wide educational, scientific, and economic programs and institutions based on voluntary co-operation of sovereign states.

Seventh: To provide through the World Federation the necessary machinery for peaceful settlement of disputes between sovereign states, as well as for gradual and peaceful change arising from new conditions in the relations between nations.

The fundamental goal of the World Federation is to prevent, by means of segregation of decisive heavy weapons and the establishment of a strong World Police, armed aggression by any state against any other, and thus to make possible lasting world peace. Elimination of the social cancer of war is also the innermost hope of the American nation and of the peoples of the world.

A GRAPHIC SUMMARY OF
THE WORLD FEDERATION PLAN

... which is, in effect,

    A Treaty of Territorial Settlement and Restoration of
    Sovereign States,

    A Treaty of Peace with the Defeated States, *and*

    A Treaty of Collective Defense (an Integrated Perma-
    nent Alliance)

Let us Examine the Plan
Step by Step . . .

The World Federation Plan provides that the world shall be divided
into

11 REGIONAL FEDERATIONS

9 shall be Sovereign Regional Federations	2 shall be temporarily Autonomous Regional Federations
PAN-AMERICAN	MALAYSIAN
BRITISH	INDIAN
LATIN-EUROPEAN	(The Autonomous Regional Federations will later become Sovereign Regional Federations upon plebiscites.)
GERMANIC	
MIDDLE EUROPEAN	
MIDDLE EASTERN	
RUSSIAN	
CHINESE	(Until it becomes sovereign the Malaysian Federation shall be under the special trusteeship of the United States; the Indian Federation shall be under the special trusteeship of Great Britain.)
JAPANESE	

Each Region is a natural economic, cultural, and psychosocial unit.
In each Region there is a reasonable balance between the needs of
industry, raw materials, and foods.

Each Region consists of one
or more SOVEREIGN STATES . . .

Some of the 11 Regional Federations consist of only one sovereign state, as in the case of the Russian or the Chinese Federation. Some consist of more than one sovereign state, as in the case of the Pan-American Federation.

Each SOVEREIGN STATE

KEEPS all its rights, including the rights

    . . . to choose its own form of government,

    . . . fix its taxes, tariffs, trade laws,

    . . . make and alter treaties,

    . . . govern itself as it sees fit;

EVEN THE RIGHT TO JOIN OR NOT TO JOIN THE WORLD FEDERATION

It GIVES UP only one right . . .

THE RIGHT TO WAGE A WAR OF AGGRESSION

The most populous Sovereign State in each Region is the

INITIATING STATE

Only the initiating state may join the World Federation on behalf of its Region.

When TWO OR MORE

    INITIATING STATES

    BECOME MEMBERS,

        The World Federation Comes into Existence

and the Regions of the initiating states which have become members are automatically member Regional Federations.

After any initiating state has joined the World Federation other sovereign states in its Regional Federation may become member states.

If the most populous state in any Region fails to join the World Federation, then after six months the next-most-populous state in that Region may join on behalf of the Region.

When the World Federation has been founded by any two or more initiating states, there shall be

TWO TIME PERIODS

The first time period is the PROVISIONAL PERIOD.

During this period the World Federation shall be governed by a Provisional Government.

Two years after it is established (or two years after the war ends; whichever is later) the first time period shall end and the Provisional Government shall cease. Then begins

The second time period, in which

the Permanent Government of the World Federation shall replace the Provisional Government.

The PROVISIONAL GOVERNMENT of the World Federation consists of a

COUNCIL OF TEMPORARY TRUSTEES

ONE TRUSTEE shall be appointed by each initiating state which joins the World Federation;

ONE TRUSTEE shall be appointed for the Malaysian Federation by the United States, acting as its Initiating State;

ONE TRUSTEE shall be appointed for the Indian Federation by Great Britain, acting as its initiating state;

and the President of the United States, or his representative, shall be an ex-officio member of the Council of Temporary Trustees.

THE POWERS

of the Provisional Government
shall be:

1. To make the treaty of peace with the Axis powers;
2. To bring relief to the states liberated from the Axis;
3. To re-establish, within one year, the sovereignty of the occupied states;

and, especially,

TO ESTABLISH THE WORLD POLICE

The World Police shall consist of

11 *National* Contingents
1 *International* Contingent

Each initiating state shall have its National Contingent, which it shall recruit, train, *and command except when any act of aggression occurs in the world,* in which case the National Contingent shall come under the command of the World Federation.

The International Contingent, called the *Mobile Corps,* shall be recruited from all member states except the initiating states and shall be armed, trained, and commanded by the World Federation Government.

The danger that any National Contingent or combination of National Contingents may be used for aggressive purposes is made impossible by the

QUOTA FORCE PRINCIPLE,

an essential element of
the World Federation Plan

Each National Contingent shall be limited to a certain *quota* of all the forces and heavy weapons which constitute the World Police.

The quotas are mathematically balanced to give every initiating state a force

SUFFICIENT FOR ITS OWN DEFENSE

but

INSUFFICIENT FOR SUCCESSFUL AGGRESSION

Here are the quotas of the National Contingents:

UNITED STATES	20%	
BRITISH	15%	
RUSSIAN	15%	
CHINESE	6%	
FRENCH	6%	
GERMAN	3%	
POLISH	3%	
TURKISH	3%	
INDIAN	3%	(Temporarily under British command)
MALAYSIAN	2%	(Temporarily under American command)
JAPANESE	2%	
	───	
TOTAL	78%	

and that leaves . . .

22% (more than any National Contingent)

for the

INTERNATIONAL MOBILE CORPS

commanded by the World Federation, and

devoted and sworn to fight against any aggressor

If any politically conceivable group of would-be aggressor nations combines against any other nation, the nation attacked, *plus the Mobile Corps* and the other National Contingents under the command of the World Federation, will have more than fifty per cent of the total world forces.

Furthermore

The heavy weapons without which modern wars cannot be successfully waged are to be

SEGREGATED

And these segregated weapons and materials of war may be manufactured only by a World Armament Trust set up, wholly owned, and controlled by the World Federation and may be used only by the World Police.

The SECURITY
of the UNITED STATES
is not solely dependent on the World Police.
In addition, the World Federation Plan sets up an

AMERICAN STRATEGIC ZONE

The United States will have, *in addition to the largest of the National Contingents,*
    Naval air bases (on a non-imperialistic basis)
        in MALAYSIA, covering the *eastern* shores of the Pacific

        in the Atlantic and Pacific islands of the Western Hemisphere.

So, even if the World Federation should in the future cease to exist, the security of the entire Western Hemisphere will be strategically greater than would be possible under any system of alliances.

THE AXIS FORCES
WILL BE EFFECTIVELY DISARMED

        While the quota table allots National Contingents to Germany and Japan;

for 24 years   The German and Japanese National Contingents shall be recruited and commanded by the International Contingent;

for 24 years   None of the World Armament Trust's segregated weapons shall be manufactured in either Germany or Japan;

and for 24 years   The Trustees appointed by Germany and Japan to the Permanent Government of the World Federation shall be subject to the approval of the other Trustees.

        Who are the Trustees? They are an essential branch of the Permanent Government which is to command the World Police.

The Government of the World Federation shall have the duty of

MAINTAINING PEACE
ARBITRATING INTERNATIONAL CONTROVERSIES
PROMOTING ECONOMIC AND CULTURAL WELFARE

The Permanent Government shall consist of

A WORLD SUPREME COURT

13 Judges {
One from each initiating state
Appointed for Life
Two, at large, from the non-initiating states

The World Supreme Court shall interpret the constitution of the World Federation, and it alone shall issue a Writ of Economic Sanctions (in case of tax evasion or treaty violation by any member state) or a Writ of War Emergency (in case of armed aggression).

A PRESIDENT

Selected for a six-year term, in rotation from the Regional Federations, the first World President being from the United States, the second from the British Federation.

The President shall defend the World Federation Constitution, and execute the World Federation laws, subject to the control of the judicial and legislative branches of the World Federation Government.

In addition to the Supreme Court and the President, the World Federation Government shall include:

A WORLD COURT OF EQUITY

13 JUDGES } One from each initiating state
Two, at large, from non-initiating states

The World Court of Equity shall deal with treaty, economic, political, or territorial disputes arising between states or regions or involving the World Federation Government.

THE WORLD TRUSTEES

13 TRUSTEES } One from each initiating state
SELECTED FOR SIX-YEAR TERMS
Two, at large, from the non-initiating states

THE WORLD VOCATIONAL SENATE

66 SENATORS } Selected by the Presidents of the
Regional Federations with the approval
of the Regional Senates, for SIX-YEAR TERMS

There shall be 6 Senators from each Regional Federation

1 representing CAPITAL (or executive management)
1   "   LABOR
1   "   AGRICULTURE
1   "   SCIENCE
1   "   EDUCATION
1   "   ARTS AND CRAFTS

The World Trustees and the World Vocational Senate shall be the legislative branch of the World Federation Government.

The World Federation Government shall have the

POWER

To *govern* (through its constitution and laws made by its legislative bodies) all territories under its direct control. These
will include the seats of its government, the bases used by
the World Police, and so forth.

To *enforce* a Writ of Economic Sanctions by such control over
trade as is necessary, and to enforce a Writ of War Emergency by the use of the World Police.

To *provide* international economic, educational, cultural, and
scientific institutions, in which, however, member states
shall be free to participate or not.

The World Federation Government has NO power

To force any sovereign state (except the defeated Axis powers)
to join the World Federation. Members of the United
Nations who do not become member states shall be treated,
in war, only as allies of the World Police.

The cost of the World Federation Government shall be borne by its
member states in proportion to their ability to pay, but shall be in the
form of dues and not of taxes which encroach upon the sovereignty
of the member states.

Each Region
(if composed of more than one sovereign state) shall have its *Regional
Government*

To administer "pooled colonies" (colonies owned jointly by the
member states of the Regional Federation);

To regulate treaty rights and co-operative economic and cultural institutions of Regional interest, within the Region.

The Regional Government shall be patterned on the World Federation Government, with

A REGIONAL PRESIDENT
Elected by the Regional Trustees

13 REGIONAL TRUSTEES

Elected by the member states in proportion to population

60 REGIONAL SENATORS

Vocational, 10 members for each vocation

A REGIONAL SUPREME COURT
of 13 Justices, selected for life

A REGIONAL EQUITY COURT
and lower Regional courts, if needed

In Regional Federations having only one sovereign state, the existing government shall be recognized as the Regional Government.

Nothing of the World Federation Plan is unalterable

except

The REGIONAL Principle (though the Regions may be changed)

and

The QUOTA Force Principle (though the Quotas may be changed)

The Constitution of the World Federation is subject to amendment; Member states may apply for transfer from one Region to another, or may even belong to *two* Regions (see Two-Way States).

The World Federation may, by due process of law, expand or reduce its functions, except that it may not encroach upon the sovereign powers reserved to the member states without their consent.

But the World Federation Plan is

COMPLETE

In every respect it is a complete blueprint which *may be put into operation immediately.*

The details of this complete blueprint are in the following pages.

THE MINIMUM REQUIREMENTS FOR A SYSTEM OF COLLECTIVE DEFENSE

A system of collective defense such as the World Federation Plan can fulfill its main objects only if it can satisfy the requirements based on a double yardstick of *acceptability* and *effectiveness*. If such a system is politically acceptable, but not effective in achieving its goal of collective defense, it is futile; and if it could be effective, but is not politically acceptable, it is equally futile.

The World Federation Plan offers a maximum of effectiveness because:

First: It establishes a separate collective government on the basis of a constitution, which is a Treaty of Collective Defense agreed to by its members, independent of the purely national interests and politics of the sovereign states, and operating without unanimous consent of its members.

Second: It possesses, independently from the sovereign states, a strictly limited but effective, enforceable power to prevent wars of aggression.

Third: It provides, on a voluntary, co-operative basis, adequate machinery for the improvement of economic, educational, and scientific standards among the peoples of the world, as well as for the peaceful settlement of disputes between nations, thereby seeking to eliminate the underlying conditions that breed wars and war lords.

Fourth: The government of the World Federation is supported by a World Police (in control of segregated decisive weapons) wholly adequate to prevent preparation for aggression or actual aggression by any politically conceivable combination of states, and wholly inadequate to jeopardize the territory or sovereignty of any state, large or small.

The system of collective security embodied in the World Federation Plan offers a maximum of acceptability because:

First: It retains, as before, the full sovereignty of every state, except the right to wage a war of aggression.

Second: It retains, in the case of the United States, its own armed forces and enhances their power against any aggressor by establishing a new American Strategic Zone.

Third: It retains, in the case of other leading states, their own armed forces, and in the case of Britain, Russia, and China it enhances the power of their armed forces against any aggressor by establishing new Strategic Zones.

Fourth: It restores or retains the full sovereignty (except for the right to wage a war of aggression) of all states which are not leading states, and enormously enhances their power to defend themselves against any aggressor by establishing a collective armed force stationed on its own collective Strategic Zone.

Fifth: It will lift, to an overwhelming extent, the immemorial, back-breaking load of the cost of wars and preparation for wars, drastically reducing taxes and releasing energy to create higher economic and spiritual standards for the world.

Sixth: It does not commit a state to permanent participation in the World Federation, since it may withdraw after a test period of twenty-five years without affecting its territorial or sovereign rights.

Seventh: It does not affect the rights of any of our allies or of neutrals who may not wish to join the World Federation, since membership in the World Federation for them is voluntary; and should they refuse to join, they are equally safeguarded against aggression from member states of the World Federation, although they cannot participate in other advantages.

Eighth: The founding of the World Federation does not require the unanimous consent of the United Nations or the consent of more than two leading powers. Thus the United States alone, with the concurrence of Britain or any other leading power, and with the support of but a few smaller states, may found the World Federation.

In the American and British democracies it will suffice that enlightened public opinion encourage or compel their governments to adopt (with modifications, if needed) the World Federation Plan. In that event two great visions will be realized: one, the vision of scores of millions in the English-speaking nations of an integrated and lasting alliance between the British Commonwealth of Nations and the United States; the other, the vision of hundreds of millions in the world of an integrated lasting alliance of all the peaceful nations against war and war lords.

Ninth: The basic conditions of the World Federation Plan express a higher synthesis of the nationalist (not fascist) and internationalist viewpoints now internally dividing the nations in their attempt to solve the problems of the coming world settlement.

Tenth: The World Federation Plan avoids any narrow ideological bias. The world cannot wait until this or that particular ideology triumphs over all the others. Since none can be conciliated, the only thing to do is to build a House of Peace in which the peoples of each sovereign state may choose or modify their own form of government and all ideologies may exist side by side.

Thus the World Federation Plan is designed to afford the maximum of effectiveness and the maximum of acceptability.

The World Federation Plan

THE ENTIRE WORLD FEDERATION PLAN is embodied in the Articles of the Constitution of the World Federation, which follows.[1]

The Constitution of the World Federation is a Treaty of World Settlement, which shall become effective upon signing and ratification in a manner usually prescribed for a Treaty of Alliance or a Treaty of Peace among sovereign states.

The Constitution, or the Treaty of World Settlement, may be adopted at any time during or after the war.

The Articles of the Constitution contain, in effect, three different treaties:

1. The Treaty of Territorial Settlement and Restoration of Sovereign States.

2. The Treaty of Peace with the defeated states.

3. The Treaty of Collective Defense (Integrated Defensive Alliance).

The provisions of these three treaties which are embodied in the Constitution of the World Federation are not grouped separately.

Only the important features of the proposed Constitution are given below, leaving a number of details to be elaborated later. It must also be remembered that this Constitution, or treaty, of the World Federation, is but a proposal to the governments of the world and their peoples. As such, it can serve only as a basis for negotiations between interested governments, out of which will come the complete and final draft of the Constitution or treaty of the World Federation.

[1] To facilitate rapid reading, the author has avoided as much as possible the legal phraseology necessary in the final text of the Constitution.

THE CONSTITUTION OF THE WORLD FEDERATION

PART ONE: THE STRUCTURE OF THE WORLD FEDERATION

Article I.

1. The world shall be divided into eleven *Regions*. Each Region shall consist of one or more sovereign states, together with their autonomous possessions and colonies, if any.

2. A sovereign state is herein defined as a state whose highest government is not controlled by another state.

3. Each Region shall become a *Regional Federation,* held together by its Regional Government.

Representatives of the sovereign member states shall form the government of each Regional Federation, with strictly limited powers.

4. Nine Regional Federations shall be sovereign and two autonomous.

The nine sovereign Regional Federations shall be: Pan-American, British, Latin-European, Germanic, Middle European, Russian, Middle Eastern, Chinese, and Japanese.

The two autonomous Regional Federations shall be the Malaysian and the Indian, under temporary trusteeship of the United States and Great Britain respectively.

5. Representatives of the member Regional Federations shall form the government of the World Federation, with strictly limited powers.

ANALYSIS: THE REGIONAL PRINCIPLE

The important connection between the Regional Principle and structure of the world government I discuss elsewhere. Here I will give the reasons for selecting the different Regions.

Each of the eleven Regions forms an economic, psychosocial, and space-political unit and, except for the Germanic and Japanese Federations, is large enough to be a self-contained unit with a reasonable balance between agriculture, industry, and raw materials. On subsequent pages provision is made for Germany and Japan. In the case of other Regions, if some of them lack an essential raw material such as coal or oil, they will have an excess of some other raw material or foods, which they can exchange through export trade for what they lack. Most of these Regions already exist politically. Japan, China, India, Russia are among them. The British Empire, sprawling on five continents, is a geographic absurdity; politically it is very much alive.

The different Regions are based not only on different economic, political, or strategic factors; they also differ psychologically. The world is *naturally* divided into approximately eleven Regions. The nations composing each of these Regions have a common complex of forces which, though not stronger than nationalism, extends beyond the frontiers of the states and distinguishes them from other Regions. These forces are the *psychosocial* forces, which form a common heritage of history, tradition, culture, law, and often language.

Except for the Pan-American and British Regions, which are more recent arrivals on the stage of history, all the other Regions existed in the past as ancient empires. Whatever the political or even racial differences between states of the same Region, and however great their passing rivalries and hatreds may be, during many centuries they have been molded into the same characteristic way of life. Today these states are still held together by their common *psychosocial patterns* inherited from empires of old. The Latin-European Regional Federation is based on the Western Roman Empire. The Germanic Regional Federation is based on the Holy Roman Empire of the Middle Ages. The Middle Europeans are the western and southern Slavs who, together with the Hungarians, Rumanians, and the Greeks, have a psychosocial pattern based on Slav, Roman, Byzantine, and Mohammedan elements. The Russian Regional Federation is composed of eastern Slavs, who spread over the vast Eurasian plain and its mountainous rim in the south, drawing into their Slav-Byzantine pattern the Mongolian races and being in turn molded by them. The Middle Eastern Regional Federation is simply the historic Arabic-Ottoman Empire. The most ancient psychosocial patterns are those of India and China. The Malaysian Regional Federation is the one whose basic pattern has been most injured by successive invasions. Only in the Pan-American Regional Federation are there two large and distinct patterns: the Latin-Indian in Central and South America, and the Latin-

Anglo-American in the North. But for vital reasons of geography and strategy (the Monroe Doctrine) they must form part of the same Federation, on the basis of the Good Neighbor policy and in expectation of a higher synthesis of the two great cultural patterns.

From the standpoint of the philosophy of history, many wars of the past were but struggles of the "ghosts" of ancient empires to reunite their dismembered states. Today, with easier communications, the same states seek to reassemble themselves within their common psychosocial, historic, and economic Regions in order better to resist oppression and aggression. The Regional structure of the World Federation Plan merely accelerates—and peacefully—this inevitable reassembly of kindred nations into larger Regional units.

PART TWO: MEMBERSHIP IN THE WORLD FEDERATION

Article I.

1. The World Federation consists of two kinds of members:
   a. Regional Federations which have joined it.
   b. Those sovereign states of the member Regional Federations which have consented to form part of the member Regional Federations.

2. No state can become a member of the World Federation unless the Regional Federation of which it is a part is also a member.

3. In each Regional Federation the largest sovereign state shall be called the initiating state. There shall be nine initiating states: United States, Britain, France, Germany, Poland, Turkey, Russia, China, and Japan. In the case of the autonomous Malaysian and Indian Federations the United States and Britain, respectively, shall temporarily act as Special Trustees and initiating states.

4. The primary function of the initiating state is to apply for membership in the World Federation in the name of and on behalf of its Regional Federation. Any initiating state can become a member of the World Federation on its own behalf and on that of its Regional Federation when it signs and adopts the Constitution of the World Federation in a manner usually prescribed for a treaty of alliance among sovereign states.

5. A *member Region* is any Regional Federation which has joined the World Federation. A *member state* is any sovereign state which has consented to participate in the government of its Regional Federation and in the World Federation.

6. No initiating state is compelled to join the World Federation except Germany and Japan, as prescribed in the Terms of Peace with the defeated states, Part Four of this Constitution.

7. No state shall be required to become a member when the initiating state of the Region of which it is a part joins the World Federation. If such a state declines to participate, it may not be coerced, but it will not share the privileges attached to membership.

COMMENT: The United States joins the World Federation on behalf of the Pan-American Region. But any other state of the Pan-American Region, such as Argentina, may refuse to participate, in which event it is treated as a non-member. This eliminates the laborious and often hopeless negotiations to secure the unanimous consent of all the member states concerned, and yet it preserves freedom of choice for each state.

8. No initiating state which is willing to abide by the Constitution can be refused admittance to the World Federation, and when it has been admitted it can neither withdraw nor be expelled.

9. In the event that an initiating state declines to join the World Federation while other sovereign states of the same Region wish to join, then the next largest of the other states of the same Region may, after a period of six months from the date of founding of the World Federation, substitute itself for the initiating state in applying for membership.

COMMENT: If Poland, as initiating state, declines to join the World Federation, then either Yugoslavia or Czechoslovakia may apply for membership six months after the founding of the World Federation if they so desire. In that event the sovereignty, territories, and all other rights of Poland will be preserved as a non-member state.

PART THREE: FOUNDING AND GOVERNMENT OF THE WORLD FEDERATION

Article I. The Founding of the World Federation.

1. The World Federation shall come into being when two or more Regional Federations become members.

COMMENT: Thus any two or more initiating states may, during or after the war, establish the World Federation by merely announcing and adopting its Constitution. The United States may found the World Federation with Britain or any other initiating state. The United States may found the World Federation with Malaysia as the second Regional Federation by restoring full sovereignty to the Philippines. In that case the Philippines becomes the initiating state, even though the Malaysian Federation still remains autonomous with the United States as its Special Trustee.

Article II. The Provisional and the Permanent Governments of the World Federation.

1. There shall be two time periods after the founding of the World Federation, namely the Provisional Period and the Permanent Period.

2. The Provisional Period shall begin immediately upon the founding of the World Federation by two or more initiating states and shall end as specified in Article IV, Sections 1 and 2 of this Part Three, after which the Permanent Period shall begin, as described in Parts Eight, Nine, and Ten.

3. During the Provisional Period the government of the World Federation shall be called the Provisional Government and shall be subject to Articles III, IV, V, VI, and VII of this Part Three.

4. All the Articles and Parts of this Constitution not specified as pertaining to the temporary duties of the Provisional Government shall be valid for both the Provisional and Permanent Governments.

Article III. The Structure of the Provisional Government.

1. Each initiating state which joins the World Federation (excepting Germany and Japan) shall appoint one Temporary World Trustee with full power to act.

2. In addition the United States, as temporary initiating state for the Malaysian Regional Federation, and Britain, as temporary initiating state for the Indian Regional Federation, shall each appoint one Temporary World Trustee representing these two Regions respectively.

3. This Council of Temporary World Trustees shall constitute the Provisional Government of the World Federation.

4. The President of the United States or his representative shall be an ex-officio member of the Council of Temporary World Trustees, with a deciding vote in the event of a tie.

5. The seat of the Provisional Government shall be in the United States, with an extraterritorial status.

Article IV. Duration of the Provisional Government.

1. If the World Federation is founded during the present hostilities, the Provisional Government shall hold office from the date of the founding of the World Federation until two years after the cessation of hostilities.

2. If the World Federation is founded after the cessation of hostilities, the Provisional Government shall hold office for a period of two years from the date of founding of the World Federation.

3. At the end of the Provisional Period the Provisional Government shall cease to exist and the Permanent Government shall automatically come into being.

COMMENT: THE PROCEDURE FOR THE ESTABLISHMENT OF THE PROVISIONAL GOVERNMENT

It would be of vital importance in winning and shortening the war, as well as in making the postwar settlement, if the World Federation were established *during the war*. In that event it is most probable that the United States and Great Britain, preferably simultaneously with Russia and China, would become the founders of the World Federation and establish its Provisional Government.

In the event that Russia and China do not choose to join for the time being, they remain allies of the World Federation, as do all other anti-Axis powers. As allies, their territories and sovereignty, as described in the Constitution, will be guaranteed as fully as though they were members of the World Federation. It will be seen that the advantages of membership in the World Federation are so great that there is little doubt that both China and Russia will immediately or eventually join.

Aside from the Axis powers, there remain as initiating states only France, Poland, and Turkey. The French Committee of National Liberation and the Polish government-in-exile may be recognized as governments *de facto,* for the purpose of joining the World Federation—subject, however, to subsequent ratification by their constitutional conventions. Turkey may also join, provided of course that she engages in the war against the Axis. Should Turkey fail to join, she may not be coerced and her postwar status shall not be affected.

Assuming that Britain and the United States are the Founder States of the World Federation, there will be four Temporary World Trustees representing the British, Indian, Pan-American, and Malaysian Regional Federations, with a combined population of nearly nine hundred million held by the integrated alliance of the World Federation. In addition will be the German and Japanese Regional Federations, whose membership in the World Federation is to be compulsory.

Article V. The World Federation and the Neutrals.
No neutral state may be discriminated against because of its failure to participate in the war against the Axis powers.

COMMENT: An individual sovereign neutral state, such as Sweden, is naturally entitled to choose its own national policy. To reproach the Swedish nation for failure to attack Nazi Germany when living under the very shadow of Nazi might is not only unjust but unrealistic. Had Sweden attacked Germany without adequate military support from the United Nations, she would have been crushed in a few weeks. As it is, Sweden has husbanded her strength and is destined to play a role which will be far out of proportion to her size. Similar considerations apply to other neutral states, such as Turkey.

Article VI. Powers of the Provisional Government during the War.
1. If the World Federation is founded during the present war, the Provisional Government shall have the following powers until the cessation of hostilities:

a. The Provisional Government shall act as a Supreme War and Peace Council in co-operation with its allies. It shall have full power (without interference in internal affairs) to act in the name of its member states and in co-operation with its allies in the general conduct of the war and in all matters pertaining to the war until the termination of hostilities.

b. No member state may negotiate a separate peace.

Article VII. Duties of the Provisional Government after Cessation of Hostilities.

During the Provisional Period the Provisional Government must fulfill the following requirements:

1. Organization of a network of Economic Agencies for the immediate relief of distressed peoples (including the defeated peoples).

2. Signing of the Conditions of the Peace Settlement with the defeated states and the enforcement of these conditions, in accordance with Part Four.

3. Carrying out the provisions of the Territorial Settlement, in accordance with Part Five.

4. Restoration of sovereignty to and the establishment of representative governments in the defeated countries and in those previously occupied by the Axis, in accordance with Part Six.

5. Establishment of the World Police and the World Armament Trust, in accordance with Part Seven.

6. Establishment of the Permanent Government of the World Federation, in accordance with Part Eight.

COMMENT: The agencies of the United Nations already functioning for the liberated countries will be incorporated under the Provisional Government of the World Federation. Also many of the economic and other war agencies, such as the Joint Shipping Board, will be incorporated in the Provisional Government.

PART FOUR: THE CONDITIONS OF THE PEACE SETTLEMENT WITH THE DEFEATED STATES.

Article I.

1. The following Conditions of Peace shall be announced by the Provisional Government and its allies as the terms of the Peace Settlement.

2. The war shall end when the Axis countries agree to join the World Federation, subscribe to its Constitution, and in addition comply with the following terms:

a. Cessation of hostilities.

b. Elimination of the Nazi, Fascist, and feudal Japanese dictatorships.

c. Total disarmament and demobilization of all existing armed forces (except for internal police) in accordance with the Quota Force Principle, as provided in Article XIV, Part Seven, of this Constitution.

d. Evacuation and resettlement of all territories which are not part of their frontiers, as specified in the World Territorial Table.

e. Restoration—over a period of ten years under the direct supervision of the World Federation Government—of expropriations and loot, or their equivalent (perishable goods and raw materials not included).

f. The surrender, for judgment by a special tribunal, of all the officials or officers directly and immediately responsible for gross violations of existing international conventions (such as mass execution of hostages, tortures, etc.). The special tribunal shall have the power to impose any penalty, including death.

COMMENT: These terms are just but not vindictive. They assure maximum future security to the victorious United Nations without crushing the millions of innocent among the defeated peoples. The promulgation of these terms by the United Nations would doubtless have a powerful propaganda effect in the Axis countries and greatly shorten the war, hastening the inevitable collapse of Hitler and his satellites. The difference between desperate German resistance (if they see no way out) and merely strong resistance (if they can be shown any way out) might be the difference, in terms of American lives alone, of several hundred thousand.

PART FIVE: THE TERRITORIAL SETTLEMENT OF THE WORLD

Article I. The World Territorial Table.

1. The World Territorial Table describes the composition of each Regional Federation and the frontiers of all the sovereign states and their possessions.

2. A more detailed definition of frontiers, as well as a more comprehensive settlement of territorial disputes, shall be left to the Permanent Government of the World Federation.

3. The general territorial settlement, as described in the World Territorial Table, when once agreed upon by the Founder States, shall not be changed except:

   a. By mutual consent of the states concerned;
   b. By plebiscite (within two years after cessation of hostilities);
   c. When a plebiscite is not feasible, by arbitration (in minor cases) of the World Equity Court.

4. The territories (or leased bases) assigned to the Pan-American, British, Russian, Latin-European, and Chinese Regional Federations are also the Strategic Zones of their respective initiating states. They are not subject to plebiscites or decisions of the World Equity Court if they involve the transfer of sovereign rights (in case of territories) or strategic rights (in case of leased bases) to another state.

5. Unless otherwise specified, the geographical frontiers of the individual states and their possessions described in the World Territorial Table are those prevailing in January 1936.

THE WORLD TERRITORIAL TABLE

Regional Federation	Sovereign States	Additions and Subtractions to Possessions and Colonies*
PAN-AMERICAN:	United States and all the Latin-American republics.	*Additions:* Japanese mandated islands and Kuril Islands (outright possessions of the United States). Territories in Western Hemisphere now held by non-American States, to be purchased and governed by the Federation.
BRITISH:	United Kingdom, Canada, Australia, New Zealand, Union of South Africa.	*Additions:* Mozambique, Djibouti, and the rest of Italian East Africa. *Subtractions:* Hong Kong, Northwest African, and Western Hemisphere possessions.
LATIN-EUROPEAN:	France, Italy, Spain, Belgium, Portugal. Special status for Vatican City (see Part Nine, Article VII).	*Additions:* British Northwest African colonies. *Subtractions:* Belgian Congo, Portuguese Mozambique, Angola, and Western Hemisphere possessions.
GERMANIC:	Germany and Austria.	*Additions:* Belgian Congo, Angola, and southern Sudan (under direct control of the World Federation for twenty-four years).

*For status of colonies see Part Nine, Article V.

THE WORLD TERRITORIAL TABLE (Cont'd)

MIDDLE EUROPEAN: Poland, Lithuania (upon plebiscite), Czechoslovakia, Rumania, Hungary, Yugoslavia (including Italian Dalmatia, upon plebiscite), Bulgaria, Albania, and Greece (including Italian Dodecanese Islands).

MIDDLE EASTERN: Turkey, Persia, Iraq, Syria, Palestine (Jewish state†), united Arabia, Afghanistan, and Egypt, including northern Sudan.

RUSSIAN: USSR, including autonomous states of Estonia and Latvia; Bessarabia up to the Prut and Danube rivers; strategic frontier with Finland, and parts of Polish Ukraine (subject to plebiscite).

CHINESE: China, including Manchuria, Formosa, and all former foreign concessions or possessions.

JAPANESE: Japan proper (frontiers of 1894, plus southern Sakhalin).   *Subtractions:* Kuril Islands.

†For status of sovereign Palestine see Part Nine, Article VIII.

THE WORLD TERRITORIAL TABLE (Cont'd)

Autonomous Regional Federations:

MALAYSIAN: Sovereign states of Philippines and Thailand (reorganized); Netherlands East Indies (under Netherlands sovereignty); Indo-China (under French sovereignty); all small Pacific islands outside the Western Hemisphere, except British and French possessions (under the sovereignty of the Malaysian Federation).

The government of the Malaysian Regional Federation, but not the governments of the sovereign states comprising it, is under special Trusteeship of the United States of America until it attains Regional sovereignty.

In selected points of the Malaysian Federation the United States Contingent of the World Police will occupy, under long-lease, non-imperialistic conditions (as in Bermuda and Cuba today), military and air-naval bases.

INDIAN: India.

Dominion or separate sovereign status of states comprising the Indian Regional Federation. The government of the Indian Regional Federation, but not the governments of the sovereign states comprising it, is under special Trusteeship of Britain until it attains Regional sovereignty.††

In selected points of the Indian Federation the British Contingent of the World Police will occupy, under long-lease, non-imperialistic conditions, military and air-naval bases.

UNATTACHED BLOC: Netherlands, Denmark, Norway, Sweden, Finland, Eire, and Korea (see Article II of this Part).

TWO-WAY STATES: Belgium, Switzerland, and Luxembourg (see Article III of this Part).

††For the structure of the Indian Federation and the rights of Britain in India see Part Nine, Article IV.

Article II. The Right of Transfer to a Region.

1. Any sovereign state which is not an initiating state may secede from its original Regional Federation and join another member Regional Federation provided:

    a. They are contiguous by land or separated by less than one thousand miles of water;

    b. A two-thirds majority of the population of the seceding state approves through plebiscite;

    c. The other Regional Federation is willing to accept the applicant.

2. Any state listed in the World Territorial Table as belonging to the Unattached Bloc may join a member Regional Federation, subject to the provisions a, b, and c of Section 1 above.

COMMENT: Austria may prefer to join the Middle European Federation. Australia may not join the Pan-American Federation because they are separated by more than one thousand miles of water; nor may Colombia join the Latin-European Federation. Of the Unattached Bloc, the Netherlands or Norway may wish to join the British or Germanic Federations; Eire may wish to join the Latin-European Federation; Korea may wish to join the Chinese Federation.

Article III. Two-Way States.

1. The states listed as Two-Way States in the World Territorial Table are those situated between two Regional Federations which have either a highly mixed population or a special economy.

2. A Two-Way State shall be a member of both Regional Federations between which it is situated, and shall send half of its representatives to each of the two Regional Federations.

3. A Two-Way State shall have equal economic rights with other member states in each Regional Federation to which it belongs, and vice versa.

4. The principle of sovereign Two-Way States may be extended to other states or districts, such as Armenia, Danzig, and Sudetenland, situated between two Regional Federations, to be decided by a plebiscite of the state concerned.

5. The same principle may be extended to certain territories

(such as Macedonia) between sovereign states of the same Regional Federation.

ANALYSIS: THE WORLD TERRITORIAL TABLE

The World Territorial Table follows the frontiers of 1936 except for changes which are either obvious or strategically necessary. Except for the United States and Canada, almost all neighboring nations have territorial disputes or designs upon each other's territories. To settle these innumerable claims would be impossible in any peace treaty. What is urgently needed is to set up international machinery for the settlement of such disputes, so taking the problem of frontiers out of the realm of power politics.

This has been done in the World Federation Plan by establishing Courts of Equity and a machinery for plebiscites under direct control of the government of the World Federation. Plebiscites are based on Wilson's principle of self-determination of peoples, with two important modifications:

1. The strategic *necessities* of a great state must be taken into consideration, within reasonable limits.

2. A different machinery from plebiscites is necessary in the case of bordering nations with a highly mixed population or economy.

There are some cases of vital strategic concern, where a great power cannot leave the security of frontiers to the decision of a plebiscite in a neighboring small state. Such is the case of the American Strategic Zone, where we cannot entrust the defense of our vital zones of the Pacific Ocean either to the Netherlands or to the future plebiscites of the natives, and must therefore control, on a non-imperialistic basis, leased bases. Except for small, rocky strategic islands, the United States gains not one inch of territory in the world settlement.

The same holds true in the case of Britain and India. The shores of India, abutting deep into the Indian Ocean, control strategically both East Africa and Australasia. That the great nations of India must be completely liberated from any economic or political tutelage is admitted by most Englishmen. But even in a fully sovereign India, Britain must retain a Strategic Zone or run the risk of dismembering the entire British Commonwealth.

I have discussed the question of the Polish Ukraine, Latvia, and Estonia elsewhere in this book. Here both strategic necessity and historical precedent require that these territories should form part of the USSR, which most likely would be ready to wage war on this issue. Without sacrificing principle or encouraging oppression, we must in some cases face strategic and political realities.

Similarly, no attempt is made in the World Territorial Table to settle the innumerable questions of different native populations *within* territories of sovereign states, except for colonial peoples for whose liberation and even sovereign status a machinery is provided in Part Nine, Article V, Pooled Colonies. But what Czechs and Moravians may do to each other and how the Serbs and Croats will get along is a matter for the sovereign Czechoslovakian and Yugoslavian states.

Except for the few specific cases of vital strategic necessity, the territorial settlement of sovereign states in the table is based on ethics and ethnics. The machinery of plebiscites has been established to determine the will of the people living in disputed territories. This machinery must be applied equally to the victorious and defeated countries. The Rumanians, the Hungarians, and the Bulgarians must receive the same fair treatment as the Poles and the Yugoslavs. It will destroy the very purpose of this war and defeat our great moral victory itself if we start by allotting millions of Germans to Poles, or Bulgarians to Serbs. Certainly neither the Polish nor the Serbian peasant seeks to exploit the German or Bulgarian peasant.

Whenever possible, in mixed territories, the World Federation shall make use of exchange of populations. There is, however, a special type of country with highly mixed population or economy where neither a plebiscite nor exchange of populations would be satisfactory. Switzerland, the oldest Federation in history, is such a country. To meet such situations adequately, a type of Two-Way Sovereign State has been established. Sudetenland is economically integrated with Czechoslovakia but psychosocially with Germany. Czechoslovakia, Germany, and especially Sudetenland would profit if Sudetenland became a Two-Way Sovereign State.

For a different reason Armenia should become a sovereign Two-Way State, in which Russia and Turkey might meet in a free zone of exchange. The case of Armenia is that of two sawed-off halves of one people belonging to two states; it should be one free people forming part of two states.

The frontier zones are the inflamed joints of the world. This new kind of state will greatly reduce the friction in frontier zones which has caused so many wars in the past.

The Unlocking of the Regions

One who devotes himself to the highly ungrateful and treacherous task of planning the affairs of the world must avoid a thousand traps. Among the deadliest of these traps is the danger of freezing the dynamic world into brutally static frontiers and social forms. It would be as disastrous to perpetuate one of several possible types of a just world as to perpetuate the status quo of the present unjust world. If it were not for the utterly destructive character of coming total wars, it might have been better to risk a dynamic world with wars than a static world without wars.

The principal safeguard against perpetuation of a static world is the insistence, in the World Federation Plan, on irrevocable sovereignty of states in all matters except wars of aggression. In this manner the scores of dynamic states that make up the world can continue their evolution or revolutions in freedom.

Provisions for the liberation of colonial peoples, and the power of the World and Regional Courts of Equity to provide for peaceful change through periodic reinterpretation of treaties and settlement of territorial disputes, should also be noted. A special safeguard is the right of any sovereign state to join any contiguous Region or, having joined, to transfer to another Regional Federation. This provision unlocks the door of any Regional Federation (except when separated by an ocean) which may refuse admission to a new member but may not prevent withdrawal of a non-initiating state.

In *Total Peace* I have established a new group of non-initiating states called the "Unattached Bloc." In the previously published *Summary of the World Federation Plan* these countries, except Korea and Eire, were included by me in the Germanic Federation, since this was economically, geographically, and psychosocially their logical

Region. Nothing has been changed by creating this Unattached Bloc, for I pointed out twice in the original draft that any non-initiating state may choose any contiguous Region and may transfer to another. But so much criticism has been directed at me for trying to "force" Germany's neighbors into the·Germanic Region that the "Unattached Bloc" has been devised.

Since the World Federation Plan makes it impossible for militarist Germany to rise again, and defends the sovereignty of all states, large or small, it makes no difference whether·Germany is a neighbor or not. But it makes a great deal of difference for the Scandinavian nations, who are starved for copper and most metals, as well as for tropical products, whether they·could have their own colonial source of raw materials which I have provided for them by attaching the Belgian Congo to·the Germanic Federation (see Pooled Colonies).

PART SIX: RESTORATION OF SOVEREIGN STATES AND ESTABLISHMENT OF REPRESENTATIVE GOVERNMENTS.

Article I.

1. The present governments in-exile and whatever non-fascist governments may arise in the defeated Axis countries may be recognized as *de facto* governments by the Provisional Government of the World Federation.

2. Within one year from the cessation of hostilities the Provisional Government of the World Federation must call constitutional conventions in each of the states previously occupied by the Axis and in the defeated states to determine the form of the new national governments and to take steps for their establishment.

3. The elections to the constitutional conventions shall be conducted in the spirit of democratic freedom and in each instance under the supervision of a special Joint Commission, composed half of representatives of the World Federation and half of representatives of the *de facto* government concerned, plus one representative of a neutral country, who shall have no vote except to dissolve a tie.

PART SEVEN: THE WORLD POLICE: THE QUOTA FORCE PRINCIPLE.

COMMENT: The Quota Force Principle may be defined as a new method of armament, composition, and distribution of the national armed forces of each state, by means of which the government of the World Federation obtains an overwhelming armed force of its own, based on a monopoly of Segregated Weapons, without jeopardizing the capacity of any individual state to resist aggression.

Article I. Definition of Segregated and Unsegregated Weapons.
1. There shall be two classes of weapons for any armed force:
    a. The Segregated, or World Weapons;
    b. The Unsegregated, or State Weapons.
2. The Segregated or World Weapons are herein defined as heavy, decisive weapons or fighting machines such as:
    a. Armored warships of type of destroyer or heavier;
    b. Heavily armored warplanes of a speed more than 250 miles per hour;
    c. Guns of 75 millimeter or higher, and heavily armored vehicles;
    d. Torpedoes and bombs of five hundred pounds or higher;
    e. All kinds of gas except tear gas;
    f. All other physical and chemical weapons of equal or greater destructive or aggressive power.
3. The Unsegregated or State Weapons are herein defined as all physical or chemical weapons of lesser destructive or aggressive power than the Segregated or World Weapons as defined in Section 2 of this Article.

Article II. Distribution of Segregated and Unsegregated Weapons.
1. The World Police shall be the only force in the World Federation which is armed with Segregated Weapons.
2. The manufacture, transportation, and possession of Segregated Weapons shall be the monopoly of the World Federation

Government, through its World Armament Trust as provided in Article XI of this Part.

3. Any sovereign state may maintain an armed force independent of the World Police, provided this force is armed only with Unsegregated Weapons and is used only for the purpose of internal policing.

Article III. Composition of the World Police.

1. The World Police shall consist of military, naval, and air forces.

2. The World Police shall be made up of twelve separate armies: eleven National Contingents and one International Contingent, or Mobile Corps.

Article IV. The National Contingents.

1. Each National Contingent shall consist of officers and men recruited from the citizens of each initiating state.

2. Each National Contingent shall be stationed only in its country of origin, with the following two exceptions:

    a. Part of the United States National Contingent may be stationed in leased bases in the Malaysian Federation and in the Atlantic and Pacific islands of the Western Hemisphere.

    b. Part of the British National Contingent may be stationed in leased bases in the Indian Federation.

3. No troops armed with Segregated Weapons, except the National Contingent of its initiating state, may be stationed at any place in a Regional Federation. No foreign troops may be moved through a Regional Federation without permission of its initiating state.

COMMENT: THE STRATEGIC ZONES

With the National Contingents distributed in this manner, each initiating state obtains as its Strategic Zone the entire Regional Federation of which it is a part. In addition the Strategic Zones of the United States and Britain are extended to include bases in Malaysia and India respectively.

4. In time of peace each National Contingent shall remain a national armed force of its country of origin, subject to the authorities of its state, who shall have the right to educate the troops in the

traditions and ideology they deem best. But in technical matters the military authorities of the state shall co-operate with representatives of the World Federation through a Joint Commission.

5. In time of war emergency each National Contingent shall become automatically, and without the necessity of approval by its initiating state, a part of the World Police, under the command of and at the disposal of the World Federation Government.

Article V. The International Contingent, or Mobile Corps.

1. The International Contingent, or Mobile Corps, shall be made up of *units of regiments* (or their naval and air equivalents) of the same nationality, recruited from all the member states other than initiating states which form part of the sovereign Regional Federations.

2. The Mobile Corps shall be stationed only in strategically located islands purchased by the government of the World Federation, and in leased bases mainly in the Two-Way States. Within these limits its forces may be moved about or concentrated at any given point. The location of the Mobile Corps shall be as follows:

Outer Ring: Spitzbergen, Iceland, Madeira, Azores, Cape Verde, Tierra del Fuego, Falkland Islands, Madagascar, Formosa, Hainan, Kuril Islands. *Inner Ring:* Korea, Armenia, Greece, Belgium.

3. In time of peace the Mobile Corps shall be under the direct training and command and at the immediate disposal of the World Federation Government.

a. The members of the Mobile Corps shall become citizens of the World Federation for the term of their enlistment, subject to the World Federation Bill of Rights, and under exclusive orders of the World Federation Government.

b. The countries of origin shall have no rights in the Mobile Corps other than participation, through a Quota Commission, in its recruitment, in accordance with Article XIV of this Part.

4. In time of war emergency the Mobile Corps shall remain under direct command of the World Federation Government.

Article VI. The Different Uses of the National Contingents and the Mobile Corps.

1. The Mobile Corps constitutes the *Shock Troops* of the World Police.

2. The National Contingents constitute the *Reserves* of the World Police.

3. In case of war emergency the first part of the World Police to be moved to quell an aggression shall always be the Mobile Corps. If more strength is needed, then the National Contingents which are nearest to the center of the disturbance shall be used.

Article VII. The Writ of War Emergency.

1. The World Police may be used only upon a Writ of War Emergency, excepting as provided in Section 6 below.

2. A Writ of War Emergency shall be issued by the World Supreme Court, and only for one or more of the following reasons:

    a. To defend a member state against any armed aggression;

    b. To stop armed aggression by a member state;

    c. To enforce the observance of the quotas of armed forces and armaments;

    d. To quell an act of mutiny or active rebellion among the troops of the World Police.

3. The World Police may not be used to enforce any other violation of the Constitution, or any economic sanctions imposed by the World Supreme Court for such other violations, unless there is armed defiance.

4. Armed aggression (or war) is herein defined as any attack with weapons of violence (Segregated or Unsegregated) when carried out by a sovereign state or its citizens against or upon the territory of another sovereign state or of any Region.

5. In all cases of armed aggression a Writ of War Emergency shall be mandatory upon the World Supreme Court, except in the case of frontier incidents if settled to the satisfaction of the attacked state.

6. The World Police may be used before the issuance of a Writ of War Emergency only in the event of a sudden aggression upon a member state. In this case the national authorities of the National Contingent, or the commanding officers of the Mobile Corps in the attacked country, shall have the right to resist without the Writ

of War Emergency, subject to subsequent approval or disapproval by the World Supreme Court.

Article VIII. Obligations of the World Police.

1. All members of the World Police shall be required to take an oath to uphold the Constitution of the World Federation and to *defend against aggression not only their own country but the World Federation and its member states.*

2. No part of the World Police shall be required at any time to participate in any military operations against its country of origin.

3. The World Police may not interfere in the internal affairs of any state, under any circumstances.

4. If any National Contingent (or the Mobile Corps) should fail to obey the orders of the World Federation Government when based upon a Writ of War Emergency, or if any National Contingent should intervene in the internal affairs of any state, such failure or intervention shall automatically constitute an act of rebellion against the World Federation.

Article IX. Equipment, Recruitment, and Training of the World Police.

1. All branches of the World Police shall receive the same equipment and be subject to the same general regulations.

2. All members of the World Police shall be highly paid volunteers, with high-school education or the equivalent, and conscious of their mission as soldiers of peace.

3. The pay of the National Contingents shall be quite adequate to attract the right type of soldiers and officers and shall be in proportion to the standard of living prevalent in the country of origin. The pay of the International Contingent (Mobile Corps) shall be uniform, rated on the standard of living of the economically more prosperous non-initiating states.

4. The term of enlistment for the troops of the National Contingents and of the Mobile Corps shall be six years, not renewable. A rotational system of enlistment shall be instituted.

5. The troops of both the National and International Contingents shall be employed, in addition to their usual duties of technical training, in works of general welfare. In the event of such disasters as earthquakes or floods, the World Federation Govern-

ment may call upon the Mobile Corps to aid in the relief of the distressed peoples. The same applies to the National Contingents, under the authorities of their respective national governments.

6. Special schools shall be established to train the men and officers for employment in governmental and public institutions. After the termination of their enlistment all members of the World Police shall have a preferential rating in the civil-service selection of officials and employees of the various branches of the World or Regional governments. An enlistment in the World Police, therefore, becomes a public career that extends beyond the term of enlistment.

Article X. Division of the World Police by Quotas.

1. To each of the eleven National Contingents and to the Mobile Corps is assigned a certain *quota* of all the troops, officers, and heavy weapons which constitute the World Police.

2. The quota of the Mobile Corps is supplied from the non-initiating states in proportion to their populations, except that, for reasons of balance, the maximum representation in the Mobile Corps allowed to any non-initiating state (such as Brazil) shall be on the basis of fifteen million population. In the event that there are not enough recruits available in any non-initiating state to fill its proportion of the Mobile Corps quota in accordance with the educational standards, the quota shall be filled from neighboring states.

3. The government of the World Federation may, from time to time, increase or decrease the *total* number of troops and/or quantities of armament of the World Police. But it shall have no power to change the quotas assigned to the National Contingents or to the Mobile Corps. Such a change can be made only by a constitutional amendment, requiring a unanimous vote of all the World Trustees, plus ratification by nine of the thirteen Regional Trustees of all Regional Federations.

COMMENT: The respective quotas of the Contingents are not equal. The quota assigned to the National Contingent of each initiating state is based mainly upon the correlation of three factors: (1) the present industrial power of the initiating state, (2) the extent of Regional territory it must defend, and (3) the psychopolitical factor.

On the following page is given a detailed table of the quotas to be assigned to each member state.

THE QUOTA TABLE OF THE WORLD POLICE

Quota	Contingent of Initiating State	Where Stationed	Regional Federation Represented
20%	United States	United States; leased bases in the islands of the Western Hemisphere and in the Malaysian Federation	Pan-American
15%	British (including English-speaking Dominions)	British Empire; bases in the Indian Federation	British
15%	Russian	USSR	Russian
6%	Chinese	China	Chinese
6%	French	France	Latin-European
3%	German*	Germany*	Germanic
3%	Polish	Poland	Middle European
3%	Turkish	Turkey	Middle Eastern
3%	Indian (provisionally selected under British Command)	India	Indian
2%	Malaysian (provisionally selected under American Command)	Malaysian Federation	Malaysian
2%	Japanese*	Japan*	Japanese
22%	International Mobile Corps All member states not listed above (non-initiating states)	Two-Way States and strategic bases owned or leased by the World Federation, as specified in Article V of this Part.	All the member Regional Federations (Collective Quota)

100%

NOTE: The percentages in this Quota Table apply to the trained man power and reserves, the composition of the High Command of the World Police, and the corresponding percentages of all the manufacturing plants, equipment, ammunition, ships, planes, and other Segregated Weapons assigned to each state.

*For the first twenty-four years the German and Japanese National Contingents shall form part of the Mobile Corps and shall not be stationed in Germany or Japan.

COMMENT: THE QUOTA TABLE OF THE WORLD POLICE

It is the declared purpose of the United Nations' governments that the world shall be policed against new aggressors by the combined forces of the United Nations. The Quota Force Principle effectuates that purpose. Over ninety per cent of the total World Police Force is assigned to the United Nations. The quota of Germany and Japan together is only five per cent, while neutral Turkey's quota is three per cent.

While the most careful consideration has been given to the quotas listed on the preceding page, the proposed table of quotas may, and probably will, be modified through negotiation between the leading powers concerned, preliminary to the founding of the Provisional Government of the World Federation. But, whatever the nature of the final agreement on the quotas to be assigned to each state, and however flexible the Constitution of the World Federation may be in other respects, it is of vital importance that the quotas should not be subjected to future changes without a grave and compelling reason. Otherwise the Quota Force Principle might degenerate into a football of power politics, with each state constantly seeking to improve its own quota at the expense of other states, for the secret purpose of aggression. Hence the stringent requirements for the constitutional amendment of the quotas, by means of which each state concerned is fully protected against unwarranted changes by other members of the World Federation.

The enormous differences between the Quota Force method of policing the world and the vague, unrealistic "policing" of the world now proposed by some statesmen of the United Nations are these:

1. The Quota Force method does not depend in any way upon the national power politics of the governments of individual nations, and cannot be upset by changes within these governments.

2. The Quota Force method embodies the principle of policing the world, but not only by the victorious nations; all the nations of the world share this privilege and responsibility.

3. The Quota Force method makes it impossible for the militarists of Germany, Japan, and other defeated nations to combine

in the future for wars of revenge or to combine with any other aggressor.

Article XI. The World Armament Trust.

The monopoly of the manufacture, transportation, and possession of Segregated Weapons vested in the government of the World Federation shall operate as follows:

1. A World Armament Trust shall be established by the government of the World Federation.

2. The World Armament Trust shall have one manufacturing division for each initiating state, to be located therein.

3. For the first twenty-four years there shall be no manufacturing division of the World Armament Trust located in Germany or Japan.

4. In each manufacturing division the production of the Segregated Weapons, as well as the reserve matériel, shall be in exact proportion to the National Contingent quota assigned to that initiating state.

5. There shall also be, in non-initiating states, a number of smaller divisions of the World Armament Trust for the manufacture of Segregated Weapons needed for the Mobile Corps.

6. All manufacturing plants for Segregated Weapons shall be purchased by the World Federation Government on behalf of the World Armament Trust and thereafter operated for its account.

Article XII. The Right of Inspection.

1. The government of the World Federation shall have the right to maintain within the territories of all member states a staff of inspectors to supervise compliance with all provisions of Part Seven of this Constitution dealing with the World Police and to report possible violations of the Quota Force Principle in connection with armed forces or the prohibition of Segregated Weapons.

2. Citizens or officials guilty of violations will be subject to extremely heavy penalties, and if the government of a member state itself is found guilty of such violation, the state will be liable to severe economic penalties.

ILLUSTRATIVE TABLE OF THE QUOTA FORCE PRINCIPLE

The *total* size of the World Police Force shall be determined by the government of the World Federation, and it may be increased or decreased as the necessity arises.

However, for purposes of illustration, let us assume that the total postwar strength of the World Police shall consist of 2,000,000 men, 50,000 warplanes, 100,000 tanks and guns, and 100 battleships or aircraft carriers, with all the other weapons in proportion. This is indeed a powerful armored force, considerably greater than would probably be necessary to maintain world security and peace in a world armed only with light weapons. Yet even this formidable force represents less than one thirtieth of the trained man power now under arms and about one tenth of the armored machines (except battleships) that will probably be produced in the world before this war is ended.

On the basis of the Quota Table, the Mobile Corps, the National Contingents, and their armament would be distributed as follows:

Initiating State	Quota	National Troops	Planes	Tanks	Capital Ships[1]
UNITED STATES	20%	400,000	10,000	20,000	20
BRITAIN	15	300,000	7,500	15,000	15
RUSSIA	15	300,000	7,500	15,000	15
CHINA	6	120,000	3,000	6,000	6
FRANCE	6	120,000	3,000	6,000	6
GERMANY	3	60,000	1,500	3,000	3
POLAND	3	60,000	1,500	3,000	3
TURKEY	3	60,000	1,500	3,000	3
INDIA	3	60,000	1,500	3,000	3
MALAYSIA	2	40,000	1,000	2,000	2
JAPAN	2	40,000	1,000	2,000	2
MOBILE CORPS	22	440,000	11,000	22,000	22
TOTAL	100%	2,000,000	50,000	100,000	100

COMMENT: FUTURE HITLERS ARE ELIMINATED

On the basis of the Quota Force Principle it will be impossible for any future dictator to carry out a gigantic program of rearmament for aggression.

[1]Capital ships now consist of battleships and aircraft carriers, but this may change later to denote any other vessel used as a capital ship.

An attempt by any government to seize or produce Segregated Weapons is a basic violation of the Constitution and Treaty of Collective Defense, automatically calling for a Writ of War Emergency and invasion of the violator state by the Mobile Corps and, if necessary, by the National Contingents of other powers. Hitler was able to carry out with impunity his program of rearmament because there was no *separate* international organization powerfully armed, owing its allegiance only to the constitution of a world government and run by officials who could not be ordered or recalled by any national government. Instead there was a remnant of the Anglo-French alliance, whose members, although in joint control of Europe, were paralyzed by the more immediate considerations of the interests of their national power politics, while the impotent League made resolutions. Under the Quota Force Principle, Hitler would have been stopped within one week instead of ten years, or else the officials of the World Federation Government would have been impeached and replaced.

Any attempt by future aggressors to arm secretly would hardly be possible, considering the legion of inspectors that would be employed by the World Federation and the fact that modern rearmament is so gigantic in scope that it cannot be concealed for long. But even if a future Hitler should succeed in an effort to rearm his country in secret and attack with his allies, he would never meet the demoralized world that Hitler met, when terrified small states hid their heads in the sands of "absolute" neutrality and the will of a powerful nation like the United States was paralyzed by political debate. Instead he would meet a highly integrated world organization with an organized World Police and overwhelming reserves. There would be no need of ambassadorial conferences behind the closed doors or dickering among the sovereign states.

ELIMINATION OF WARS BETWEEN INDIVIDUAL NATIONS

On the basis of the Quota Force Principle, it is impossible to cite any situation in which one state could successfully attack another. Unless the Mobile Corps *and all* the National Contingents refuse to act (which psychologically is out of the question), an aggressor nation must be heavily outnumbered.

This, of course, will have a most beneficial effect upon the individual nations. France, for instance, will no longer have to fear an attack from Germany. Not only will she have twice the amount of armored forces as Germany, under the quota, but the formidable Mobile Corps, more than seven times stronger than the German Contingent, will be her perpetual ally against aggression. Thus it will not matter to France that Germany's population and industrial power are so crushingly superior.

The same applies to China, whose National Contingent (six per cent) will be three times as strong as that of Japan. China will not even have to fear an attack by Russia (fifteen per cent), since she will have for her immediate defense an Armored Force of twenty-eight per cent, composed of the Chinese National Contingent of six per cent plus the Mobile Corps of twenty-two per cent—not to count the other National Contingents. The tragedy of Poland, wedged between powerful hereditary enemies to the west and east, also will disappear. The innumerable wars between the nations of the Balkans will be eliminated. Fratricidal wars, such as those between Bolivia and Peru, will never be revived.

Even if the United States, with its quota of twenty per cent and great distance from the nearest bases of the Mobile Corps, should, for example, invade Mexico, the power of the Mobile Corps is such that the aggression would be short-lived. The United States would not get much further than Mexico before it met the bulk of the Mobile Corps, while other National Contingents would begin to concentrate in the Pacific. The United States would lose its magnificent Malaysian bases and its foreign trade would be destroyed.

The International Contingent by its very nature will always move against an aggressor and never in an aggressor's favor. It not only consists of carefully selected and trained troops but is made up of units of regiments of the same nationality, representing two score of smaller states. The homes and families of its troops are in those states, and there is nothing that any dictator could offer that would satisfy all of these states enough to induce them to risk their own destruction. Even if the Mobile Corps should betray the World Federation, it would have to face a coalition of all the remaining National Contingents who, for vital reasons of power politics, could not permit the tyranny of small states any more than the domination of a great power. The Quota Force Mechanism operates, so to speak, on a gyroscopic principle by automatic balance of military, psychosocial, and political forces.

ELIMINATION OF WARS BETWEEN COALITIONS

The Quota Mechanism not only eliminates military dictatorships and wars between individual nations; it eliminates wars between alliances or coalitions of nations. *On the basis of the Quota Force Principle, it is impossible to cite any politically conceivable combination of nations which could conduct a war of aggression against the remaining nations of the World Federation without being decisively outnumbered.*

Let us assume a most powerful (though a very unlikely) combination of nations some years after the World Federation is founded: The United States, Great Britain, and France decide to rebel against the World Federation and to conquer the world. *Without* the Quota Force Principle there is no question that this coalition of powers could easily dominate the world. *With* the Quota Force Principle, the joint quota of these three nations would be only forty-one per cent. Against them there would be lined up armored forces of planes, tanks, and warships totaling fifty-nine per cent, of which twenty-two per cent, the Mobile Corps, would be the Shock Troops. Before England and France (twenty-one per cent) would have time to develop their industrial potential into a military potential they would be overwhelmed, and the United States, with its twenty per cent, would be isolated.

Let us reverse the situation and assume a communist-dominated Europe and Asia, in revolt against the World Federation and the Anglo-Americans. *Without* the World Federation, a communist Japan, China, Poland, Russia, Germany, France, and Turkey against the Anglo-Americans would automatically result in a third world war. If the democracies were divided within or between themselves, they would probably lose such a war; and even if they were united, the issue would be in doubt. *With* the World Federation, the quotas of the rebel communist nations would total only thirty-eight per cent, against the sixty-two per cent total of the Mobile Corps, the Anglo-Americans, and the other Contingents of the World Police.

The decisive importance of the Mobile Corps as a balance wheel in the various combinations of National Contingents is apparent. The quotas of the United States, Britain, and Russia and the quota of the Mobile Corps are so balanced that a war of aggression by two of these countries could not succeed against the third plus the Mobile Corps. It is practically impossible to form any combination of aggressor nations which could prevail against the Mobile Corps and only a few other initiating states.

As part of the World Federation, neither the United States, Britain, nor Russia would ever fight alone if attacked; and because of their large quotas, each could form a nucleus of resistance against the aggressors, which would probably prove decisive. *Without* the Quota Force Principle, none of these powers could ever be assured of support from other nations; nor could any of them successfully resist the many aggressor combinations that could be and certainly would be organized against these immensely wealthy nations. *With* the World Federation, its Constitution becomes a perpetual Treaty of Alliance, binding together these three great powers, and binding each of them to the collective power of all the smaller nations.

Let us now assume a situation in the not too distant future, twenty-seven years hence, when both Britain and the United States are threatened by a Trotskyite Russia (superior in power to the United States), militarist China-Japan, and neo-Nazi Germany. It could not happen earlier, because Germany and Japan will be effectively disarmed by the World Federation. A deal is made to divide the world in three parts, and Russia, who will exact a lion's share and who no longer needs to fear industrialized Germany, consents. *Without* the World Federation, Britain will at once lose India, the Middle East, the Mediterranean, and we must lose Malaysia. After the British Isles are besieged and taken, we will lose, to start with, Latin America. The end for our *small* population of one hundred and fifty-eight million will then be in sight. Even if the Germany-Russia-China-Japan axis decides not to attack Britain and the United States for a few more years, we would still be crushed under the ever-mounting load of armaments against the machines plus tremendous man power of the axis. *Without* the Quota Force Mechanism, we cannot very well insist on disarming our former allies—Russia or China—and keep them disarmed. They will therefore have twenty years in which to prepare at leisure.

With the Quota Force Mechanism, the World Federation breaks up the potential Axis threat in embryo by preventing any state from taking even the first step in rearmament. During twenty-seven years the World Federation also builds trained reserves of the World Police and organizes the collective defense of the world on a permanent basis. Should conflict break out anyway, the neo-axis will have only twenty-six per cent against the World Federation and Anglo-American seventy-four per cent. Two or three precious months will be ample time, with modern planes, to annihilate the aggressors.

Finally, let us take the United States alone, assuming that Britain's power is neutralized by an internal revolution while we are being attacked by Germany, Russia, China, and Japan. *Without* the World Federation we would be easily overwhelmed. *With* the Mobile Corps and Malaysia, we would have forty-four per cent against the neo-axis twenty-six per cent, again a decisive superiority.

In conclusion, two great powers like the United States and Britain will be in dire jeopardy a quarter of a century hence without the World Federation and the Quota Force Principle. With the World Federation and the Quota Force Principle they will indefinitely retain their present relative standing in the world.

How to Disarm Germany and Japan

Some may advance this objection to the Quota Table: the Axis powers, far from being totally disarmed, are allowed (in the case of Germany and Japan) to have their own National Contingents. At first glance this seems to contradict the specific promise of the Atlantic Charter to disarm the Axis powers. Actually, the Quota Force Principle not only disarms the Axis powers far more effectively than if they were stripped of every soldier and gun, but makes it possible to keep them disarmed for generations.

It must be realized, of course, that these specially selected German and Japanese Contingents for twenty-four years are part of the Mobile Corps, under the full control of the World Federation; that these Contingents, as part of the Mobile Corps, are stationed not in Germany or Japan but in the Mobile Corps bases, and that no production of weapons in Germany or Japan will be permitted for twenty-four years.

Let us now consider Germany, which for nearly a century has been the chief culprit in European wars of aggression, after the twenty-four-year period is over and she regains peacetime control of her National Contingent. *Without* the Quota Force Principle, the adequate disarmament of Germany (or of any other power) could be maintained only by means of foreign troops of occupation, permanently stationed in the strategic centers of Germany itself. But the permanent occupation of a virile and powerful country like Germany could never be realized in practice. There would be the relentless pressure of the Germans themselves, internally united by hatred of a foreign master. There would also be, in due time, growing political pressure within the United Nations, demanding the recall of the costly troops of occupation. Furthermore, there would be inevitable rivalries and fears among the former allies, and behind-the-scenes "arrangements" with Germany. One by one, or all together, the armies of occupation would withdraw and leave a void in Germany—a void which would be quickly filled by vengeful Germans, especially those of the militarist class.

With the Quota Force Principle, Germany will not only be disarmed, but will be kept disarmed by a *new kind of permanent army of occupation*. This occupying army, composed of Germans themselves, will be maintained, not against the opposition of the entire German people, but with the enthusiastic consent of most of them. The German National Contingent (three per cent) will fulfill the duty of defending its fatherland against aggression from without, and also perform the function of serving as a watchdog to prevent the formation of another, rival army within. That portion of the German quota which is composed of the peace-loving, idealistic type of German who in the past has contributed so much to civilization, will be the staunchest ally of the World Federation and the most relentless foe of the militarists within the country. Those volunteers who are not so idealistic will, in their own selfish interests, seek to prevent the establishment of a rival army. In any case, this three per cent of highly paid Germans in the World Police, while strong enough and wise enough to crush any future militarist attempts within their own country, will never be strong enough to threaten their neighbors with wars of aggression. Finally, a legion of inspectors, responsible only to the World Federation Government, will see to it that in Germany, as elsewhere, the provisions of the Quota Force Principle are relentlessly enforced.

The Quota Force Mechanism provides not only the means for an effective disarmament of Germany and Japan, but, what is more important, the *only* means of keeping them permanently disarmed.

THE NATIONAL CONTINGENTS

The most striking characteristic of the Quota Force Principle is to be found in its method of using the national armies of the initiating states. Each National Contingent of the World Police becomes a double-purpose army: In peacetime it is, as heretofore, a *national* armed force, trained and commanded by its own citizens and stationed exclusively in its country of origin for the purpose of *defense* against any aggression. In the case of war emergency the National Contingent becomes an *international* armed force, maintained and commanded by the Government of the World Federation for the purpose of *attack* against aggressors.

This type of national armed force is based on an entirely new conception. The National Contingent does not "belong" to its initiating state. Though recruited from the state's citizens and stationed in its territory, it is *lend-leased* by the World Federation to the initiating state for the purpose of guaranteeing the latter against the possible tyranny of the World Federation Government or the possible military dictatorship of the World Police. Hence the detailed and specific provisions as to the nationality, recruitment, and peacetime command of these National Contingents.

But the main purpose of the National Contingents is to create an ever-ready international police force powerful enough to prevent successful aggression by any state or combination of states. It is with this understanding that the volunteers are trained, and it is to this higher purpose that they dedicate themselves.

This double use of a national army is psychologically possible only because of the great strength of nationalism inherent in modern states. For instance, it is psychologically certain that the United States soldiers, selected and trained by the American Government, would never turn against their mother country to support any tyrannical action of the World Federation or to further the cause of a *foreign* dictator. On the other hand, since the United States National Contingent is also a part of the World Police, paid by the World Federation and made up of professional soldiers bound by oath and training to support the Constitution of the World Federation, this Contingent would not hesitate to move against any foreign country guilty of aggression, when commanded to do so by the World Federation. Thus the American Contingent would defend both the World Federation and the United States.

This question may be raised: What is to prevent a leading power from seizing control of its National Contingent to use it for purposes of conquest, or to prevent its constitutional use by the World Federation?

It is highly improbable that any government could thus seize control of its National Contingent. Something akin to a revolutionary conspiracy would be required for it deliberately to break the solemn pact of defensive alliance which binds all member states together, and thus become an aggressor against the World Federation. Any attempt at conquest would create a divided public opinion within the country, and a divided National Contingent. It could not possibly succeed against the overwhelming forces of the other National Contingents and the Mobile Corps.

All National Contingents are controlled by the same powerful psychosocial forces: On orders of the World Federation Government they will *attack* an aggressor anywhere, for they have been selected and trained and are paid for that purpose, and they will *defend* their own countries against any aggressor, because they are rooted in their nations.

Let us reverse the situation and consider whether a possible conspiracy within the World Federation Government could secure sufficient military force to unjustly attack and overwhelm an individual state, despite its National Contingent.

The World Federation Government is prevented from becoming tyrannical precisely because of the nationalistic structure of the National Contingents. An attempt to launch an unjustified attack against one nation is a threat to other nations. It is certain to meet with resistance not only from the National Contingent of the attacked state, but from other Contingents as well.

In addition, the structure of the World Federation Government itself makes it very difficult for a nation or combination of nations to conspire against the others. The officials of the World Federation Government are not ambassadorial representatives of their states or Regions, subject to orders or recall. They owe their allegiance during a fixed term of office only to the Constitution of the World Federation; they are subject to speedy impeachment and removal from office either for abuses of power or for failure to act. The checks and balances in the Constitution are so arranged that no single branch of the World Federation Government can control it. Therefore any conspiracy would require that a majority of the World Supreme Court join with a majority of the World Trustees and the President of the World Federation to violate the Constitution in the selfish interest of a nation or Region. Even if such a conspiracy did take place, the enormous forces of opposition generated within the World Federation Government itself and in the World Police would make its success impossible.

Thus the inner contradiction involved in the problem of world peace has been solved. An international armed force has been created which is powerful enough to stop any aggression, and yet, by means of the National Contingents, each leading power retains the means to defend itself against *any* aggression—even against the possible tyranny of the World Federation.

THE INTERNATIONAL MOBILE CORPS

For the first time in history the smaller nations of the world, which have a population of roughly three hundred million, will acquire a powerful collective armed force for their own defense and also for the defense of all other member states and of the World Federation itself. It will be seen from the Quota Table that the collective quota assigned to the small nations exceeds the individual quota of any single initiating state. Thus the Mobile Corps becomes more powerful than any National Contingent. Existing sovereign states, such as Brazil or Norway, and revived sovereign states, such as Korea, will receive the immediate protection of the Mobile Corps against any future aggression. The protection of any small state has now become entirely possible, due to modern communications and transportation, by means of which the decisive heavy weapons can be quickly concentrated anywhere in the world. The same Industrial Revolution that has virtually disarmed all the weaker nations can rearm them in the service of lasting peace.

It is psychologically certain that the Mobile Corps will always be on the side of the World Federation and *against* any aggressor nation or any rebellious National Contingent. The World Federation is the only and the *last* bulwark of freedom and security for the smaller nations. These nations have no imperialistic ambitions. They seek to survive—not to conquer. So that the Mobile Corps may be bound even more strongly to the World Federation, its regiments have been taken from the control of their states of origin (except for recruiting) and placed, in war or peace, under the direct control of the World Federation. The regiments of the Mobile Corps, though composed of troops and officers of the same nationality (thus avoiding the destruction of the national spirit, as in the case of a "foreign legion"), are stationed outside their countries of origin and owe their allegiance only to the government of the World Federation.

For all these reasons the immediate and most powerful defense of the World Federation against aggression or rebellion is placed in the hands of those nations whose very existence depends on the World Federation—the weaker nations. By means of the Quota Force Mechanism, these weak nations, which *individually* could not maintain even a fraction of such force, *collectively* become the greatest military power in the world.

The Mobile Corps, even to a more decided extent than the National Contingents, will operate as a double purpose force: to defend the family of the smaller nations against aggression by powerful neighbors, and to be the first to defend an initiating state against aggression.

Why the Quotas Are Equitable

There may be some who will find apparent injustices in the Quota Table.

In the case of China, for example, it would seem that this heroic nation of five hundred million people should be entitled to more than six per cent of the world's armed forces. Actually, the very size of her population is the main reason for China's relatively low quota. China not only has a very small industrial capacity and a territory which is fairly easy to defend, but she possesses an enormous homogeneous population. She will have trained forces for internal policing at least four times the size of those of the United States. Such a police force, even without Segregated Weapons, will be, *in effect,* a supporting infantry.

The ideal distribution of the World Police might seem to be the assignment of an equal quota to each of the eleven Regional Federations. But this would be totally unrealistic. In computing the quotas one must keep in mind not only the factors of territory and industrial capacity but the psychopolitical factors as well. If each Region had an equal quota of the world's armed forces, the poorer Regions (which are in great majority) might seek to combine for an attack against the few prosperous Regions. In the face of such a dangerous prospect no statesman of the United States, Britain, or Russia could seriously advocate the adoption of the World Federation or any similar Plan.

After the surrender of the Axis powers, Russia, Britain, and the United States will have virtual military control of the world and a monopoly of the production of heavy weapons. If the peoples and the governments of these three powers are to be asked *voluntarily* to surrender their monopoly of heavy weapons for the benefit of all nations, they must be offered in exchange at least a minimum guarantee of military security, other than the good will of the rest of the nations. On the other hand, if we are to have lasting peace, the other nations of the world must be offered equally effective military guarantees against future aggression by these three powers, individually or in combination.

For these reasons the quotas assigned to the United States, Britain, and Russia (fifty per cent in all) have been calculated so as to strike a satisfactory balance of power between the individual strength of their National Contingents—more than adequate for defense, inadequate for attack—and the collective strength of the rest of the world.

On the basis of their existing industrial potentials and vast territories to defend, the combined military strength of the United States and Britain should be nearer seventy-five per cent of the world's armed forces than thirty-five per cent. But that would mean Anglo-American military control, which the rest of the world would not long tolerate. The quotas of the United States and Britain, therefore, were **made** low enough to guarantee the rest of the world against possible Anglo-American tyranny and yet high enough to assure the Anglo-Americans, jointly or even separately, an adequate defense against possible aggression by any conceivable combination of the other powers of the world. The high quota of fifteen per cent for Russia is more than adequate to defend her against combines of aggressor nations.

In the deeper sense of future reality, it is perhaps best for the peace of the world that the United States, Britain and Russia should be the ones with a preponderance of quota strength. These three powers have not only an idealistic but a selfish interest in preserving peace. Each has a *lebensraum* of continental dimensions. The economy of each is expanding inwardly, not outwardly. Each is threatened by powerful rivals—rump superstates like Germany, which lacks *lebensraum,* or embryonic superstates like China, which lacks technology.

Thus the Quota Force Principle is supported on its two opposite poles: by the most powerful nations, because they have everything; and by the smallest nations, because they wish to preserve what they have.

Article XIII. The Cost of the World Police.

The cost of the organization and full maintenance of the World Police shall be apportioned among the member states as follows:

1. Each initiating state shall pay the amount equal to the quota of the National Contingent and armament assigned to it.

2. Each initiating state shall pay, in addition, an amount equal to one twenty-second of the quota of the International Contingent and armament assigned to it.

3. All the non-initiating states shall each pay their share of the remaining eleven twenty-seconds of the quota of the International Contingent and armament in proportion to the number of their nationals in the International Contingent.

4. In the autonomous Malaysian Regional Federation the Netherlands, France, the Philippines, and Thailand shall pay one half the cost of the Malaysian National Contingent and the United States the other half; in the autonomous Indian Regional Federation the natives shall pay one half of the cost of the Indian National Contingent and Britain the other half.

COMMENT: The United States, for example, pays twenty per cent of the total cost of the World Police, and in addition pays an amount equal to one twenty-second of the twenty-two per cent which is the quota of the International Contingent. Assuming two million men in the World Police, the cost for the United States would be the upkeep of four hundred thousand men of her National Contingent, plus the upkeep of twenty thousand of the International Contingent. Half of the cost of the International Contingent Quota (eleven per cent) will be paid by the non-initiating states. In this manner any initiating state, such as the United States, not only reduces enormously the burden of armament which she would have to bear if no World Police were instituted, but in addition obtains, for a fraction of the cost, the perpetual service against any aggressor of the most powerful armed force in the world—the International Contingent. At the same time the smaller states secure the service of their collective International Contingent, without which they could not survive, at a fraction of the cost.

Article XIV. Procedure for World Disarmament and Organization of World Police.

The organization of the World Police shall take place during the Provisional Period, and shall proceed as follows:

1. Immediately upon cessation of hostilities, the Provisional Government of the World Federation shall appoint one Quota Commission for each initiating state and one for the Mobile Corps.

2. The Quota Commissions for the initiating states shall be composed half of appointees of the Provisional Government and half of appointees of the government of the initiating state concerned. The Quota Commission of the Mobile Corps shall be composed of one representative from each member non-initiating state and an equal number appointed by the Provisional Government.

3. In every country the respective Quota Commissions, in cooperation with the officials of the state, shall proceed to demobilize and disarm all the existing forces armed with Segregated Weapons. Segregated Weapons shall be deposited in special arsenals and ports.

4. At the same time the Quota Commissions shall proceed to recruit, examine, and arm with Segregated Weapons the volunteers for the World Police, in exact proportion to the quota of troops and armaments assigned to each state.

Exception: In the case of the initiating states Germany and Japan:

    a. The Quota Commission shall be named entirely by the Provisional Government of the World Federation, who shall proceed to the recruitment of their National Contingents;

    b. During twenty-four years their National Contingents shall be under full control of the government of the World Federation and shall be deemed to be an added quota (three per cent for Germany and two per cent for Japan) of the International Contingent, which shall have the right to station its other armed forces on the territories of Germany and Japan.

    c. During twenty-four years there shall be no production of Segregated or Unsegregated Weapons whatsoever on the territories of Germany and Japan, and the production of their five per cent of armaments shall be arranged elsewhere, in the plants supplying the International Contingent;

    d. During twenty-four years a selected number of industrialized plants in Germany and Japan (such as Krupp), which in the past specialized in the production of armaments, shall be managed by a Special Agency of the World Federation for the account of the German and Japanese governments, for non-military production, and their production shall be turned entirely to the rebuilding of the areas originally invaded by Germany and Japan.

COMMENT: By the procedure described in this paragraph it is possible to achieve two revolutionary changes within one year from the termination of hostilities: (1) the disarmament of all the individual nations, and (2) the establishment of the National Contingents and the Mobile Corps of the World Police. This can be done without encroaching upon the freedom or essential sovereignty of any nation. As a result the economic reconstruction of the world can proceed, not in an atmosphere of power politics among the victors and hatreds among the defeated peoples under American, British, or Russian troops of occupation, but within the political and military framework of freedom and order, satisfactory to the victors and the vanquished alike.

Article XV. The Quota Force Principle and Non-Member States. The quota of Armed Forces and Segregated Weapons assigned to each state shall be applied regardless of whether or not the state is a member of the World Federation. The procedure shall be as follows:

1. In the case of non-initiating states which remain outside the World Federation, they shall be forbidden to possess, manufacture, or transport Segregated Weapons. In exchange the World Federation shall guarantee them against any foreign aggression.

2. In the case of any initiating state which is not a member of the World Federation, a special Quota Limitation Treaty shall be negotiated. By the terms of this treaty the initiating state may maintain at its own expense its own independent armed forces and may manufacture Segregated Weapons, provided it does not exceed the quota assigned to it, and provided it permits full inspection by representatives of the World Federation.

3. In the event that a non-member initiating state refuses to sign such a treaty, the World Federation Government need not use coercion. The quotas can be maintained by a proportionate increase in the total armed strength of the World Federation's member states.

COMMENT: The Quota Force Principle operates like a defensive alliance among the member states, except that the military rights and duties of each member are determined in advance and except that, through the machinery of the World Federation, the alliance is made irrevocable.

It is of fundamental importance that no state should be allowed to break down the Quota Force Principle by exceeding its quota of armed forces armed with Segregated Weapons. The application of the Quota Force Principle must be made world-wide if lasting peace is to be assured.

The only real difficulty in applying the Quota Force Principle to non-member states arises if an allied initiating state, such as Russia, refuses either to join the World Federation or to enter into a Quota Limitation Treaty. It is possible that Russia, mindful of her bitter prewar experiences with the capitalistic countries and suspicious of their future intentions, might adopt a policy of total isolation until convinced that the World Federation is designed for her benefit as well as for that of other nations. Since it is unthinkable that the United Nations should take a hostile attitude toward a former ally whose heroism has contributed so much to their cause, another solution is provided in Section 3 above. There could be no objection on Russia's part if the World Federation should increase its own total armed strength, parallel to Russian increases, so as to maintain the Quota Force Principle. Since the structure of the World Federation makes it impossible for any member state to engage in wars of aggression, Russia will soon become convinced that her military security is best maintained by the Quota Force Principle, and she will abandon any attempt to upset it.

Furthermore, because of the Quota Force Principle, there is another decisive advantage to membership in the World Federation which will eventually cause Russia and every other country to join. This is the cost of military security. By means of their National Contingents the United States, Britain, and Russia acquire larger armed forces of their own than they would probably have after the war if they maintained separate armies; strong forces are given to the other initiating states; and a powerful collective army is created for the smaller states of the world. Yet the total armed strength will be but a fraction of the fifteen or more million men previously held under arms even in peacetime, and the cost to the individual nations will be enormously reduced.

By pooling their resources and overhead each of the seventy-odd nations will have for its defense a far more powerful armed force than heretofore, at a fraction of the previous cost—thus saving billions of dollars yearly. If we add to this the backbreaking load of war expenditures, the saving may well mean a new civilization, with an undreamed-of standard of living for all.

This completes the presentation of the Quota Force Principle. In essence the Quota Mechanism regulates the transfer of the monopoly of Segregated Weapons and armed forces from the individual nations into the hands of a co-operative of all nations. Only in this manner can the world achieve lasting peace. A tremendous load will be lifted from the shoulders of humanity. And the social cancer of war will be checked by the organized forces of peace.

PART EIGHT: ORGANIZATION AND POWERS OF THE PERMANENT GOVERNMENT OF THE WORLD FEDERATION

For purposes of clarity it is assumed that the World Federation will contain the full complement of eleven member Regional Federations. However, in the event that the World Federation contains less than eleven member Regional Federations, all the articles and provisions of this Constitution shall remain in force except that in the matter of selection of the government of the World Federation and the number of representatives, and in the matter of voting, an adjustment shall be made to correspond to the reduced number of member Regional Federations and member states.

Article I. The Three Branches of the Permanent Government.

1. The *executive branch* of the World Federation Government shall be headed by the World President, with his Cabinet. The World President shall have a six-year term, not renewable.

2. The *legislative branch* of the World Federation Government shall consist of two houses: The World Trustees and the World Vocational Senate.

    a. All members of the legislative branch shall have six-year terms, not renewable.

    b. The House of World Trustees shall be composed of thirteen members, one from each initiating state and two, at large, from the non-initiating states.

    c. The World Vocational Senate shall be composed of sixty-six members, six from each Regional Federation, representing in equal proportion Capital (or executive management), Labor, Agriculture, Science, Education (secular and religious), and Arts (including Crafts).

3. The *judicial branch* of the World Federation Government shall consist of a World Supreme Court and a World Equity Court.

    a. The World Supreme Court shall be composed of thirteen members, for life terms (with retirement provision), one from each initiating state and two, at large, from the non-initiating states. It shall be the final interpreter and custodian of the Constitution of the World Federation.

b. The World Equity Court shall be composed of thirteen members, for life terms (with retirement provision), one from each initiating state and two, at large, from the non-initiating states. It shall deal, either directly or through appointed arbitrators, with all treaties and with all economic, political, or territorial disputes arising between states or Regions or involving the World Federation Government.

4. The capital of the World Federation shall be located on extraterritorial grounds in the initiating state from which the current World President is chosen. When it moves, the previous capital shall become an endowed world university.

COMMENT: The slight disadvantage of moving the capital every six years is more than compensated for by bringing the World Federation into the heart of every Region and by periodically creating world centers of culture.

Article II. The Selection of World Federation Officials.

1. The World President shall be chosen, except in one case, from each initiating state in turn.

a. The first President of the Permanent Government of the World Federation shall come from the United States. The second World President shall come from the British Regional Federation; the third, exceptionally, shall be selected by all the member states which are not initiating states Thereafter the Latin-European and the other Regional Federations shall choose the World President in turn, moving eastward.

b. After the first term of office the World President shall be elected either by a majority vote of all the voting inhabitants of the Regional Federation from which he is chosen or by a majority vote of the Regional Senate with the approval of the Regional President.

2. The World Trustee, Justice of the World Supreme Court, and Justice of the World Equity Court from each initiating state shall be selected by the head of that state, with the approval of its legislative body.

3. The two World Trustees, two Justices of the World Supreme Court, and two Justices of the World Equity Court representing all the non-initiating states shall be selected as follows:

a. The Regional Trustees of each Regional Federation which are chosen by the non-initiating states of that Region shall appoint delegates to a World Electoral Convention.

b. There shall be thirteen delegates to the World Electoral Convention in all, appointed in proportion to population of the non-initiating states; except that, for reasons of balance, the maximum representation allowed to any non-initiating state (such as Italy) shall be on the basis of fifteen million population.

c. This World Electoral Convention shall elect (and not from their members) the two World Trustees, two Justices of the World Supreme Court, and two Justices of the World Equity Court representing all the non-initiating states.

d. In the event that the Regional Governments are not yet in operation and there are no Regional Trustees, then the heads of the governments of the various non-initiating states shall jointly choose the representatives for the World Federation Government.

4. The procedure described above shall apply in the selection of the third World President from all the non-initiating states.

5. The President of each Regional Federation shall select six World Senators, one representing Capital (or executive management), one representing Labor, one representing Agriculture, one representing Science, one representing Education, and one representing Arts. The appointment of these Six World Vocational Senators must be approved by a majority vote of the Regional Senate. A rotational system shall be instituted so that the terms of one third of the Senators shall expire every two years.

6. For the first twenty-four years the German and Japanese members of the World Trustees, World Supreme Court, and World Equity Court must be approved by the other World Trustees.

7. All officials and employees of the World Federation shall become citizens of the World Federation for the duration of their office. They shall not be responsible to the governments of their countries of origin, and may not be prosecuted by any state for their acts during their term of office. However, they are impeachable and subject to heavy penalties by the World Federation for abuse of office or for

failure to act promptly and with due diligence in carrying out their duties as prescribed in the Constitution.

8. After the first term of office each initiating state or Regional Federation may adopt any alternative method for selecting its World Trustees, World Senators, or World Justices, provided such method is based on popular election. The same provision shall apply to all Regional Governments.

Article III. The Powers of the World Federation Government.

1. The Powers of the World Federation Government over member states and Regions are of three kinds:

> a. Powers enforceable by means of the World Police, requiring a Writ of War Emergency issued by the World Supreme Court.
>
> b. Powers enforceable by means of economic sanctions (blockades, extra tariffs, etc.), requiring a Writ of Economic Sanctions issued by the World Supreme Court. When economic sanctions so imposed are resisted by arms, such resistance shall automatically constitute an act of armed aggression, subject to a Writ of War Emergency.
>
> c. Powers based upon the consent of one or more member states, under the legislative control or supervision of the World Vocational Senate and the executive power of the World President.

2. The powers which are enforceable by means of the World Police are:

> a. The prohibition of armed aggression by any member state or Region.
>
> b. The prohibition of the manufacture, transportation, or possession of Segregated Weapons by any member state or any Region.
>
> c. The administration of the World Police and the World Armament Trust, in accordance with the Quota Force Principle, Part Seven.
>
> d. The right to maintain in the territories of sovereign states World Federal Courts and inspectors for the sole purpose of enforcing the prohibition of the manufacture or transportation of Segregated Weapons by private organizations or state officials. The World Federation Courts in each country must

be based on the Bill of Rights, including trial by jury made up of native citizens.

3. The powers which are enforceable by economic sanctions are:
a. Collection of dues from member states for the maintenance of the government and various institutions of the World Federation. Assessment of dues shall be based upon each state's proportion of national wealth or annual income; or, if it appears both desirable and feasible, upon rental values of land or any other proportionate method of valuation. No tax or levy which is discriminatory against a member state or encroaches upon the sovereignty of a member state may be imposed by the World Federation. If the dues are not paid within three months of the stipulated date, the government of the World Federation may levy upon the imports and exports of the delinquent state to the extent of its delinquency.
b. Supervision of the rights of the native inhabitants of Pooled Colonies to self-rule and fair treatment, in accordance with Part Nine, Article V.
c. Administration of international communications, including the allocation of radio wave lengths.
d. Supervision of certain important straits, canals, and waterways so that no nation may be barred from passing through these waterways and no discriminatory rates may be charged to any state or the citizens of any state.
e. The conduct of plebiscites in sovereign states to determine the will of the people in regard to joining a Regional Federation; the conduct of plebiscites in autonomous Regional Federations and in Pooled Colonies to establish sovereignty; the conduct of plebiscites (under jurisdiction of the World Equity Court) to settle territorial disputes, in accordance with Part Five. All plebiscites shall be conducted by means of Plebiscite Commissions established jointly with the governments of the states or territories concerned.
f. Under the World Equity Court:
(1) Arbitration of all economic or territorial disputes between member states or Regions, except as limited by Part Five, Article I, Section 4.
(2) Periodic reviewing (every twenty-four years and upon

complaint) of treaties to rectify obvious injustices when due to changed conditions;

(3) Negotiation of Priority Treaties;

(4) Enforcement of all treaties or agreements between member states, Regional Federations, and the World Federation.

(5) Lower Equity Courts, under supervision of the World Equity Court, shall settle all disputes arising between citizens or corporations of different Regions or between them and the governments of member states.

(6) The power to grant to any member state of the World Federation, upon application to and approval of the World Equity Court, the right to a sealed road (rail or auto) across the territory of another member state, leading to a sea outlet on the basis of extraterritoriality. The same outlet may also serve for commercial aviation.

COMMENT: Russia may build an outlet to the Persian Gulf; Sweden, to a warm port through Norway; or Bolivia, through Peru. This provision will eliminate one of the most common causes of war.

4. Those powers which are based upon the consent of one or more member states: When such consent has been obtained it shall acquire the status of a treaty or agreement between the World Federation Government and the particular member state.

a. The establishment (by legislation) of a World Bank, a World Commodity Corporation, and other corporations to deal with exchange, trade, etc. The dues from member states to the World Federation which are paid in money shall be cleared through the World Bank and its exchange; the dues which are paid in goods or raw materials shall be cleared through the World Commodity Corporation. It shall be the fundamental purpose of the World Federation's economic agencies to raise the general living standard of the nations of the world and to eliminate excessive trade barriers.

b. The power to provide the necessary legislation and money for the administration of various international universities and scientific research institutions; labor, consumer, and co-operative organizations; international institutions to deal with problems of unemployment, health, populations, immigration, conservation of natural resources, fisheries, and wild life; international standards of weights and measures, calendar, and currency; as well as other international organizations for the relief of distressed or undeveloped peoples and for the general welfare of mankind.

c. The maintenance of special institutions and teachers (from secular schools and religious institutions of all denominations) whose duties shall be to conduct, simultaneously and in every country, a program of education for world citizenship. Special emphasis shall be placed on inculcating in the youth of the world a consciousness of their duty to preserve peace among the nations.

d. The appointment of a special commission to work for official recognition and establishment of a neutral international language, to be taught in the schools of the world as a secondary language, and eventually to become the official language of the World Federation.

e. The appointment of a special commission to draw up a minimum World Federation Bill of Rights, which will become embodied in the Constitution of the World Federation and under which all citizens of the World Federation shall be governed. The national governments of all the member states shall be asked—but they shall not be coerced—to subscribe to this Bill of Rights.

f. A sum equal to at least one fourth of the total annual budget of the World Federation (which includes the total amount spent by the initiating states on their National Contingents) shall be spent on the various international organizations above described. The World Senate shall have the exclusive right to make appropriations, up to the sum available.

COMMENT: THE POWERS OF THE WORLD VOCATIONAL SENATE

The World Federation will probably require an annual budget of about four billion dollars—an enormous sum, but only a fraction of the amount now spent on wars and preparations for wars. Moreover, one quarter of this four-billion-dollar budget will be expended yearly by the Vocational Senate for the general welfare of mankind.

The powers of the World Vocational Senate provide machinery for the long-term economic reconstruction of the world. While Freedom from War is being safeguarded by the World Police, the agencies of the World Vocational Senate can proceed to promote peaceful co-operation in economic activity among the nations of the world. Thus higher standards of living may be attained by all, and Freedom from Want can be gradually extended to all peoples. The economic tensions and strains between and within nations can be reduced, thereby removing one cause of aggression.

Another function of the World Vocational Senate, a function of the utmost importance, is a world-wide program of peace education. This program can be successful only if carried out simultaneously in all countries. *Without* the World Federation, one nation (such as France) may teach pacifism while another (such as Germany) exalts military virtues, the result being the psychological disarmament of the former country, and its consequent defeat and possible enslavement by the militarized nation. The ultimate hope of permanent peace lies in persistent, world-wide education of youth and higher standards of living for all.

5. *Territories.* The government of the World Federation may possess its own territories and govern them as though it were a sovereign state. But the extent of these territories shall be strictly limited to the needs of the Federation's institutions (as in the case of the District of Columbia), and the inhabitants of these territories shall be governed on the basis of the World Federation Bill of Rights.

Article IV. Procedure for Decisions, Amendments, Impeachments.

1. All decisions (except amendments to the Constitution) of the World Supreme Court, World Equity Court, World Trustees, and Regional Trustees shall be made on the basis of nine out of thirteen votes.

All decisions of the World Senate and Regional Senates shall be made on the basis of a majority vote.

COMMENT: The provision for decisions of the courts and trustees gives added protection for minorities. In the case of the Senates, since the composition of these bodies is different, the minorities are adequately protected.

2. *Amendments:* The Constitution of the World Federation may be amended by an affirmative vote of not less than nine World Trustees and thirty-four World Senators, subject to ratification by not less than seven Regional Federations, on the basis of an affirmative vote of not less than nine Regional Trustees and thirty-one Regional Senators in each Region.

> *Exceptions:*
>
> a. Those Articles dealing with the Quota Force Principle, the procedure for amendment of which is specified in Part Seven, Article X, Section 3.
>
> b. Articles dealing with the sovereign rights of a member state—its form of government, internal affairs, and taxation—and with the number and composition of the Regions, require the same procedure for amendment as in the case of the Quota Force Principle.

3. *Impeachments:* All provisions of the Constitution shall be mandatory upon all the members of the government of the World Federation. Failure to act with due diligence in all essential matters and abuses of power shall be impeachable offenses. The World Supreme Court, concurrently with any four Chief Justices of the Regional Supreme Courts, shall act immediately upon complaint as a Council of Impeachment for the highest officials. A member of the World Supreme Court, in turn, may be impeached and penalized by a special court composed of eleven Chief Justices of the eleven Regional Federations.

Any high official of the World Federation Government may be impeached: (a) upon complaint of four Regional Presidents, supported by a vote of eight Regional Trustees of each of the four Regional Federations; (b) upon the complaint of the World President, eight World Trustees, and thirty-four World Senators, or (c) upon the complaint of four Regional Chief Justices. Impeached officials shall be suspended from office for a period of trial.

COMMENT: In the League of Nations the sins of omission were far more disastrous than the sins of commission. Hence the automatic, mandatory nature of the Constitution of the World Federation. Hence also the extension of the usual conception of impeachment and a new machinery for its operation, so as to protect the Constitution and the minorities of the Regional Federations against abuses or inaction by the majorities.

PART NINE: ORGANIZATION AND POWERS OF THE REGIONAL GOVERNMENTS

ANALYSIS: THE SOLUTION OF THE DILEMMA OF SOVEREIGNTIES

A question will be raised: Why not form this government by simple representation from sovereign states? Why do we need the Regions to form the government of the World Federation? In the answers to these questions lies the whole solution of the Dilemma of Sovereignties.

The problem is to create a world government representing seventy-odd sovereign states in such a manner that the world government would be strong enough to enforce the prohibition of war, yet unable to encroach upon the essential sovereignty and interests of individual states. This is essentially a problem of representation.

Until now it was believed that there were only three different ways in which the sovereign states could be represented in any kind of world government or assembly of a league. None of these three ways or solutions solves the problem.

The first is the League of Nations type of solution, where the full sovereignty of each state is religiously preserved and where no important action can be taken by the government of the League without unanimous consent. This means that Bolivia can veto the proposals of the United States since Bolivia, being a juridically equal sovereign state, has one vote and the United States also has one vote. As a result we have a world government which is powerless to sneeze, let alone carry out the gigantic task of the prohibition of war.

The second solution is Clarence Streit's Federal Union principle, according to which the world government is made up of democratically elected representation on the basis of population. In the League of Nations solution the absolute sovereignty of each state is retained, leading to a world government that is no government at all. In Streit's solution the sovereignty of states (and nationalism) is completely abolished, leading to an all-powerful world government that may well become a tyranny. For reasons previously explained, such a world government is much worse than no government at all.

The third and last solution is that of Walter Lippmann's "nuclear" alliance of three great powers who would "manage" the world organization and become its "nuclear" government. This amounts to a world co-dominion of three sovereign states, each jealous of the other. The sovereignty of the remaining smaller states will become fiction, depending entirely upon the good will of the bosses. The smaller states will be "represented" but they might as well pack up and go home, for except by promoting coalitions or rivalries among the bossing powers, there is no effective way in which they can assert their sovereignty over the dominant powers who have the bigger armies and therefore the final say. The "nuclear" alliance solution of a world organization has not even the few virtues of the League of Nations type (where at least all sovereign states had a juridically equal voice) and none of the advantages of Clarence Streit's solution (where at least the people of the largest states, not their governments, would have a say in the world government). Thus all three solutions are either ineffective or politically unacceptable or both, and none of them can solve the vital dilemma of just and effective representation.

In all these cases the solution of the problem of representation in the world government is sought either on the basis of the juridical equality of sovereign states (the League of Nations type) or on the basis of domination by a few more populated or more powerful states over the rest (Streit and "nuclear" alliance types). As a result all the peace planners are bashing their heads either against a blank wall of the juridical equality of all states (preferring world justice) or against the opposite blank wall of domination by a few states (preferring world order). Nor could any compromise be reached between these two solutions since one excludes the other *in toto*.

The solution exists, however. It consists in a new method of representing the sovereign states in a world government whereby the juridical equality of all sovereign states is preserved, the greater interests of leading powers are protected, the rights and freedom of the smaller powers are safeguarded, and yet the world government is all-powerful within its strict limits of the enforcement of matters pertaining to the prohibition of war.

This method consists in dividing the sovereign states of the world into two separate groups of states: a group of all the larger states and a group of all the smaller states. The historical and actual group of leading or initiating states consists of the United States, Britain, France, Germany, Poland, Turkey, Russia, China, and Japan. The rest of the sovereign states belong to the group of smaller states. Italy is only the second strongest state of the Latin-European Region, yet must be included, for the purposes of representation in the world government, among the "smaller" states.

These two separate groups of states are represented *separately* in the world government. Each leading state selects its own World Trustee and other representatives, while the group of all the small states selects collectively their own proportion of World Trustees and other representatives in the world government. This proportion for the small states is roughly twenty per cent of the total representation in the world government, because the total population of the small sovereign states, which is nearly four hundred million, numbers roughly twenty per cent of the total population of the world. The remaining eighty per cent, or about one billion six hundred million, is made up largely of the populations of leading states and of as yet undeveloped peoples.

The small states elect collectively two World Trustees out of thirteen and two members of the Supreme and Equity World Courts. Only in the Vocational Senate, which has no enforceable powers and which is selected by the entire Region and not by the initiating states, they have no separate representation.

But it is not enough to give to the small states a proportionate representation and a juridically equal vote. It is necessary to give them a collective armed force, which is the International Contingent. Its twenty-two per cent is slightly higher than one fifth of the total of the armed forces, in order to balance the combined quota of the strongest initiating state and the Malaysian Contingent, which is also twenty-two per cent. Later, as new sovereign states are formed from today's undeveloped nations, they too will be represented either in the group of small states or in the group of leading states.

This principle of separate representation of two groups of

sovereign states gives us a kind of representation in which the vital interests of all the leading states are safeguarded without injuring the vital interests of any small state.

Such is the new and, I believe, final solution of the Dilemma of Sovereignties. One can devise variants of this solution, but the principle of organization into separate groups of sovereign states with proportionate representation and juridical equality must remain. In my original plan I had no separate representation for smaller states in the House of World Trustees or in the World Supreme Court. That was because I believed that the principle of separate representation was adequately safeguarded by the establishment of the International Contingent recruited from the small nations. Since then I have come to the conclusion that the management of the International Contingent of the World Police must not be entrusted exclusively to the World Trustees selected by initiating states only, and that the group of small states must be represented separately in all branches of the government except the Vocational Senate. This change made the world government more complex but even safer than before.

I now can answer the second question: Why do we need the Regions to form the government of the World Federation?

Exactly the same world government could be formed directly by separate groups of leading and small states without bringing in the Regional Principle. Such a variant seems more simple. Actually there are many reasons why it would be less acceptable and less effective than a system of integrated Regional governments topped by the world government.

I have already pointed out that the eleven Regions of the world are, with one or two exceptions, natural economic, space-political, and psychosocial units. Most of the leading states in these Regions exercise a powerful economic influence over their neighboring states in the same Region and in turn depend upon the good will of the small states. In many ways their relations are of Regional character and cannot be adequately regulated by the world government. On the other hand, they are too complex and too diversified to be regulated without serious friction by direct state-to-state relations.

This world is still too large for a central government to attend to its needs. Without the Regional Federations, seventy-odd sovereign nations would continue their semichaotic relations in a climate of quarrels and strife; the world would be much more disjointed; and the ideal of world citizenship would be removed to a dimmer future. Nations must learn how to co-operate with their neighbors before co-operating with the world.

In addition to the revolution in communications, other economic and strategic reasons make the trend toward groupings larger than nations irresistible. Nations like China and Russia are already in an advanced stage of integrated regionalism. With their enormous man power they will dominate the world economically if not strategically. This is one of the many reasons why a Regional machinery, embryonic to start with, is indispensable to help integrate other economically or psychosocially kindred groupings.

The small states will also find in a Regional structure their best insurance against the overwhelming power of the leading states.

I sought to interpose between the seventy-odd sovereign nations and the World Federation Government an intermediate mechanism, which reduces the cumbersome number of sovereign nations to workable political units without diminishing in any way the rights of each state. This intermediate mechanism is the Regional structure where each of the eleven Regional Federations becomes both an operating unit within the World Federation and a cohesive force between the member states composing it. The problem was to find a larger area than the frontiers of a state, a sort of common denominator, for a group of sovereign states. Such a larger "molecular" unit or Region could not be formed on the basis of ideological or purely racial affinities, since most national states contain various ideologies and races. Nor could it be formed on the artificial basis of the "economic zones," since such arbitrary zones would necessarily require the suppression of national frontiers and of national states—a politically impossible task in our lifetime. As for the division by continents or subcontinents, the lines drawn are merely geographic.

But I did not have to look that far for nearly perfect Regional units where the nations were already strongly held not only by economic or geographic factors, but also by the psychosocial forces. These Regions stared at me from the map of the world.

Article I. The Regional Constitutions.

1. Each Regional Federation shall have its own constitution within the framework of the general Constitution of the World Federation.

2. In the case of Regions containing only one sovereign state—Russia, China, and Japan—their then existing governments shall be recognized as Regional Governments. In the case of the British Commonwealth of Nations its existing structure and relationships shall also be recognized.

3. In the case of Regions containing two or more sovereign states there shall be a minimum Basic Constitution, patterned after the World Federation Constitution, the object of which is to hold the Region together and yet preserve the sovereign rights of the member states.

Article II. The Basic Constitution for Regions containing two or more sovereign states shall provide for:

1. An *executive,* consisting of a Regional President elected by the Regional Trustees for a six-year term, not renewable. The presidency and the capital alternate or rotate (depending on the size of the initiating state) every six years among the principal member states of the Regional Federation.

2. A *legislature,* consisting of thirteen Regional Trustees, elected in proportion to the population of the member states; and a Regional Senate (Vocational) of sixty members representing (ten each) Capital (or executive management), Labor, Agriculture, Science, Education, and Arts. Each member state shall be represented by a number of Regional Senators proportionate to its population. Each Regional Senator shall be recommended by a recognized national association of the member state he represents and appointed by the chief executive of that member state with the approval of its legislature.

3. A *judiciary* of thirteen justices, selected for life (with a retirement provision), forming the Regional Supreme Court. A Regional Equity Court shall also be provided for. These courts shall constitute the lower courts of the World Federation and shall deal with intra-Regional matters not reserved for the World Courts.

Article III. The Powers of the Regional Government under the Basic Constitution.

1. Administration and development of Pooled Colonies, if any, as described in Article IV following.

2. Legislation and administration of preferential economic advantages between member states of the same Regional Federation (similar to the interrelations existing within the British Empire). This includes the *right of first refusal,* which is the right to supersede, on the same terms, any state or citizen outside the Region in any negotiated treaty or concession.

3. The right to levy limited tariffs on intra-Regional trade between member states for the maintenance of the Regional Government and its institutions.

4. The right to negotiate treaties with individual member states regulating immigration from other Regional Federations, intra-Regional trade and labor, and inter-Regional imports and exports, with a view to eventual free trade. The consent of each member state shall be required in each case.

No member state shall be prevented from making its own economic agreements, imposing tariffs, etc., with any other sovereign state, subject to the limitations set forth here.

5. Administration by the Regional Senate of various intra-Regional economic, educational, and other institutions, similar to those controlled by the World Vocational Senate.

6. Each Regional Federation may amend its Basic Constitution by an affirmative vote of two thirds of its member states, so as to achieve a closer co-union—as, for instance, common currency, customs, commodity, and public works organizations.

COMMENT: Different Regional Constitutions are necessary because of the great differences in the psychosocial patterns of the Regional Federations and in their levels of economic and political development. Furthermore, the member states within each Region also differ to a certain extent, and separating many of them are accumulated historical hatreds and suspicions. For this reason the powers of the Regional Governments are even more limited than the powers of the World Federation Government, and there is very little that the Regional Government can do without the consent of its member states. Nevertheless, the structure and organs are there for the future development of a closer partnership between the member states. The amendment provision offers wide scope for the natural evolution of the governments of the various Regional Federations and enables each Region to evolve the constitution best fitted to its needs.

Following is the suggested modification of the Basic Constitution as it applies to the autonomous Indian Regional Federation.

Article IV. The Status of India.

1. The autonomous Indian Regional Federation shall possess full Dominion status. It may attain the status of a sovereign Regional Federation by arrangement with Britain or (automatically) upon a World Federation plebiscite based on a reasonable minimum educational standard. It shall consist of at least two sovereign states: the Hindu (now led by the Congress party) and the Mohammedan (the Pakistan plan). In addition there may be smaller sovereign states such as the princes' states, or states with highly mixed Mohammedan and Hindu populations. All these states shall be held together by a common foreign policy, customs union, currency, police force, and other Federation institutions of common weal. In other respects each state shall be sovereign.

2. The Indian Regional Government shall consist of thirteen Trustees: seven chosen by the sovereign Hindu state, four by the sovereign Mohammedan state, and two by the smaller sovereign states. At least half of the sixty Vocational Senators shall be selected by the larger Hindu state. Until separate Regional sovereignty has been attained, the President shall be selected by the British Crown but shall have only nominal powers. The executive power shall be vested in a Prime Minister, selected by the Regional Trustees and Vocational Senate and responsible to them. After Regional sovereignty has been attained the executive power shall be vested in a Regional President, selected as prescribed in the Basic Constitution for sovereign Regions.

3. Until separate Regional sovereignty is attained, Britain shall have the economic rights of a member state in the Indian Federation, but no political power. She shall also retain command of the Indian National Contingent of the World Police and in addition may have her own military and air-naval bases in India, garrisoned by part of the British National Contingent.

4. The World Federation shall guarantee the establishment of the Indian Regional Federation either during or immediately after

the war. It shall also undertake to provide complete cultural and religious freedom for all the minorities within the Indian sovereign states.

COMMENT: The Indian problem, like most historical problems, is a complex of contradictory psychosocial interests. The Indian complex consists of three problems: the Hindu, the Mohammedan, and the British.

1. The Hindu majority would never consent to the breakup of the essential unity of the Indian subcontinent, which would mean the fragmentation of its six-thousand-year-old psychosocial pattern. Therefore Sir Stafford Cripps's proposal for the division of India into two or more entirely separate Dominions was entirely unacceptable to them.

2. The Mohammedans would never consent to remain in the role of a perpetual minority party, especially within the Hindu system of dominant castes.

3. The British, while probably prepared to give fullest political and economic concessions, could not consent to transfer effective military control of India into other hands—certainly not in time of war. In the British Commonwealth of Nations, India forms a strategic central body; the military bases in India can control eastern Africa and the Pacific as far as Australasia. A militarily independent India, in spite of the noble intentions of her present leaders, *might* throw her weight on the side of Britain's enemies. Furthermore, no country in the world is inherently better suited for a native fascist dictatorship than this caste-ridden, chaotically divided, yet rapidly industrializing subcontinent. Democracy is a hollow word where millions of humans are "untouchable."

This is not an argument in favor of continuing Britain's domination of India. But until the World Federation substitutes international law for power politics, the vital strategic interests of Britain in India must be safeguarded.

Within the framework of the World Federation and of the Indian Regional Federation a solution of this complex of problems is now possible. It is only with the arrangement described in the preceding Article or with some similar arrangement that the three basic contradictions of the Indian problem can be resolved: the necessity of maintaining India's fundamental psychosocial unity; the just demands of the Hindu majority in parts of India and of the Mohammedan majority in other parts of India, each for a free and sovereign status; and those strategic and economic interests of Britain in India which are not based on imperialistic domination.

Article V. The Principle of Pooled Colonies.

1. The assignment of important colonial territories is described in the World Territorial Table, Part Five of this Constitution.

2. *Compensation for Colonies:* A fair purchase price, to be determined by the World Equity Court and based upon actual value, shall be paid by a Regional Federation which acquires colonies to the member state of another Regional Federation which was the former possessor, provided the latter was not an aggressor state.

3. *The Pooling of Colonies:* All the colonies or possessions of the member states of the Latin-European Regional Federation shall be pooled together and administered by the government of the Latin-European Federation, with rights of trade, immigration, and access to raw materials open equally to all the citizens of the member states of the Latin-European Federation. The same arrangement shall prevail for the British Federation and its colonies, and for the Pan-American Federation and its purchased possessions.

4. The colonies assigned to the Germanic Federation in the World Territorial Table shall be administered directly by the government of the World Federation for a period of twenty-four years. But the citizens of the Germanic Federation shall have free rights of trade, immigration, and access to raw materials in these colonies. Belgium, as former possessor, shall have a preferred status in the administration of the Belgian Congo. After a period of twenty-four years has elapsed the administration of these colonies shall be placed in the hands of the government of the Germanic Federation.

5. *The Rights of Colonial Populations:* All the Pooled Colonies shall have self-rule. Any colony of more than three million inhabitants may become a sovereign state within the same Regional Federation upon a plebiscite based on a reasonable educational standard.

6. The administration of the Pooled Colonies by the Regional Governments shall be under strict supervision of the World Federation Government. It shall be the duty of the World Federation Gov-

ernment to undertake that the natives are given fair treatment in the development of their economic and educational standards.

7. The World Federation Government shall have full power to intervene to enforce the provisions of this Article.

COMMENT: THE PROBLEM OF AFRICA

By eliminating the crazy-quilt map of Africa and by the substitution of three great blocs—the western bloc assigned to the Latin-European Federation, the central bloc assigned to the Germanic Federation, and the eastern bloc assigned to the British Federation—the first important step toward eventual unification of Africa will have been taken. The enormous potential resources of Africa offer enough for the natives and for the immigrants, provided the exploitation of natives is abandoned. The Regional Governments, under the supervision of the World Federation Government, will assure higher living standards and education for the natives, and their eventual sovereignty. The granting of immediate independence to the African people, of whom the great majority are totally illiterate, would simply result in their ruthless exploitation by native caciques or inherently fascist politicians of the worst breed.

The proposal to transfer the African and all other colonies to a world organization, immediately after the war, is unrealistic. It would not be acceptable either to victorious Britain or to revived France, and it would be an almost insurmountable obstacle to the establishment of the World Federation. Even if such a proposal were accepted, such a world organization, in possession of the world's colonies, would become a malevolent seat of power politics and intrigues among the nations. The Constitution of the World Federation, with its Regional structure and Pooled Colonies, offers the best protection and hope for the liberation of the natives. And there is good reason to hope that future development of the African continent will permit the establishment of a twelfth Regional Federation—the African.

Article VI. The Principle of Priority Treaties.

1. Japan shall have adequate access to raw materials and exports of the Malaysian and Chinese Federations through special Priority Treaties negotiated under the supervision of the World Equity Court.

2. The Priority Treaties may not exceed one third of the total

foreign trade of the neighboring Federations, and they must be based on competitive prices or goods with any other state or Region.

3. The principle of Priority Treaties may be extended to other Federations in need of indispensable raw materials, such as the Germanic and Middle European Federations.

COMMENT: THE "HAVE-NOT" NATIONS AND RAW MATERIALS

By the pooling of colonial resources in the Latin-European and Germanic Federations, together with the method of Priority Treaties, the problem of raw materials for the principal "have-not" nations, Germany and Italy, will be substantially solved. In addition the common colonial interests will operate in the Latin-European and Germanic Federations as a powerful cohesive force for peace and unity among their member states, just as, in the earlier history of the United States, there was a common heritage in the West.

In the case of Japan there are no sparsely populated rich lands near her. The method of Priority Treaties offers at least a partial solution during the period of hatreds generated by her own war lords. But this may not be enough. The worst thing for the cause of lasting peace is to leave any nation, however great the misdeeds of her rulers, in an economic strait jacket. The best solution of the problem of Japanese-Chinese relations would be a permanent customs union between these two Regional Federations, with equal and unrestricted rights of trade and settlement within the territories of both peoples. It is true that in the first stages of such a union Japan, which is more advanced industrially, would profit more. But as China's own industrialization accelerated (and the customs union would contribute to this end), the eventual and more lasting economic advantage would lie with China. It is to be hoped that the wisdom and generosity of the Chinese people will overcome the Himalayan heights of hatred that bar such a solution at present. A customs union between these two branches of the Mongolian race—one a land power and the other a sea power—would be of enormous benefit to them both. Nor would there be any objection from outside nations on grounds of power politics, since the Quota Force Principle removes any danger of aggression by the reunited Mongolians. The sovereign state of Korea would, of course, be part of this customs union. In this manner, while each of the Mongolian states and Regions would preserve its personality, all would be reunited in a vast zone of free trade and peaceful co-operation.

Article VII. Status of the Vatican City.

The Vatican City shall be a state within Rome, with extra-territorial access to its own seaport. The Vatican City shall have all the attributes of a sovereign state and it shall be protected against aggression as in the case of other member states. But it shall not be required to join the Latin-European Regional Federation or any other Federation.

Article VIII. The Status of Palestine.

A special commission appointed by the government of the World Federation shall decide during the Provisional Period on one of the two following solutions to the Jewish problem in Palestine:

1. *First Solution:* Palestine shall become a Jewish sovereign state in the following manner:

> a. A sufficient part of the Mohammedan and Christian populations of Palestine shall be transferred to another territory in the Middle East so that there shall be a Jewish majority remaining in Palestine. This transfer shall be effected only with the consent of the groups concerned.

> b. Equivalent or better land and living conditions shall be provided for the transferred non-Jewish populations, together with a reasonable bonus.

> c. The expenses of this transfer shall be borne half by the Jewish state and half by the World Federation.

> d. The special religious rights of non-Jewish churches in Jerusalem, as well as the rights of minorities, shall be fully safeguarded.

> e. The creation of the Jewish Palestine state shall in no way affect the rights of citizens of Jewish extraction in other states.

2. *Alternative Solution:* In case the number of non-Jewish residents of Palestine who consent to emigrate from Palestine is not sufficient to permit the establishment of a Jewish majority, then Palestine shall become a ward of the World Federation itself. The government of the World Federation shall be Palestine's own sovereign state until such time as, through intensified postwar immigra-

tion of the now uprooted Jews, Palestine acquires a Jewish majority and, upon a plebiscite, its separate sovereignty is established.

COMMENT: It is impossible now to foresee the actual conditions that will justify the adoption of either of these two solutions.

Despite the attachment of the Arabs to Palestine, it is reasonable to assume that a large number of both Arabs and Christians will consent to emigrate if sufficient inducement is offered. On the lands thus vacated, it will be possible to settle the hundreds of thousands of homeless Jews now herded in the ghettos of Europe, thus forming a Jewish majority in Palestine and a sovereign Jewish state.

Nothing short of a sovereign Jewish state, the advocates of the first solution say, can remove the Jewish question from the agenda of civilized mankind. But such a solution is possible only within the double framework of the World Federation and of the Middle Eastern Federation.

The Jewish problem really arose with the destruction of the Jewish corporate state in Palestine in the first century. This resulted in the intensification of the Jewish spiritual state throughout the world. The solution does not lie in beating down with senseless persecution the fierce flame of spiritual nationalism. It lies in the reestablishment of the Jewish political state, which will operate as a safety valve for the ancient psychosocial forces of the Jews. The Jewish law must be re-embodied in its own national vessel, and the Jewish nation must be granted its own passport to the family of nations. Then the historic Jewish problem will dwindle to the size of, say, the Italian, Irish, or Polish "problem" in the United States.

However, Palestine is a sacred land to the Jews, the Moslems, and the Christians alike. If Palestine becomes the ward of the World Federation, then any citizen of the world can go there if he chooses, and every citizen of Palestine will become a citizen of the world. This alternative solution, also, can be made possible only through the establishment of the World Federation.

Article IX. The Structure of the Pan-American Regional Federation.

In the Pan-American Regional Federation the presidency and the capital shall alternate between the United States and each of the six largest Latin-American republics. Whenever the United

States selects the Regional President, the Latin-American republics shall select, in all, seven of the thirteen Regional Trustees. Whenever a Latin-American republic selects the Regional President, the United States shall select seven of the thirteen Regional Trustees. Representation in the Regional Supreme Court and Equity Court shall be similarly determined. Half the Vocational Senators shall be from the United States and the other half from Latin America.

COMMENT: In the case of the American Regional Federation we are dealing with the largest number of sovereign states of any Region (twenty-one), and we are also dealing with two widely different psychosocial patterns—a bloc of one hundred and thirty-eight million North Americans and a bloc of one hundred and twenty million Latin Americans. Yet these two vast blocs of peoples can be harmoniously integrated within one Region, without jeopardizing the sovereignty of the smallest of states.

By the means described in this paragraph, the Latin-American republics obtain an *absolute equality of power* with the United States, maintaining a perfect equilibrium between the North and South American continents, and implementing with strong, practical machinery the Good Neighbor policy and Pan-American ideals.

The method of representation is a very important point. If the Pan-American Supreme Court interprets and enforces treaties between the American states, instead of our State Department dealing separately with the weak Latin-American republics, it will be of enormous advantage not only to our diplomacy but to our business interests. For then American investments will not be at the mercy of local politicians of different countries, but in the hands of the Equity Court of the Pan-American Federation, with equal representation from North and Latin-American blocs. Within the Pan-American Federation the Latin-American nations, with their enormous physical resources, can freely co-operate with the United States in the common task of creating a higher synthesis of the best elements of the Latin-American and North American cultures.

Article X. The Structure of the Malaysian Regional Federation.

The Malaysian Regional Federation shall have a modified Basic Constitution, wherein the United States, as Special Trustee, shall be temporarily represented in its Regional Government until the eventual plebiscite establishes a separate sovereign status. The United States shall select the Regional President and half of the Regional Senators. The House of Regional Trustees shall consist of four Trustees representing the Philippines (sovereign); four representing the Netherlands East Indies (under Netherlands' sovereignty); two representing Indo-China (under French sovereignty); two representing Thailand, which shall become a sovereign democratic state, organized along the lines of the Philippines; and one from the smaller Pacific islands.

Unlike other Regional Governments, the Vocational Senate of the Malaysian Federation shall have equal powers with the Regional Trustees. The concurrent vote of no fewer than thirty-one Senators or the vote of no fewer than nine Trustees, together with the approval of the President, shall be final. The vote of thirty-one Senators and nine Trustees shall override the veto of the President.

Added powers shall be given the government of the Malaysian Federation for the establishment of a Regional police force, customs union and currency, and for the development of the economic and educational standards of its peoples. The capital shall at first be in Manila; and the Philippines, as the most progressive sovereign state, shall play the leading role in assisting the United States of America (under supervision of the World Federation) to establish a sovereign United States of Malaysia as quickly as educational standards permit.

In the Netherlands East Indies the Netherlands shall retain her essential sovereign rights, except the right to maintain military or air-naval bases. Furthermore, as a condition of the return of these colonies, she must agree to give self-rule and fair treatment to the native populations, to observe the Priority Treaties, and to cooperate in the Malaysian Regional Government. The same shall apply to the rights of France in Indo-China.

Until separate Regional sovereignty is attained, the United States, as Special Trustee, shall retain command of the Malaysian National Contingent of the World Police, and in addition may have her own military and air-naval bases in Malaysia, with part of the American National Contingent stationed there.

ANALYSIS: THE AMERICAN STRATEGIC ZONE

The American Strategic Zone consists of two zones, the inner and outer zones. The Western Hemisphere, under the Pan-American Regional Federation, is the inner zone, and the Asio-Pacific region, under the Malaysian Regional Federation, is the outer zone.

The American fortified bases in the Pan-American Federation (inner zone) are:

Group 1. Bases on United States territory, together with the bases previously leased in Bermuda, Cuba, Trinidad, etc.

Group 2. Bases on the pooled territories of the Pan-American Federation—those in the Western Hemisphere now held by non-American states, which are to be purchased and governed by the Pan-American Federation. They include: Falkland Islands, British, Dutch, and French Guianas, the Netherlands West Indies, Martinique, and Guadaloupe.

The American fortified bases in the Malaysian Federation (outer zone) are:

Group 1. Bases on islands mandated to Japan by the League of Nations. These islands are to become the outright possessions of the United States.

Group 2. Leased bases on territories of the Malaysian Federation. They include: Philippine Islands, Netherlands East Indies, Indo-China, and Thailand, as well as bases on some smaller Pacific Islands of strategic importance.

In each case the military, naval, and air bases shall be occupied by troops of the United States National Contingent of the World Police. No other troops armed with Segregated Weapons (except the Malaysian National Contingent in Malaysia, temporarily under United States command) shall be stationed in the entire American Strategic Zone.

In addition the bases of the Mobile Corps (International Contingent) are so arranged that they become, in effect, a third zone of defense for the United States or for any other state.

If the World Federation Plan is adopted, the American Strategic Zone (as well as the Strategic Zones of other leading powers) will become an important feature of the Quota Force Principle. If the World Federation Plan is *not* adopted, and nationalism and power politics continue to prevail, the establishment of the American Strategic Zone will become absolutely indispensable. For in such a world the strategic defense of the Western Hemisphere could not long be maintained unless the United States had full control of the western Atlantic and the eastern Pacific. Full control could be exercised only by occupying a chain of military and naval-air bases in the outlying islands of the western Atlantic and eastern Pacific, *and* on parts of the continent of Asia.

If the Pan-American and Malaysian Federations are not established, the American Strategic Zone can still be set up as follows:

The United States shall lease bases, on long-term, non-imperialistic conditions such as now prevail in our present bases in Bermuda or Cuba, in all the territories enumerated above as part of the American Strategic Zone. In addition the United States shall also lease bases in the following territories, which in the World Federation Plan would be occupied by the Mobile Corps:

Iceland, Greenland, Azores, Madeira Islands, Canary Islands, Cape Verde, Hainan, Formosa, Korea, and Kuril Islands.

Furthermore, the United States shall also lease bases in New Caledonia, Timor, and the Ryukyu Islands.

The principle of leased bases permits the United States to defend the vital approaches to the American continent and at the same time preserves the sovereignty and freedom of the state whose territory is leased. The United States does not interfere in the internal affairs of the country containing the base, and the rights of the United States will be limited to the territory of the leased bases and the necessary means of transportation if its bases are located overland. There is one notable exception in the case of bases leased from the Netherlands in the East Indies and from France in Indo-China. There the United States should have the right of supervising the policy toward native populations.

The island of Hainan flanks Indo-China, and Formosa flanks Japan and the Philippines. Both islands are indispensable to anchor the American Strategic Zone in the mainland of Asia.

The islands of Hainan, Sumatra, Luzon, and Formosa form a highly important strategic "Big Dipper" whose handle extends northward through Ryukyu Islands and over Japan to the Kuril Islands, connecting with the Aleutians. At the same time the southern crescent of the Dutch East Indies connects with Timor, New Caledonia, the Marshall Islands, Hawaii, and Alaska to complete the strategic circle around the heart of the Pacific.

States in possession of these islands will not be allowed to maintain on them armed forces or fortified bases that may endanger the security of the American bases.

The Malaysian Region and Our Allies

There are five victorious powers among our war allies who will be affected by the establishment in the Malaysian region of the outer American Strategic Zone—Britain, Russia, China, the Netherlands, and France.

Britain: No British is included in the Malaysian Zone. None of her economic interests are affected, since the American bases are solely strategic. To Britain, and especially Australia and New Zealand, a strong United States in Asia should be an invaluable strategic asset. We seek none of her territories, and indirectly we powerfully support her strategic position. Economically, the crushing defensive load that Britain must carry in Asia will be considerably lightened since she will not need all the costly defenses that she would have needed if there were no American Strategic Zone.

Thus a strong America in Asia is not only extremely valuable insurance for Australia and New Zealand (who will have much to say about this matter) but is also a great advantage to England.

Russia: Russia's attitude will depend upon whether she views the American Strategic Zone from the standpoint of her long-term or her short-term interest. It is definitely in Russia's real interest to have a strongly based United States in Asia. This will insure her own eastern flank against possible future aggression by industrialized Asiatic powers, in the same manner that the American western flank will be insured by a strong Russia. If Russia, however, views the American Strategic Zone from the standpoint of her short-term interests, then she is likely to oppose, at least indirectly, its establishment.

Such short-term interests will be motivated by purely Russian power politics. In the first place, Russia has a formal twenty-year alliance with Britain. She would naturally support her ally. Besides, neither Russia nor Britain would have a free hand in China with the United States close by. It may well be that if Russia and Britain come to an understanding about their respective "zones of influence" in Europe, there is no reason why they shouldn't come to an understanding about their "zones of influence" in the Far East. That would complete a double political encirclement: The United States, the most powerful state in the world, would be encircled by the two next most powerful states, Britain and Russia; China, the most populous state in the world, would also be encircled in Asia. And the isolation of the United States and China, which the geopoliticians of Germany and Japan failed to realize, will have been accomplished by the power politicians of Britain and Russia.

I do not mean to say that such are the plans of the British and Russian governments. But the logic of the situation is there, and at times it is hard for even the best-intentioned of governments not to follow the line of least resistance. It is our task to make this the line of maximum resistance and thereby preserve our national interests and the respect of both Britain and Russia.

Our answer to possible Russian objections, therefore, would be similar to our answer to Britain. We want a strong Russia, and we have no objections to a Russian Strategic Zone that would adequately protect her frontiers. Russia should have no objections to a non-imperialistic American Strategic Zone. What happens in Asia is just as vital to our national security as it is to Russia or Britain. Both Britain and Russia have a ringside seat in Asia. The American state cannot be kept in the gallery thousands of miles away.

China: Except for a small clique of budding Chinese imperialists, both the Chinese government and the people will welcome the United States as their new neighbor. There is no question about the fear of China that we may withdraw from Asia, leaving China between the devil and the deep sea. What China will need more than anything else is time to recuperate and the friendship of America.

Japan was able to invade China only because the balance of power in the Far East broke down. Russia after the First World War was helpless, and later needed all her strength to face Germany; Britain was Japan-appeasing; while America, though deeply sympathetic, was reluctant to take active steps against Japan thousands of miles away. China would welcome, therefore, the American move into Asia, if for no other reason than the mere presence of the United States on the spot, thereby adding a third effective great power in the play of balance politics.

While the interests of Britain, Russia, and China are involved in the American Strategic Zone only indirectly, the Netherlands and France are affected directly.

The Netherlands: The Dutch East Indian colonial empire lies between the continents of Asia and America in the heart of the American Strategic Zone. Unless the United States controls all the strategic bases of the Dutch East Indies, the whole concept of the American Strategic Zone is useless. The future American position in Asia will be strategically indefensible if we are to rely on the bottleneck of a few bases in the Philippines or east of the Philippines. Without the bases of the Dutch East Indies, the United States will be, in effect, thrown back into the vast emptiness of the eastern Pacific. The Pacific shore of the American continent will be indefensible once future enemy powers seize the Dutch East Indies as a base for their operations. We had enormous difficulties with a relatively weak Japan. Imagine what would happen if future powers many times stronger than Japan should advance against us from the Dutch East Indies.

Our problem is to find a just solution whereby the United States controls the fortified places of the Netherlands East Indies, wins over the friendship of the natives, and preserves the friendship of the politically intelligent Netherlanders. This solution exists if the Netherlands will lease to the United States the strategic bases required, and will agree to co-operate in military matters pertaining to external defense. The Netherlands should further agree to carry out a thorough reform in administration of the native populations, establishing a true dominion status (see Malaysian Federation). We would in turn agree to maintain in other respects sovereignty of the Netherlands over East Indian possessions and not to interfere in their internal affairs.

There should be no objection whatsoever on the part of the Netherlands government to such an agreement with the United States. In fact, such an arrangement should be more than welcome, since the Netherlands retains her sovereignty over the East Indies and at the same time secures a powerful protection against future aggressors. What Britain did for fifty destroyers, as a gesture of good will, the Netherlands should do in exchange for the heavy sacrifice in American lives and billions of dollars that we must yet spend in order to regain this precious pearl of the Orient for the benefit of the Netherlands. It would seem, therefore, that an arrangement could be made of great mutual benefit to the Netherlands and the United States. The Netherlands would not only retain her East Indies possessions intact, but would secure the permanent and powerful support of the United States in their defense against aggressors at a cost far less than if she were to carry the backbreaking load of defense on her own shoulders. The United States would secure the indispensable bases for the defense of the American continent.

Unfortunately, things are not that simple in power politics. There are certain financial interests which have a powerful influence on the Netherlands government-in-exile. These Dutch interests, closely allied with the rubber and oil interests of the City of London, are fundamentally inimical even to American big business, let alone the larger interests of the American nation. They are almost certain to oppose the "violation" by the United States of the Netherlands sovereign rights. They naïvely imagine that the vast empire of the East Indies is still their private hunting preserve, and that somehow they can manage to foil the American nation by appeals to the traditional friendship and admiration we all have for the Dutch people. They will invoke the absolute sovereignty of the Netherlands over the East Indies and suspect our motives. For special reasons of their own they will try to convince the Netherlands government to refuse to lease military bases under any conditions, and they will insist that the defense of the East Indies be left entirely in the hands of the Netherlands government. In a matter that might involve our very existence, the United States cannot entrust her interests to any weak foreign state, however friendly. This would be political folly, for it might develop into strategic suicide. If we should do so, we would be strategically at the mercy of the Netherlands government. A friendly government may be changed overnight into a government hostile to us. A government may be dominated by certain vested interests and follow the lines of power politics of another great power. There may be, at some future time, fascist cliques in cahoots with our enemies, as was the case of Vichy France in Indo-China. Even a friendly government may fail to prepare adequate defenses for the East Indies and commit blunders that would do us irreparable strategic harm.

For strategic reasons of our own, we will be forced to defend the

Netherlands East Indies against future aggressors. But for the Netherlands to insist on unlimited sovereignty while knowing that she could not regain or hold her possessions without our help is tantamount to a policy of juridical holdup, to which we would be very stupid to submit. This is especially so in view of the fact that such an attempted holdup would be made only in order to keep the United States out of the Netherlands East Indies, so that a few thousand Dutch plantation owners and stockholders might continue, in the name of sovereignty and democracy, to exploit millions of natives whose friendship we need as much as we need strategic bases.

I am well aware that in the United States, strong opposition exists to any kind of restoration of Netherlands sovereignty in the East Indies. Both liberals and conservatives correctly observe that the days of vast Dutch and Portuguese empires existing in the benevolent shadow of the City of London are limited. "Our American boys," they say, "have not died to regain the East Indies from the Japanese conqueror for the benefit of Dutch and British bankers. Both from the selfish American standpoint and for the sake of humanity, it might be better to abolish Dutch rule, establish complete independence of the Malaysian people, and make an arrangement with them, rather than with their Dutch masters, for the American strategic bases. Certainly few tears will be shed over the demise of Dutch colonial imperialism."

There is much strength in this argument, but I am opposed to it. This is not because the United States is committed, as some Dutch statesmen claim, to restoration of their colonial possessions. The United States has no such commitment, explicit or implicit. It is one thing to liberate heroic Holland from her status as a German colony and restore her full sovereignty. It is quite another thing to perpetuate, through heavy American sacrifices, the prewar status of the colonial people under Dutch domination. The reason I am in favor of retaining a conditional Dutch sovereignty in the East Indies is to be found in the principle that underlies my whole approach to the problem of world settlement. I seek a world settlement which is just, humane, and capable of evolution toward even higher goals and final solutions. In order to achieve its purpose this world settlement must be, at the same time, realistic. To be realistic, one must seek solutions on the basis of a higher synthesis of conflicting historic interests—

solutions which are both effective and acceptable. This does not mean sacrifice of an essential principle or an essential requirement. It does mean recognition within reasonable limits of a historic, economic, psychosocial, geographic, and strategic reality.

The contrast in strength between Japan in attack and the Netherlands East Indies in defense was pitiable. The population of the Netherlands East Indies is somewhat greater than that of Japan proper. The natural resources of the Netherlands East Indies are immensely greater than those of Japan. Consequently the Dutch government had extraordinary opportunity to develop a free, prosperous, and powerful empire. This unique opportunity was bartered away on the stock markets of Amsterdam and London, while the East Indies lay defenseless.

No one disputes the heroic courage and the outstanding achievements of the Dutch nation. Americans have the friendliest feelings for Holland. But this friendship does not include acquiescence by the American nation in the selfish and greedy policy of various Netherlands governments which in the past left the defense of the East Indies wide open to an aggressor.

The Netherlands government-in-exile announces that things will be different in the future, and promises a kind of dominion status. There is no reason to doubt these good intentions. But even the best of the Netherlands governments could not change the imperious necessity for the United States to take defense of the East Indies into its own hands. I said "imperious necessity" and not "imperialistic." Our interest in the East Indies is, and must remain, strategic. If we can preserve the historic sovereignty and economic interests of the Netherlands without losing our strategic bases and without perpetuating the exploitation of the natives, then there is no reason why we should injure materially the interests of the Netherlands state.

A certain period of time must elapse before the native populations could achieve the minimum economic and educational standard needed to save them from falling into the clutches of local politicians and despots. A reformed Dutch administration could greatly help there. The colonial past of the Dutch ruling class in the East Indies shows crimes of stupidity and ignorance rather than of malice. There were brilliant Dutch administrators who accomplished a great deal, considering the limitations of their psychological climate. And with the assistance of the United States, there are good hopes that the dream of a Dutch-Indonesian Commonwealth, futile in the past, might become reality in the future. There is room enough in the Dutch East Indies for the Hollander and for the Malaysian, once the incubus of colonial exploitation is removed. Both the Malaysian and the Dutch peoples will profit greatly from mutual help and joint contribution to a free and democratic Dutch-Indonesian Commonwealth. The Dutch, ceasing to be masters, can become what they should have been in the past—teachers and friends.

Any politically intelligent Hollander will perceive that such an arrangement with the United States would be an ideal solution for the real Netherlands interests in the East Indies. The problem of defense against inevitable future aggressors will be permanently solved.

The United States could thus become not only a friend but a permanent ally of the Netherlands East Indies, without seeking economic advantage. But if it is a question of choice between our strategic requirements and Netherlands absolute sovereignty, then absolute sovereignty must go. If it is a choice between free development of the natives and Dutch imperialism, then imperialism must go.

France: Similar considerations apply in the case of France in Indo-China. There also we must occupy as part of the American Strategic Zone leased air-naval bases on the shores and fortified places inland. France must agree to pursue a policy toward the natives leading toward their liberation under a dominion status. In exchange we will recognize the economic rights of France in Indo-China.

To France, Indo-China is merely a source of economic profit. To us it is a vital anchorage of our strategic chain of bases indispensable to the defense of the Pacific approaches to our continent. Without this anchorage on the continent of Asia, the western end of our strategic chain would be left in the sea, so to speak, on the islands of the East Indies. To France such an arrangement should be highly satisfactory, since she retains her essential sovereignty and at the same time solves the otherwise unsolvable problem of the defense of Indo-China against future aggression.

Thailand should be temporarily occupied by United States troops and her Japanese puppets eliminated. We should then pursue a policy similar to our policy in the Philippines. As soon as possible we shall establish a democratic Thailand Republic and enter into an arrangement for the lease of American bases.

The islands of Hainan and Formosa must be under full Chinese sovereignty except for the leased territory on which American bases are to be established. Similarly with the sovereign state of Korea.

If the World Federation is not established, the structure of the American Strategic Zone is necessary for our safety.

A fortified base is not only a strategic obstacle but a time unit. A chain of fortified bases is a precious chain of time units that may mean the difference between the destruction of a state and its salvation.

By means of these strategic bases we can become a world power for militant peace, with feet firmly planted in the heart of the Pacific, on the islands girdling the shores of Asia, and on the mainland itself. Then we can prevent war lords of the future from seizing the vast resources of the Asiatic states and plotting the conquest of the world. Our action can be immediate and effective, since we will not be blocked by supine buffer states enmeshed in petty power politics and legalistic technicalities of sovereignties which they could not defend themselves and which, if they fail to defend, threaten our own ruin.

However, it is obvious that maintenance of the American Strategic Zone by this country acting alone would require a tremendous establishment and wide dispersal of American armed forces and a vast expenditure of American money. Although it would give us strategic advantages in future wars, it does not guarantee that we would not have to wage wars, or insure future generations against loss of life.

All Americans genuinely concerned with world peace, weighing this grim necessity for maintenance of a far-reaching strategic zone against the possibility of maintaining peace by a workable system of collective defense, will prefer the latter alternative. Seventy-four per cent of the people of the United States and seventy-five per cent of the informed leaders of opinion have so expressed themselves. But, despite this popular demand for an "international police force," what are the actual chances for government action?

What Are the Chances That
the World Federation Plan Will Be Accepted?

A system of world settlement, however desirable, is of little value unless it has a chance of being adopted. Psychologically, that plan or system is most likely to be adopted which not only fulfills a long-felt need but which does so with the minimum amount of opposition within the nations and among them. On this basis the World Federation Plan, in spite of its new approach and great scope, has a remarkably good chance of being adopted. It was expressly designed to be approved by practically all the nations of the world. To illustrate this, let us consider the position of the powers which will play the leading roles in the world settlement after Axis defeat.

Great Britain: It has become evident, even to many Englishmen, that the British Empire as constituted today cannot long survive. The sprawling empire is threatened on every side by vast blocs of industrialized nations, and the dangers, far from decreasing after this war, will increase—there will be threats from revived Europe and from new industrial giants such as China and the Middle East, or even India.

A permanent partnership with the United States is the only lasting solution to Britain's postwar problems. But anti-British feelings in the United States, and suspicions of the British ruling class, make it very doubtful that the United States Government would be supported in a power-politics alliance. Even if such an alliance were pushed through by political maneuvering, it could not possibly last.

The World Federation Plan removes any American objection to postwar co-operation with Britain and makes a true co-union of the English-speaking commonwealths practicable through an integrated, perpetual alliance embodied in the Plan. It guarantees the existence of the British Commonwealth of Nations, and offers to Britain a unique opportunity to resolve her inner contradictions without danger of future aggression.

Russia: To Russia the World Federation Plan offers a guarantee of collective security against aggression from Europe or Asia. Within her own Strategic Zone, protected by her own quota of armed forces, Russia is free to continue her great experiment unmolested, and yet is welcomed into the family of nations on a basis of absolute equality. There is no other way in which Russia can feel lastingly secure in

the postwar world against the threat of a coalition of capitalist powers. The government of Soviet Russia is too realistic to trust the good
intentions of the Anglo-Americans after their common enemy has
been defeated. Unless Russia obtains *effective guarantees* of postwar
security (as she will under the World Federation Plan), she too, in
self-defense, will have to resort to power politics, seeking to profit by
every disorder or war among her neighbors. Thus Russia might be a
constant threat to the nations of Europe and Asia.

The World Federation Plan offers Russia and her neighbors irrevocable guarantees of security. Such a solution of the Russian problem
would do more to unite Russia with her allies than a hundred solemn
treaties.

China: The World Federation Plan assures the termination of a
national nightmare which began with the Boxer Rebellion—the partition of China. The Plan enables her to reassemble her severed parts
and become a whole and prosperous nation, with a vast Strategic
Zone of her own. It permanently guarantees her sovereignty and
finally liberates her from the threat of white domination—economically and militarily. Furthermore, the World Federation enables
China to develop industrially without exciting the fears of other
great nations. Without the World Federation, power politics might
dictate that other nations should sooner or later strike at China, to
prevent her five hundred million people from becoming too powerful industrially, and therefore militarily. For China, as well as for
other nations, the World Federation, with its Quota Force Principle,
is the only practical and lasting substitute for power politics.

Other Nations: It is not necessary to enumerate in detail the equally
great advantages offered to other nations. Turkey will once more become the central state of the ancient Arabian Empire, now revived in
the Middle Eastern Federation. Poland, squeezed from the west and
the east by the Germans and the Russians, will realize the dream she
has treasured since medieval times. But instead of trying to hack her
way by force to the Baltic and the Black seas, she will find the way
open through voluntary co-operation with her sister nations, notably
a restored Czechoslovakia, Yugoslavia, and Greece, in the Middle
European Federation. France, Italy, and Spain, separately, would be
doomed to vassalage under the Germans or the Anglo-Americans.
Reunited in a powerful Latin bloc, they will resume their historic

civilizing role. France, with her vast possessions and non-increasing population, will gain by taking her natural allies into partnership and giving them a common stake to defend.

As for the smaller nations of the world, the enormous advantages of the World Federation have been discussed elsewhere. Without the World Federation, each small nation would either have to seek a powerful protector (and pay heavily for that protection) or eventually perish. Under the Quota Force Principle, the weak individual nations can become the strongest collective power on earth—an impregnable bulwark of lasting freedom and peace.

United States: It would be simpler to list the gains to the United States:

1. An *integrated* Pan-American Federation and permanent collective-defense alliance.

2. An *integrated* Malaysian Federation and permanent collective-defense alliance.

3. Security in a vast, new American Strategic Zone of four hundred million people, held in amity and co-operation through these Federations.

4. A permanent, *integrated* collective-defense alliance with the British Commonwealth of Nations.

5. A permanent, *integrated* collective-defense alliance with Russia, China, and all the states who desire to join us.

6. A permanent, *integrated* collective-defense alliance with smaller sovereign states of Europe, Africa, and Asia.

Most precious of all: the liberation of the peoples of the world now oppressed, and continuation of the American way of life and lasting peace in security for all.

All this the United States gains with but a fraction of the cost of this war and without doing injury or injustice to a single nation.

To the materialists, and to the incurable cynics about world peace, it may be pointed out that by entrusting its destiny to the World Federation Plan the United States runs no risk whatsoever. If the promise of lasting peace is betrayed, the American nation will still have the "insurance" of the American Strategic Zone. Together with her neighbors—four hundred million strong—America will be powerful enough to remain isolated or to throw a decisive weight against future aggressors. But if it becomes clear that the World Federation and its Quota Force Principle are operating smoothly, then even the most hardened cynic must admit that there will no longer be the precautionary need for the American Strategic Zone.

There will be some who may object to the World Federation Plan, not on any specific grounds, but with the general argument that the whole system is too new and untested by history. Let them be reminded that in the year 1291 the selectmen of three tiny Swiss cantons met in a field and took an oath of perpetual alliance against the war lords who threatened their peace and freedom. The alliance grew and endured for more than six centuries, in spite of wide differences in language, religion, and economic structure. This was because each canton retained its full freedom but created a special organism—the Federation—to carry on the common defense. What the Swiss did on a microscopic scale the United Nations can now do on a world scale.

I said before that the Industrial Revolution which carried so much hope for humanity also carried the seeds of its own dissolution; I say now that these seeds can be destroyed. The hope for humanity lies in industrialized America. Our power, though ephemeral, is immense. It is the power to organize the whole world for the twentieth century with the same bold and humane spirit with which our founding fathers organized our world in the eighteenth century.

The time is short in which to lay the foundations for the peace to come. The battle of peace must be planned *now*. Every day lost in preparation decreases our chance of winning and increases the chance for future wars.

Every thoughtful man is aware of the enormous power of an idea. But in order to become an active force, the greatest idea needs time to become known, understood, and developed as a movement. The World Federation Plan is an idea which can germinate rapidly in favorable soil, because never before in history has there been such yearning for freedom from war. Once this Plan is made known to a sufficient number of people, it will become a powerful, perhaps an irresistible, force on the side of victorious peace.

"What Can I Do to Help?"

Today many experts, as well as laymen, are convinced that the World Federation Plan will help to write a workable treaty of peace, if it can be made known to the American people and to the people of other countries. This can be done only by general discussion and by educational propaganda. To promote such discussion and education the World Federation, Inc., a non-profit membership corporation, with a charter issued by the state of New York, has been organized. It is strictly non-partisan, abstaining from political or ideological activities and disinterested in the internal affairs of any nation. Those devoting their time to establishment of the World Federation Plan believe that they are contributing to the greatest and most beneficial revolution in history. They trust that even if the Plan is not adopted in detail, its presentation to the public and to governments will lead to the development of an even better plan, to the lasting good of humanity.

The files of the World Federation hold many valued letters of encouragement and commendation of the Plan, a number of them signed by names nationally or internationally famous. But of them all perhaps the most moving came from a lieutenant in the United States Army, serving overseas. He wrote:

"I'm celebrating being alive after a year's foreign duty in this war. By way of celebration, I'm inclosing a money order for twenty-five dollars, with the request that if you are as sick of periodic futile slaughters as I am, and Culbertson's plan for a world settlement makes more sense in your mind than beautiful slogans, you spend the money for copies of his summary and mail them out to editors, women's clubs, commercial clubs, senators, representatives, governors, etc., with a little note to the effect that we expendables will accept our fate without bitterness when the one hundred and twenty-eight million of you at home show us that by your action some such plan and organization has been achieved. To date we are going nowhere except to hell with a lot of fine promises."

There is no denying the magnitude of the task of establishing the World Federation. But the American people have never been afraid of the *size* of the truth.

In the First World War two million young Americans crossed the Atlantic. They returned victorious. Their fathers, being unprepared, lost the peace. This time millions of other young Americans are crossing the oceans. Once more they will win the battles of war. Again their fathers are unprepared for the battle of peace. The World Federation Plan is offered so that *"it shall not happen again!"*

Index